Myths of Exile

The Babylonian exile in 587–539 BCE is frequently presented as the main explanatory factor for the religious and literary developments found in the Hebrew Bible. The sheer number of both 'historical' and narrative exiles confirms that the theme of exile is of great importance in the Hebrew Bible. However, one does not do justice to the topic by restricting it to the exile in Babylon after 587 BCE. In recent years, it has become clear that there are several discrepancies between biblical and extra-biblical sources on invasion and deportation in Palestine in the 1st millennium BCE. Such discrepancy confirms that the theme of exile in the Hebrew Bible should not be viewed as an echo of a single traumatic historical event, but rather as a literary motif that is repeatedly reworked by biblical authors.

Myths of Exile challenges the traditional understanding of 'the Exile' as a monolithic historical reality and instead provides a critical and comparative assessment of motifs of estrangement and belonging in the Hebrew Bible and related literature. Using selected texts as case-studies, this book demonstrates how tales of exile and return can be described as a common formative narrative in the literature of the ancient Near East, a narrative that has been interpreted and used in various ways depending on the needs and cultural contexts of the interpreting community. *Myths of Exile* is a critical study which forms the basis for a fresh understanding of these exile myths as identity-building literary phenomena.

Anne Katrine de Hemmer Gudme is Professor with special responsibilities at the University of Copenhagen. She has published several articles on rituals in the Hebrew Bible and the book *Before the God in his Place for Good Remembrance* (2013) on votive practice.

Ingrid Hjelm is Associate Professor at the University of Copenhagen. She is the author of *The Samaritans and Early Judaism* (2000) and *Jerusalem's Rise to Sovereignty* (2004), in addition to a considerable number of articles within the field of Samaritan studies, the history of ancient Israel and the Hebrew Bible. She is general editor of the Copenhagen International Seminar series.

COPENHAGEN INTERNATIONAL SEMINAR

General Editors: Ingrid Hjelm and Thomas L. Thompson
both at the University of Copenhagen
Editors: Niels Peter Lemche and Mogens Müller,
both at the University of Copenhagen
Language Revision Editor: James West
at the Quartz Hill School of Theology

Available:

JAPHETH BEN ALI'S BOOK Of JEREMIAH
Joshua A. Sabih

THE EMERGENCE OF ISRAEL IN ANCIENT PALESTINE
Emanuel Pfoh

ORIGIN MYTHS AND HOLY PLACES IN THE OLD TESTAMENT
Lukasz Niesiolowski-Spanò

CHANGING PERSPECTIVES I
John Van Seters

ARGONAUTS OF THE DESERT
Philippe Wajdenbaum

THE EXPRESSION "SON Of MAN" AND THE DEVELOPMENT Of CHRISTOLOGY
Mogens Müller

BIBLICAL STUDIES AND THE FAILURE Of HISTORY
Niels Peter Lemche

BIBLICAL NARRATIVE AND PALESTINE'S HISTORY
Thomas L. Thompson

"IS THIS NOT THE CARPENTER?"
Edited by Thomas L. Thompson and Thomas S. Verenna

THE BIBLE AND HELLENISM
Edited by Thomas L. Thompson and Philippe Wajdenbaum

RETHINKING BIBLICAL SCHOLARSHIP
Philip R. Davies

REPRESENTING ZION
Frederik Poulsen

Forthcoming:

REWRITING PETER AS AN INTERTEXTUAL CHARACTER IN THE CANONICAL GOSPELS
Finn Damgaard

SYRIA-PALESTINE IN THE LATE BRONZE AGE
Emanuel Pfoh

HISTORY, ARCHAEOLOGY AND THE BIBLE FORTY YEARS AFTER "HISTORICITY"
Edited by Ingrid Hjelm and Thomas L. Thompson

BIBLICAL INTERPRETATION BEYOND HISTORICITY
Edited by Ingrid Hjelm and Thomas L. Thompson

THE JUDAEOKARAITE RECEPTION OF THE HEBREW BIBLE
Joshua A. Sabih

Myths of Exile
History and Metaphor in the Hebrew Bible

**Edited by
Anne Katrine de Hemmer Gudme and
Ingrid Hjelm**

LONDON AND NEW YORK

First published 2015
by Routledge
2 Park Square, Milton Park, Abingdon, Oxon OX14 4RN

and by Routledge
711 Third Avenue, New York, NY 10017

Routledge is an imprint of the Taylor & Francis Group, an informa business

© 2015 A. Gudme and I. Hjelm, editorial and selection matter; individual chapters, the contributors

The right of the editors to be identified as the authors of the editorial material, and of the authors for their individual chapters, has been asserted in accordance with sections 77 and 78 of the Copyright, Designs and Patents Act 1988.

All rights reserved. No part of this book may be reprinted or reproduced or utilised in any form or by any electronic, mechanical, or other means, now known or hereafter invented, including photocopying and recording, or in any information storage or retrieval system, without permission in writing from the publishers.

Trademark notice: Product or corporate names may be trademarks or registered trademarks, and are used only for identification and explanation without intent to infringe.

British Library Cataloguing-in-Publication Data
A catalogue record for this book is available from the British Library

Library of Congress Cataloging in Publication Data
Myths of exile : history and metaphor in the Hebrew Bible / edited by Anne Katrine de Hemmer Gudme and Ingrid Hjelm. -- First [edition].
pages cm. -- (Copenhagen international seminar)
Includes index.
1. Jews--History--Babylonian captivity, 598-515 B.C.--Biblical teaching.
2. Exile (Punishment)--Biblical teaching. 3. Bible. Old Testament--Criticism, interpretation, etc. 4. Metaphor in the Bible. I. Gudme, Anne Katrine de Hemmer, 1980- editor.
BS1199.B3M98 2015
221.6--dc23
2014042046

ISBN: 978-1-138-88689-6 (hbk)
ISBN: 978-1-315-71451-6 (ebk)

Typeset in Times New Roman
by Taylor & Francis Books

Contents

List of figures	ix
List of tables	x
List of contributors	xi
List of abbreviations	xii

Introduction ANNE KATRINE DE HEMMER GUDME AND INGRID HJELM	1

PART I
Creating exilic identities

11

1	Exile as the great divide: Would there be an 'ancient Israel' without an exile? NIELS PETER LEMCHE	13
2	God leading his people: Exodus' *longue durée* FABIO PORZIA	28
3	Exile and return and the closure of the Samaritan and Jewish canons INGRID HJELM	51
4	Constructions of exile in the Persian period CIAN POWER	65
5	Exile as pilgrimage? INGRID HJELM	79
6	Psalm 137: Exile as hell! NIELS PETER LEMCHE	89

viii *Contents*

PART II
Motifs of exile and return 99

7 Sheep without a shepherd: Genesis' discourse on justice and
reconciliation as exile's *raison d'être* 101
THOMAS L. THOMPSON

8 Idol-taunt and exilic identity: A Dalit reading of
Isaiah 44:9–20 125
DOMINIC S. IRUDAYARAJ

9 Exile and emergent monotheism: Learning loyalty
from Jeremiah 42–44 137
ROB BARRETT

10 The return from exile in Ezra-Nehemiah 150
ROBERTO PIANI

Index of sources 162
Index of authors 170

List of figures

2.1	Seal from Megiddo	33
2.2	Ivory from Megiddo	34
2.3	Cylindrical seal from Beth-Shean	34
2.4	Seal from Beth-Shean	35
2.5	Seal from Southern Palestine	36
2.6	Seal from Southern Palestine	37

List of tables

10.1	The pairing of "gold and silver" in the Hebrew Bible	153
10.2	2 Kings 23:22 and Nehemiah 8:17	158
10.3	Nehemiah 8:1, Joshua 8:31; 23:6; 1:7–9	159

List of contributors

Rob Barrett worked on a Sofja-Kovalevskaja research project on early Jewish monotheisms from 2009 to 2012, is author of *Disloyalty and Destruction: Religion and Politics in Deuteoronomy and the Modern World*, and is now Director of Forums and Scholarship at The Colossian Forum.

Ingrid Hjelm, Associate Professor, Department of Biblical Studies, Faculty of Theology, University of Copenhagen, is the author of *Jerusalem's Rise to Sovereignty: Zion and Gerizim in Competition* and *The Samaritans and Early Judaism. A Literary Analysis.*

Dominic S. Irudayaraj holds graduate degrees in Biblical Studies and Computers. He taught at Herat University, Afghanistan and at Andhra Loyola College, India. He is currently a doctoral student at Jesuit School of Theology of SCU, CA.

Niels Peter Lemche was Professor of Theology at the University of Copenhagen 1987–2013 and is a founding member of the 'Copenhagen School'. His work has concentrated on Israelite history and, more recently, on the Old Testament as a Hellenistic book.

Roberto Piani is Biblical and Theological Adviser to the Catholic Church in Bremen, Germany and Licentiate (2009) in Sacred Scripture at the Pontifical Biblical Institute, Rome, Italy. He is a contributor to the journal *Aggiornamenti Sociali*, Milan, Italy.

Fabio Porzia, Master in Old Testament Exegesis at the Pontifical Biblical Institute in Rome (Italy), is currently a PhD student at the University of Toulouse – Jean Jaurès (France) and the University of Florence (Italy), working on the development of the Jewish identity during the first millennium BCE.

Cian Power is a doctoral student at Harvard University's Near Eastern Languages and Civilizations Department. Cian's dissertation examines the attitudes of the authors of the Hebrew Bible towards language and languages.

Thomas L. Thompson is Professor Emeritus from the University of Copenhagen. He is the author of *The Historicity of the Patriarchal Narratives* (1974); *The Bible in History* (1999); *The Messiah Myth* (2005); *Biblical Narrative and Palestine's History* (2013).

List of abbreviations

ABD	*Anchor Bible Dictionary* (Freedman 1992)
AF	*The Kitāb al Tarīkh of Abu'l-Fath* (Stenhouse 1985)
ANET	*Ancient Near Eastern Texts* (Pritchard 1969)
AT	*The Greek Alpha Text of Esther*
BASOR	*Bulletin of the American Schools of Oriental Research*
BHS	Biblia Hebraica Stuttgartensia
BZAW	*Beihefte zur Zeitschrift für die alttestamentliche Wissenschaft*
CBQ	*Catholic Biblical Quarterly*
CBR	*Currents in Biblical Research*
CIS	*Copenhagen International Seminar*
DCH	*Dictionary of Classical Hebrew* (Clines 1993)
EA	"El-Amarna letters" (Knudtzon 1907–1915)
HDT	*Hittite Diplomatic Texts* (Beckman 1999)
IEJ	*Israel Exploration Journal*
JBL	*Journal of Biblical Literature*
JR(G)	John Rylands (Gaster)
JSJ	*Journal for the Study of Judaism*
JSOT	*Journal for the Study of the Old Testament*
JSOTS	*Journal for the Study of the Old Testament Supplements*
KAI	*Kanaanäische und aramäische Inschriften* (Donner and Röllig 1962–64).
KJV	The King James Version of the Bible
LXX	The Septuagint
MM	*Memar Marqah* (Macdonald 1963)
MT	Masoretic Text
NEA	*Near Eastern Archaeology*
NRSV	The New Revised Standard Version of the Bible
Or	*Orientalia*
RB	*Revue Biblique*
REB	The Revised English Bible
SJOT	*Scandinavian Journal of the Old Testament*
SP	The Samaritan Pentateuch

TDOT	*Theological Dictionary of the Old Testament* (Botterweck and Ringgren 1986)
ThZ	*Theologische Zeitschrift*
TM	*Tibåt Mårqe* (Ben-Hayyim 1988)
VT	*Vetus Testamentum*
ZAW	*Zeitschrift für die alttestamentliche Wissenschaft*
ZDMG	*Zeitschrift des deutschen morgenländischen Gesellschaft*

Introduction

Anne Katrine de Hemmer Gudme and Ingrid Hjelm

When scholars speak about 'the Exile' in biblical studies they almost univocally mean the Babylonian exile in 587–539 BCE rather than any historical and literary exiles mentioned in ancient literature. The Babylonian exile is frequently put forward as the main explanatory factor for religious and literary developments that can be found in the Hebrew Bible. In many ways, it has become *the* single event around which most scholarly interpretations of the Hebrew Bible revolve. Sometimes it seems as if the Exile is even the main reason we have such a collection of writings as the Hebrew Bible (cf. e.g. Sanders 1976: 188). In recent years, however, biblical scholars have begun to question the monolithic nature of the Exile in both biblical scholarship and in regard to the content of the Hebrew Bible. A cursory reading of the Hebrew Bible makes it clear that there is no such thing as *the* Exile in the texts. Even if the Babylonian exile (587–539 BCE) looms large in biblical literature, there are in fact narratives about several major exiles in the Hebrew Bible. In chronological order these are the deportation of *all* the inhabitants of the Kingdom of Israel by the Assyrian king Shalmaneser (ca 722 BCE; cf. 2 Kings 17; Hjelm 2004: 32–41); then follows the first deportation from Jerusalem to Babylon during the brief reign of the Judaean king Jehoiachin (598/597 BCE; cf. 2 Kings 24:10–17); a succeeding second deportation follows the fall of Jerusalem (587/586 BCE; cf. 2 Kings 25:1–21); and, finally, Jeremiah 52 presents a voluntary flight to Egypt (582 BCE; cf. Ahn 2010: 1–8).

The theme of exile is certainly of great importance in the Hebrew Bible; the sheer number of both 'historical' and narrative exiles confirms this, but one does not do justice to the topic by restricting it to the exile in Babylon after 587 BCE. There are several discrepancies between biblical and extra-biblical sources on invasion and deportation in Palestine of the 1st millennium BCE. In contrast to biblical foci on themes of the cessation of the kingdoms of Israel and Judah and a total deportation of their populations at the hands of the Assyrian and Babylonian monarchs in the 8th and 6th centuries BCE, many other invasions and exiles took place in these regions from the mid-9th to the 2nd century BCE. Of the exiles mentioned in the Hebrew Bible only one is truly testified in extra-biblical sources, namely that of 598/97 to Babylon, while the second exile (587/86) and the flight to Egypt (582) mentioned in 2

Kings 25 and Jeremiah 52 have no extra-biblical verification. The exile following the fall of the Kingdom of Israel did not take place during Shalmaneser as related in the Book of Kings, but two years later during the reign of Sargon II. It was of limited consequence for the region (Becking 1992; further ref. in Hjelm 2005). Some 27,280 people were deported and probably replaced by Midianite tribes (Knauf 1988). 2 Kings 17:24 lists five different peoples as newcomers to the area, but such is not mentioned in any Assyrian sources and apart from meagre onomastic evidence (Lawson Younger 2004),[1] almost nothing of the material culture of the region can be attributed to any of the regions mentioned in the Bible (Stern 2001: 45; Lawson Younger 2004: 255). Assyrian city planning and architecture were mostly restricted to military and administrative centres displaying considerable signs of Neo-Assyrian influence and found in great numbers throughout Palestine (ref. to this in Hjelm 2005).

Major deportations, however, followed Sennacherib's conquest and devastation of Judaea in 701 BCE. Some 200,150 persons were afflicted by it when not only a major part of the population had been deported, but several Judaean cities handed over to the loyal Assyrian vassal kings of Ashdod, Ekron and Gaza (Na'aman 1993; Lipschits 2003). The event was commemorated in the Hebrew Bible as a major victory (Hjelm 2004: ch. 2–3), because Judah's king and capital (Jerusalem) remained intact. Hezekiah's kingdom, however, was greatly diminished and subjected to heavy vassalage. In addition, although Israel's kingship was replaced by Assyrian governors, the city of Samaria's rebuilding and role as provincial capital made it politically and economically superior to the diminutive vassal kingdom of Judaea. That the kingdom of Judaea had also fallen victim to the Assyrian occupation and shared with Phoenicia, Lower Galilee, the Shephelah of Judaea and the southern coastal areas the fate of being subjected to several population replacements from the time of Tiglat-pileser III onwards (Oded 1979: 26–32, 116–35; Na'aman 1993; Stern 2001: 130–31; Hjelm 2005), is not a story cherished by the authors of the Hebrew Bible. Neither are the historical consequences of these upheavals of any real concern. The cessation of the Israelite kingdom is also the cessation of its history in the Books of Kings and Chronicles. Although land achievement plays such a considerable role in the Hebrew Bible, the narratives basically concern its protagonist's ethnic, familial and religious conditions and development. Social and historical structures are used as canvasses for biblical authors' sermons, discussions and narratives about Yahweh's elected people. In- and out-groups are declared faithful or unfaithful depending on each author's perspective and goal.

Such aspects also pertain to the relationship between biblical descriptions of exile and its consequences and the information about the so-called exilic period that can be gleaned from archaeological and extra-biblical material. It has become increasingly clear that the biblical accounts of exile and return are far removed from what can be reconstructed about the historical exiles and the lives and experiences of the inhabitants of Israel and Judaea and their descendants in the first millennium BCE. In 1996, Hans Barstad concluded that the myth of the empty land is indeed a myth, and, following Kenyon and Barkay, he even considered it possible that a larger number of the populace remained in the city of Jerusalem (so also Ofer 1994 and Barstad 2003: 9).[2] Such, however, has been disputed by Carter (1999 and 2003), Lipschits (2003: 328–29) and Stern (2004) who have reservations that more than a tiny minority lived there in the Babylonian and the beginning of the Persian period.[3] According to these scholars "the Babylonians completed the devastation begun with the Assyrians and left the land 'virtually depopulated'" (Stern 2004: 274), while "Jerusalem and its environs were thoroughly razed by the Babylonians, and there is no evidence of any settlement there whatsoever until the Persian period" (Lipschits 2003: 365). By the mid-4th century most of Yehud was inhabited by Edomites, not Jews (Stern 2004: 274), and it was, in fact, only in the beginning of the Hellenistic period that Jerusalem expanded to a size larger than that of a minor temple city (Stern 2001: 581; 2004: 274; Lipschits 2003: 330). Only the tribal area of Benjamin, north of Jerusalem seems to have been minimally affected by the Babylonian conquest (Zorn 2003: 438). So Judaea might, in fact, have been 'the empty land', which Israel never was (Becking 1992; further ref. in Knoppers 2004 and Hjelm 2005).

Documents pertaining to the Judahite/Yehudite settlements in Mesopotamia in the Babylonian and Persian periods make it very clear that several of the deported families managed to make a living in their new surroundings and decided to stay there (Zadok 1979; Pearce 2011). In short, the Exile, which was in fact several exiles, was neither as all-encompassing as some biblical texts lead us to believe, nor as clear-cut and finite as it is sometimes presented both in the Hebrew Bible and in biblical scholarship. One should take into account also the many narrative 'exiles' in the Hebrew Bible such as the patriarchs living as strangers in the land in Genesis, the Exodus from Egypt and the Israelite struggle with the local Canaanites in the book of Judges (cf. Levin and Ben Zvi 2010: 2). With a lower dating of the production of biblical literature to the Persian and Hellenistic periods one must consider also the forced and voluntary exiles to Egypt during Ptolemy I and Antiochus IV narrated in *Letter of Aristeas*, 1 and 2 Maccabees and Josephus, as part of the canvas.

Similar problems relate to biblical discussions of return, which basically is viewed as a Judahite return to Jerusalem in the Persian period, 'forgets' the return of other peoples, but envisions a return of Israel's tribes in a reunified Jerusalem. Several deportation texts from Tiglat-pileser III to Esarhaddon mention that people have been brought from Palestine to Mesopotamia and Elam, and several Assyrian and Babylonian rulers (e.g. Esarhaddon, Ashurbanipal Nabonidus and Nebuchadnesar II)[4] claim that they brought people and their gods back to their homelands. In addition, language of 'return', which conveys construed identities on replaced peoples was part of ancient Near Eastern deportation ideology.[5]

The above mentioned discrepancies confirm that the theme of exile in the Hebrew Bible should not only be viewed as an echo of traumatic historical

4   *A.K. de Hemmer Gudme and I. Hjelm*

events, but also as a literary theme that is taken up and reworked in a variety of ways by the biblical authors in order to build specific identities and to express ideology. There is not one Exile in the Hebrew Bible, there are many, and there is not one interpretation of or portrayal of Exile in the biblical texts, there are as many as there are biblical authors – sometimes even more.

This volume represents a movement away from an understanding of the Exile as a monolithic historical reality that lies behind the texts of the Hebrew Bible and proposes in its stead a critical and comparative approach to motifs of estrangement and belonging in the Hebrew Bible and related literature. By following the current trend in biblical research on exile and abandoning *the* Exile in favour of the many exiles, displacements and departures, the essays in this volume offer a varied and dynamic view of the many myths of exile in the Hebrew Bible.

Part 1, "Creating exilic identities", explores the widespread use of exilic metaphors and myths in biblical and related ancient Near Eastern literature. The essays in the first part of the book demonstrate how tales of exile and return can be described as a common formative narrative in the literature of the ancient Near East, but also a narrative that is interpreted and used in various ways, depending on the needs and context of the interpreting community. These six essays form the basis for understanding myths of exile as identity-building literary phenomena in their cultural contexts.

In "Exile as the great divide: Would there be an 'ancient Israel' without an exile?", Niels Peter Lemche explores the biblical myths of the Babylonian exile and the subsequent return to the land as well as the origins of the tradition of a united people of Israel. Lemche initially concludes that the tradition of a united Israel has no basis in any historical reality in Iron Age Palestine. The earliest possible time that such a tradition could emerge is after the fall of Judaea in 597/87 BCE. According to Lemche, the formation of 'exilic' traditions in the Hebrew Bible and related literature indicates that it happened as late as the Hellenistic period. Lemche answers the question posed in the title as he concludes that the Babylonian exile did not in fact create an exiled people or nation. It was the other way around. The biblical authors who created the stories about the people of Israel did not belong to a people living in exile because they had no other choice and no option to return. They were Jews living in the Jewish Diaspora in the Hellenistic Period and they created the story about the forced exile in order to explain why they and their kinsmen were not living in the promised land of their fathers. This story also includes a utopian hope for the future, when every Jew has returned to his ancestral home, a hope which to some extent is still alive today.

In "God leading his people: Exodus' *longue durée*", Fabio Porzia uses iconographic exegesis to investigate the biblical motif of God leading his people. By comparing texts from the Hebrew Bible with pictorial and textual evidence from the ancient Near East, Porzia traces similarities between the Egyptian iconographic motif of the Pharaoh, who leads defeated enemies into captivity, and the biblical motif of God who leads his people into freedom.

Porzia concludes that the motif of the God/king leading a people belongs to an Eastern Mediterranean *koiné*, which the Hebrew Bible taps into and even inverts. The God of the Exodus-formulas is modelled on the Pharaoh or the ancient Near Eastern king in general, but with one important difference: the Pharaoh leads enemies into slavery and submission to Egypt. The God of the Exodus leads his people away from exactly those things. With this analysis Porzia shows how collective memory can transform a political linguistic code, which was initially primarily related to geographic entities such as cities and lands, into a myth relating to a divinely chosen people and thus contributes to the formation of an ethnic and 'national' identity.

In "Exile and return and the closure of the Samaritan and Jewish canons", Ingrid Hjelm takes up the literary motif of the journey in ancient literature in general and in the Pentateuchal traditions in particular. In biblical literature, the journey is frequently combined with either a voluntary or forced exile and in the Hebrew Bible this exile is often presented as a punishment for disobedience. Hjelm compares the literary traditions of the Samaritans and the Jews with regard to the journey's end in the Pentateuchal traditions and beyond and she traces the differences between the Samaritan and Jewish traditions about Joshua and the events that follow upon the arrival in the land. Hjelm concludes that although the two traditions differ significantly in their representations of the culmination of the desert wanderings, they both conclude with an admonition to keep the law and thus they both create a cultic continuum by tying together the narrative patterns of journey, settlement and adherence to the law.

In "Constructions of exile in the Persian period", Cian Power investigates the many and varied attitudes towards the Babylonian exile in Persian period biblical literature. Power examines 'Third Isaiah', the books of Haggai, Zechariah, Ezra and Nehemiah, 1 and 2 Chronicles and Esther, asking questions such as: How long did the exile last? Who went into exile? And how significant was the exile for Judaea? Power's analysis shows that there are significant disagreements between these texts with regard to the duration of exile, the status of those left behind and the importance of the exile for the future of the people of Israel. Power concludes that the understanding of the exile in Persian period Yehud was not formulated at once. Biblical literature contains several different voices and opinions on exile, which biblical scholarship must remember to detect and appreciate in order to get a better understanding of the individual texts' constructions of exile and their nuances.

In "Exile as pilgrimage?", Ingrid Hjelm continues her exploration of the journey motif in the Pentateuchal tradition and poses the question: Were the wanderings in the wilderness a success or a failure for the Israelites? How should we interpret the fact that Moses and his generation never, in fact, make it into the Promised Land? Hjelm proposes an allegorical reading, where the journey through the desert can be seen as a pilgrimage to the Holy Land, which can be likened to a sanctuary; the temple as the adytum in its middle, the land itself as the holy precinct, which is fenced off by a border,

6 *A.K. de Hemmer Gudme and I. Hjelm*

and the wilderness as the surrounding chaotic and profane world. The journey through the wilderness is depicted with surprising ambiguity in the Pentateuchal tradition. It is a place and a time where Israel travels with and is close to their God, but is also a place plagued by mutiny, discontent and doubt. Hjelm concludes by suggesting that the new generation that enters the land in the Book of Numbers may not be a failure at all, but rather a group of pilgrims reaching their goal enlightened and transformed, having left their disobedience and disbelief behind in the desert.

In "Psalm 137: Exile as hell!", Niels Peter Lemche offers a thorough reading of a motif – which can be found, for instance, in Psalm 137 – where exile is perceived as a hellish prison, where the captives can lament their fate, yearn for their home and plot revenge over their captors. Lemche moves on to consider another version of the motif – which can be found for instance in Lamentations, the Prophets and in the Deuteronomistic history – where exile is hell and a punishment for sins. Lemche then compares these memories of exile in the Hebrew Bible with what we know about the several historical exiles in the Iron Age. Lemche stresses that there never was a massive return to Yehud and Jerusalem and that the biblical representations of exile are literary constructions. The texts remember Jerusalem as Paradise and Babylon as Hell although this most certainly was never the case.

Part 2, "Motifs of exile and return", encompasses four case-studies of selected Hebrew Bible texts. In these examples, myths of exile and return are put to specific and varied use and the explanatory potential of literary motifs of exile and return are amply demonstrated.

In Chapter 7, "Sheep without a shepherd: Genesis' discourse on justice and reconciliation as exile's *raison d'être*", Thomas L. Thompson leads the audience on a grand journey through Genesis' all-encompassing theme of justice and reconciliation. Thompson's chapter takes its departure from a previously published article on the story of Cain's murder of Abel in Genesis 4 (Thompson 2011). Here he introduces a series of narrative themes that, being particularly rich in their potential for the development of Samaritan-Jewish allegories, reflect utopian elements of myths of exile and return. The story's reiterations maintain and feed a number of central plotlines of the Pentateuch, which in the present chapter are identified as (1) the leitmotif of the cursed land bringing exile and estrangement. This is a narrative thread that begins first in the curse of Adam in Genesis 3:17–19, and is reiterated and thematically expanded in a number of texts from the Primeval narratives and the beginning of the Abraham narrative; (2) the theme of 'brothers fighting brothers' (Hjelm 2003), which is linked closely to the stereotypical motif of the younger supplanting the elder, first brought forward in the prophetic allegorical conflict of Jacob and Esau's birth narrative (Gen 25:19–34); (3) the thematic opposition of revenge and reconciliation, which is a theme that dominates ancient Near Eastern discourse on blood-guilt; and (4) the dark side of the great ancient Near Eastern theme of the king as shepherd of his people. What is the fate of the sheep when they have lost their shepherd? This last theme builds up to an investigation of the pivotal and wide-ranging discourse on the ethical righteousness of Yahweh in his royal role as judge of this world. Thompson's investigation of this theme revolves around questions of divine irascibility and the fear and terror implied in Yahweh's covenant discussed in light of divine and royal figures in ancient Near Eastern literature. The discourse, central to the Abraham stories (Gen 18:25), ultimately succeeds in giving both a critical and comprehensive closure to Genesis as a coherent literary whole. It consists of three variations of a story, which begins in exile and the abuse of the generous host and closes in the reconciliation of shepherds quarreling. This discourse is garnished by tales of conflict, injustice and reconciliation in the Jacob narratives with an additional three narratives about women and sexuality. Together they effect a transvaluation of ethics, which is first illustrated in the story of Lot's daughters in Genesis 19:30–38, but becomes systemic in three bridge narratives, which bind the Jacob narratives to Genesis' resolution in the Joseph story. These narratives – namely, the Dinah story, the story of Tamar and that of Potiphar's wife – ultimately succeed in giving both a critical and comprehensive closure.

Dominic S. Irudayaraj's chapter, "Idol-taunt and exilic identity: A Dalit reading of Isaiah 44:9–20", interprets Isaiah's mockery of Babylonian idol making through lenses of resistance literature from low caste Dalit communities in India. Much like the exilic experience, Dalit history is marked by experiences of trauma, when Dalits have been denied their rightful place within the Indian social system. Relegated to the periphery of society, perceived as polluted and polluting, and therefore deemed untouchables, Dalits have endured crises for centuries. Dalit literature embodies features of resistance, ridicule and reversal, which not only protest against hegemonic discourses, but also construct Dalits' fractured and fragmented identity. It evidences what happens when a marginalized group's repeated attempt to regain its denied status meets with disappointments. The group then resorts to what is within its power to do. It seeks to formulate counter-discourses, through which the group's hopes and anxieties are given expression. Much like Isaiah's anti-Babylonian diatribe, Dalit literature embodies a tone of ridicule, scorn, mockery and protest. It belittles what is held in esteem by the high castes and aims at undermining their dominant worldview. *Reversal* is employed to both critique the hegemonic narratives and, in the process, construct a narrative that infuses a different and meaningful perspective to the same reality. Irudayaraj's comparable reading of Isaiah 44:9–20, with this literature's use of *resistance*, *ridicule* and *reversal*, underscores the prophetic novelty by which the prophet constructs the identities of a 'defeated' deity, a dispersed community, and a de-centred prophet for his exilic audience.

Rob Barrett's chapter, "Exile and emergent monotheism: Learning loyalty from Jeremiah 42–44", discusses how monotheism is promoted in Jeremiah 42–44 in the author's recollection of his audience's past history, which is both a forensic analysis of something that went horribly wrong and potent rhetoric that points forward to something right. Jeremiah's rhetoric functions by

8 *A.K. de Hemmer Gudme and I. Hjelm*

pitting the protagonist prophet against a range of out-group opponents with the purpose of persuading the in-group readers of the book to heed to the prophet's words. Barrett's analysis of Jeremiah's narrative analogy in chapters 42–44 is given as an example of the book's subtle argument about Yahweh's uniqueness. Jeremiah's double discussion of the remnant seeking protection both from Egypt and the Queen of Heaven creates a conceptual category for alternative powers to Yahweh. These alternatives include other gods and political powers, but entrusting oneself to any of these powers is a fatal mistake. Jeremiah's discourse portrays the identity of the survivors of Jerusalem's destruction as a people who trust in Yahweh's power alone. His literary recollection of the failed past is no disinterested, disembodied recounting of dispassionate history, but a medium through which a successful future can be imagined.

Roberto Piani's chapter, "The return from exile in Ezra-Nehemiah", challenges the often claimed similarity between the missions of Ezra and Moses, which establishes Ezra as a *Moses redivivus*. Such claim rests on an over-interpretation of Pseudepigraphic and Talmudic sources' reverence for Ezra as a Moses figure, who would have been worthy of receiving the Torah for Israel had Moses not preceded him. However, the biblical Ezra in Nehemiah 8 is not presented simply in the image of Moses. The first part of the Book of Ezra might contain general allusions to the Exodus narrative, but Piani finds no explicit connection between the characters of Moses and Ezra in the text. Consequently, the overall image of the return from exile as depicted in Ezra and Nehemiah seems to be more than just a second Exodus. Piani rather proposes to see Nehemiah 8 as a text that views Ezra as not only a legitimate successor to Moses, but also to Joshua and Josiah, and with strong ties to the Levites. Biblical traditions emphasize for each of these characters distinctive aspects of the Torah: Moses with its revelation, Joshua and Josiah with its (faithful) transmission, and Ezra (and the Levites) with its transmission and interpretation. Piani's reading has consequences for whether one views the return from exile as a radical new beginning, which points forward to the oral Torah, or whether Ezra should, in fact, be viewed as shaped in continuity with the past. In such view, he is better understood as *one of the agents* of the Torah, promoting the written Torah as a determent identity factor. Emphasizing the role of the Torah of Moses, the biblical authors legitimized and authorized Ezra and his group as trustworthy successors to Moses, Joshua and Josiah.

Notes

1 Lawson Younger's attempt at identification of the peoples and their gods mentioned in 2 Kings 17 does not give evidence that these have been deported to Palestine.
2 For further references, see Knoppers 2004: 152.
3 See discussion in Knoppers 2004 and Hjelm 2005.
4 Ref. to these texts in Thompson 1992: 346–50 and Hjelm 2005.

Introduction 9

5 In a recent monograph, John Ahn has proposed a more nuanced and precise terminology in relation to the study of exile in the Hebrew Bible. Ahn, who draws inspiration from contemporary research on migration, advocates 'forced migration' instead of the more commonly used 'exile' and encourages biblical scholars to discern between for instance 'displacement' and 'internal displacement' (Ahn 2010: 27–46). Although Ahn certainly has a point, especially when it comes to analyzing and interpreting specific historical cases of displacement and migration, we have decided not to adopt his terminology in this volume, mainly because the scope of the volume is exile and return as a literary motif, not as a historical reality.

Bibliography

Ahn, J. 2010. *Exile as Forced Migrations: A Sociological, Literary, and Theological Approach on the Displacement and Resettlement of the Southern Kingdom of Judah.* Berlin: De Gruyter.

Barstad, H.M. 1996. *The Myth of the Empty Land. A Study in the History and Archeology of Judah during the "Exilic" Period.* Oslo: Scandinavian University Press.

——2003. "After the 'Myth of the Empty Land': Major Challenges in the Study of Neo-Babylonian Judah". In *Judah and Judaeans in the Neo-Babylonian Period.* O. Lipschits and J. Blenkinsopp (eds). Winona Lake, IN: Eisenbrauns: 3–20.

Becking, B. 1992. *The Fall of Samaria: An Historical and Archaeological Study.* Leiden: E.J. Brill.

Carter, C.E. 1999. *The Emergence of Yehud in the Persian Period: A Social and Demographic Study.* Sheffield: Sheffield Academic Press.

——2003. "Ideology and Archaeology in the Neo-Babylonian Period: Excavating Text and Tell". In *Judah and Judaeans in the Neo-Babylonian Period.* O. Lipschits and J. Blenkinsopp (eds). Winona Lake, IN: Eisenbrauns: 301–22.

Hjelm, I. 2003. 'Brothers Fighting Brothers: Jewish and Samaritan Ethnocentrism in Tradition and History'. In *Jerusalem in Ancient History and Tradition.* T.L. Thompson (ed.). London and New York: T&T Clark International: 197–222. Arabic edition in *Al-Quds, Urūshalīm al-'adūr al-qadīma bīn altūrāh wa al-tārīkh* (*Al-Quds, The Ancient City of Jerusalem between Tradition and History*). T.L. Thompson and S.K. Jayyusi (eds). Beirut: Centre for Arab Unity Studies: 275–306.

——2004. *Jerusalem's Rise to Sovereignty. Zion and Gerizim in Competition* (*JSOTS* 404; *Copenhagen International Seminar* 14). London and New York: T&T Clark.

——2005. "Changing Paradigms: Judaean and Samarian Histories in Light of Recent Research". In *Historie og Konstruktion. Festskrift til Niels Peter Lemche i anledning af 60 års fødselsdagen den 6. september 2005.* M. Müller and T. L. Thompson (eds). Forum for Bibelsk Eksegese 14. Copenhagen: Museum Tusculanum: 161–79. In English.

Knauf, E.A. 1988. *Midian: Untersuchungen zur Geschichte Palästinas und Nordarabien am Ende des 2. Jahrtausends v. Chr.* Wiesbaden: Harrassowitz.

Knoppers, G.N. 2004. "In Search of Post-Exilic Israel: Samaria after the Fall of the Northern Kingdom". In *In Search of Pre-exilic Israel. Proceedings of the Oxford Old Testament Seminar.* J. Day (ed.). JSOTS 406. London and New York: T&T Clark International: 150–80.

Lawson Younger, Jr., K. 2004. "The Repopulation of Samaria (2 Kings 17:24, 27–31) in Light of Recent Study". In *The Future of Biblical Archaeology: Reassessing*

10   *A.K. de Hemmer Gudme and I. Hjelm*

Methodologies and Assumptions. The Proceedings of a Symposium August 12–14, 2001 at Trinity International University. J.K. Hoffmeier and A. Millard (eds). Grand Rapids, MI and Cambridge, UK: W.B. Eerdmans Publishing Company: 254–80.

Levin, C. and Ben Zvi, E. 2010. *The Concept of Exile in Ancient Israel and Its Historical Contexts.* Berlin: De Gruyter.

Lipschits, O. 2003. "Demographic Changes in Judah between the Seventh and the Fifth Centuries B.C.E.". In *Judah and Judaeans in the Neo-Babylonian Period.* O. Lipschits and J. Blenkinsopp (eds). Winona Lake, IN: Eisenbrauns: 323–76.

Na'aman, N. 1993. "Population Changes in Palestine Following Assyrian Deportations". *Tel Aviv* 20/1: 104–24.

Oded, B. 1979. *Mass Deportations and Deportees in the Neo-Assyrian Empire.* Wiesbaden: Reichert.

Ofer, A. 1994. "'All the Hill Country of Judah': From a Settlement Fringe to a Prosperous Monarchy". In *From Nomadism to Monarchy: Archaeological and Historical Aspects of Early Israel.* I. Finkelstein and N. Na'aman (eds). Jerusalem: Israel Exploration Society: 92–121.

Pearce, L.E. 2011. "'Judean': A Special Status in Neo-Babylonian and Achemenid Babylonia?" In *Judah and Judaeans in the Achaemenid Period: Negotiating Identity in an International Context.* O. Lipschits, G.N. Knoppers and M. Oeming (eds). Winona Lake, IN: Eisenbrauns: 267–77.

Sanders, J.A. 1976. "Exile". In *The Interpreter's Dictionary of the Bible.* Vol. 1. Nashville: Abingdon.

Stern, E. 2001. *Archaeology of the Land of the Bible. II. The Assyrian, Babylonian and Persian Periods (732–332 B.C.E.).* New York: Doubleday.

——2004. "The Babylonian Gap. The Archaeological Reality". *Journal for the Study of the Old Testament* 28: 273–77.

Thompson, T.L. 1992. *The Early History of the Israelite People. From the Written and Archaeological Sources.* Leiden: E.J. Brill.

——2011: "Genesis 4 and the Pentateuch's Reiterative Discourse: Some Samaritan Themes". In *Samaria, Samarians, Samaritans: Studies on Bible, History and Linguistics* (Studia Judaica 66, Studia Samaritana 6). J. Zsengeller (ed.). Berlin: de Gruyter: 9–22.

Zadok, R. 1979. *The Jews in Babylonia during the Chaldean and Achaemenian Periods according to the Babylonian Sources.* Studies in the History of the Jewish People and the Land of Israel Monograph Series 3. Haifa: The University of Haifa.

Zorn, J.R. 2003. "Tell en-Nasbeh and the Problem of the Material Culture of the Sixth Century". In *Judah and Judaeans in the Neo-Babylonian Period.* O. Lipschits and J. Blenkinsopp (eds). Winona Lake, IN: Eisenbrauns: 413–47.

Part I
Creating exilic identities

1 Exile as the great divide
Would there be an 'ancient Israel' without an exile?

Niels Peter Lemche

It is really remarkable how biblical studies have developed over the last generation. When I studied theology – in the heyday of classical historical-critical scholarship – early Israel explained everything. The formation of Israel and Israelite identity belonged to this period and to the dominating societal model of the time, the *amphictyony*, a league of twelve tribes.[1] Students would flunk at the examination in the Old Testament if they were not able to explain in detail every function of this sacral tribal league. Israel's traditions about its origins all belonged to the amphictyony where such holy traditions were nourished, not at the campfire among shepherds but within the sacral confines of the amphictyonic institutions. There might never have been a historical Abraham or Jacob as maintained by mainly German scholars,[2] or there might have been one as argued by their American colleagues,[3] but everyone was in agreement that the traditions about Abraham existed within the context of Israel's sacral league. The amphictyony was simply the *axis mundi* and everything turned around this centre.

Now, as argued years ago by Thomas Kuhn, dominating paradigms are bound one day to become too 'heavy' when they are used to explain everything and end up explaining nothing but their own existence (Kuhn 1962). As a consequence, they simply break down and sometimes leave no traces after them. This was very much what happened to the amphictyony. Around 1970, several scholars including this author (Lemche 1972) began asking questions in earnest about this amphictyony (a few, such as Otto Eissfeldt (1935 and 1975), Sigmund Mowinckel (1958) and Georg Fohrer (1966), had never succumbed to the impact of the hypothesis). This happened on the basis of historical-critical readings of the biblical historiography pertinent to the pre-state period. The amphictyony had to go because it was not found in biblical stories. However, the consequence was that scholars had to look for another period to pin the Israelite historical tradition. And the logical choice was the period of the united monarchy of David and Solomon. Here scholars following Gerhard von Rad placed the original home of the Yahwist and Israelite history writing (von Rad 1944).

The issue was to find a situation when all Israelite tribes were still together, and the period of David and Solomon seemed to be the last possible chance

14   *N.P. Lemche*

of finding a historical home for Israelite unity, at least in pre-Hasmonean times. After Solomon, the Israelite tribes split into two sections, Israel and Judah. The common Israelite tradition would have to originate in a time when a unity was supposed to exist. In the royal centre of Jerusalem, hectic activity took place when scribes and *Gelehrter* were commissioned to write the 'national' history of the newly established kingdom. In itself this theory about the origins of Israelite historiography was not a bad idea. There are indeed plenty of examples of historians getting such assignments, the period of Augustus being perhaps the most obvious, when Livy sat down to write his enormous history of Rome.[4] Livy was part of the intellectual circle around Augustus and simply had to cope with the anti-imperial sentiments still strong in higher Roman society. More modern examples have to do with the rise of modern history writing after the French revolution when a new kind of society was looking for its legitimation (Lemche 2008: 34–35).

History repeats itself. It was not long before the idea of a home for Israelite historiography at the court of David and Solomon came under attack, simply because the very existence of this court was questioned. The same happened to the reality of the image of the early Israelite monarchy as found in the Old Testament, which now went down the drain, taking with it also its major figures, David and Solomon. There was no royal city of Jerusalem when David and Solomon were supposed to have ruled from Jerusalem over a major kingdom stretching far into Syria (Palmyra).[5]

Much of the discussion about Israel's origins was founded on archaeology and the interpretation of what was found on the ground. Thus the American model of the Israelite conquest – very close to the story told by the Book of Joshua – rose and fell with the interpretation of the archaeology on which it was founded.[6] The same happened to the imperial city of Jerusalem in David's and Solomon's time. The very archaeology which should have supported the existence of the great centre of Jerusalem turned out to be a broken cane when it became clear that there were no traces of a great city here in this period. The long discussion, which was mainly conducted between Israeli archaeologists, more or less ended in a kind of stalemate when Israel Finkelstein gave in and said that maybe David was some local chieftain roaming the mountains of Judea (Finkelstein and Silberman 2006: 58–59). However, it was hardly so that this chieftain had an elaborate court where great histories were written down.

Now the catastrophe struck: Where did this unity between Israel and Judah, i.e. between all twelve of Israel's tribes, originate, when there was not a society embracing all parts of ancient Israel? Evidently there were no historical reasons for its existence. There was no institution in the pre-state period where such an idea of unity might have been kindled. Neither did anything turn up in the Iron Age allowing for an Israelite feeling of identity between all its components. The centuries following the alleged break-up of this alleged united monarchy never provided any occasion when such a pan-Israelite identity was in effect. On the contrary, the historiography of 1 and 2 Kings describes a continuous conflict between Jerusalem and Shechem, soon substituted by Samaria, as a kind of continuation of the conflict that previously existed in the Amarna Age, symbolized by the characters of Abdi-Ḥeba from Jerusalem and Lab'aya from Shechem.[7] This enmity between the north and south pops up again in the conflicts between Samaria and Jerusalem in the Persian (although only literarily attested in Nehemiah's story about the rebuilding of the walls of Jerusalem, Nehemiah 3–4; 6) and Hellenistic periods and is perpetuated in the conflict between Jews and Samaritans into Roman times.

Israel and Judah were never united during the Iron Age. It is a totally imagined unity belonging to another period. It is not reflecting any historical reality and should be left out as a paradigm for explaining historiography in the Old Testament or for that matter the history of ancient Palestine.

Now it is time to move down again to the next point in history during which the idea of an Israelite unity may have arisen. Logically this should be the exile, a period without Israelite and Judean presence in Palestine, or so it is argued in the Bible. From a historical point of view this is nonsense. The tiny stratum of *literati* – an expression nailed by Ehud Ben Zvi – from Judah, by all means a minor political entity in the southern mountains, may have been lifted from Jerusalem and Judah to Babylonia, but there was no exile from the former area of Samaria dating to the beginning of the 6th century. On the contrary, the former territory of the kingdom of Israel was left in peace by Nebuchadnezzar who had no problems with Samaria.[8] The deportation after the Assyrian conquest of Samaria was limited to, according to Sargon II, some 27,290 persons, perhaps about one tenth of the total population.[9]

Whether or not the descendants of people from Samaria merged with newly arrived deported people from Judah after 597/87 is unknown. Thus we cannot say that the idea of a united Israel arose by combining northern and southern traditions in the years following 587. Further, it should also be remembered that the Assyrians, over a period of two hundred years, carried out several deportations from many places, some of a much larger scale than the ones that hit Samaria and Jerusalem (Oded 1979; Lawson Younger 1998). It is not wrong to imagine the Assyrian empire as a melting pot not only of people but also of traditions from all over the ancient Near East. The population of the Assyrian core landscape around the city of Assur was never very large.[10] However, if the Babylonians brought some stray 10,000 or fewer immigrants from the west it would not have mattered much. Babylon alone counted for perhaps up to 200,000 people.[11] If biblical historiographers have something to contribute, the importance of the small number of deported people was mitigated somewhat by the decision to settle these people in one place in Mesopotamia close to the Khabur river, the Tel Abib of Ezekiel, which does not undermine the fact that the best sources for their life come from the Murašu archives from Nippur in Central Mesopotamia.[12]

Biblical tradition tells us that these were the true remains of the ancient population of Jerusalem and Judah, who at their return to the old land had a

16   *N.P. Lemche*

considerable task left to clean the land of its foreign population who had no right to the place where they were living. Biblical tradition says that after Cyrus' conquest of Babylon, the Jews were allowed to return to the land of their fathers, and so they did (2 Chron 36:22–23). History – and the Bible – says that this was far from true but makes it clear that during the following Persian period there was a comprehensive Jewish population in Mesopotamia.[13] To be sure, the Babylonian exile ended around 1950 CE when the Jewish population of Iraq was airlifted to Israel.[14] The same happened in Egypt, where – again according to scripture – there was a considerable community of refugees from Jerusalem and Judah, a society which did not return but settled in Egypt and became rather dominant in the newly founded Greek city of Alexandria in the Hellenistic Period.

Did the exile create these societies? In a way the answer is yes, but did it as a physical fact create the idea of the world popular in emerging Jewish societies outside of Palestine between 600 and 300 BCE? That was definitely the case, although we should give up the idea of seeing this exile as a punishment that forced early Jews to stay in foreign countries. Rather we should speak of a Jewish diaspora (in Hebrew *golah* means both exile and diaspora) as a place of Jewish communities that for the most part had no intention to 'return' to poor Palestine. Studying the living conditions in a Hellenistic city explains why they may not have found the perspective of moving to the naked hills of Judah very inviting.

In the Old Testament we find a plethora of traditions about origins from many places – some Palestinian, some Egyptian, some Mesopotamian, some relating to Phoenicia and Syria, and some deriving from Greek tradition. The writers who put these traditions together into (later) biblical literature were educated people – the literati. But did everything happen in one place? And where did it happen? In Jerusalem? The answer must be: Certainly not. There was hardly any city here of importance before the late Persian or the Hellenistic period. The Tel Aviv archaeologists say that Jerusalem only began to grow in the first part of the 2nd century BCE.[15] But then in Samaria? Samaria is a strong candidate because the city and its society were not destroyed.[16] The Assyrians conquered the place but did not destroy it, and Nebuchadnezzar had no interest in punishing Samaria for something of which it was not guilty.[17] In 325 BCE inhabitants of Samaria burned the Greek governor Andromachus and the city itself was turned into a Macedonian colony.[18] A new Samarian urban society arose at Gerizim next to ancient Shechem, at a time when it was the largest urban centre in central Palestine (cf. Magen 2007).

The dominant northern tradition found in biblical literature may owe its existence to the literary activities in the major 'Samarian' centres. Nowadays the Samaritans share their tradition with the Jews, including the Pentateuch. In spite of its Samarian origins, the Samaritan Pentateuch includes the same traditions as its Jewish counterpart, including also traditions that may have had very little to do with Samarian reality, such as the tradition about the return from Egypt after an exile there lasting for several hundred years. For this reason, we find in the Pentateuch, as it is handed down to us, a mixture of Judean and Samarian traditions, sometimes expressed via stories and information presenting an image of conflicting interests. An early study illustrating the animosity between Shechem and Jerusalem based on biblical stories can be found in Eduard Nielsen's almost sixty year old dissertation on Shechem from 1955 (Nielsen 1955).[19]

So, how many traditions did the Samarians provide for the Pentateuch? The answer is: In Genesis quite a few. And it continues in both Joshua almost exclusively referring to the territory of the Samarians, Judges, and the beginning of 1 Samuel. Then, how many traditions did the south provide for the authors of the Pentateuch? This time the answer is surprising: In Genesis, outside of the Abraham stories, not very many. Thus there is not a word about Jerusalem, although the definitely very late note about Abraham and Melkizedek in Genesis 14:18–20 may represent an endeavour to make up for the deficit.

However, when we arrive at the end of Genesis and move on to the Book of Exodus, we are in Egypt where the Samarians never were.[20] Again the conflict between the north and the south comes up here and there, as in the story of Joshua's scouts in Numbers 13–14, explaining why the Israelites had to travel around in the desert for forty years before they were allowed to enter Canaan from the east instead of from the south which would have been a natural choice if they came from Egypt.

The exodus story is pivotal when it comes to understanding the formation of the idea of the exile. Contrary to the rest of the Pentateuch, we also have a *terminus ante quem* for the formation of this story, in the first half of the 2nd century BCE, when the Jewish tragedian Ezekiel from Alexandria wrote his play on Exodus.[21] The extant fragments of Ezekiel's drama display a marked similarity with passages in the Book of Exodus, although we can never be sure that they are reflecting Ezekiel's own text. The quotations may have been standardized by later authors who quoted lines from Ezekiel in their own writings, making them conform to the text of the Septuagint.[22]

However, the general plot is clear, and Ezekiel definitely knew the story of the Exodus and was interested in presenting it to his audience in a dramatic way. Here we have some building blocks for the formation of the tradition of the first Israelite exile, the one in Egypt. Another building block is found in Josephus (*Contra Apionem* 1.16ff.) where Josephus launches a furious attack on Manetho (most likely dating to the 3rd century BCE) for his description of the expulsion of the Hyksos, understood by Josephus to be the Israelites. Normally biblical scholars are very reluctant to see the exodus narrative as a variant of the Egyptian story about the expulsion of the Hyksos people.[23] The historical background for this event lies back at the beginning of the Late Bronze Age (before 1500 BCE), so there can be no discussion of the primacy of the Egyptian tradition.

We do not have Manetho's own text of the expulsion of the Hyksos but only the résumé of Manetho in Josephus, and Josephus' résumé is, if anything,

18   *N.P. Lemche*

extremely biased. Thus we do not know if Manetho was at all referring to his contemporary Jews or simply included in his Egyptian history the ancient legend about the Hyksos. Because of this we cannot even say whether or not Manetho knew of the Jewish exodus-tradition or whether this tradition of the exodus depended on Manetho and represented rewritten Manetho. However, in the case that Manetho really was the basis on which the exodus tradition in the Bible was formed, we have a clue to the background on which the Jewish ideas of the exile in Egypt and later escape from Egypt were formed. We do not have to refer to any discussion about the historicity of the event. It never happened.

Now it is understandable that a story about travelling from Egypt to the land of Israel might have been in existence among early Jews living in Egypt. After all, their world was not a closed one and Egyptian tradition knew stories about both private people and Egyptian officials travelling to Palestine and Phoenicia, including plain fiction.[24] Although the rulers of Egypt in the Persian period were already at odds with the Persian Empire, the borders were not closed for the exchange of material goods, ideas, and human travellers. The situation continued after Alexander's death. Here the Greek rulers of Egypt were involved in several wars with their Seleucid colleagues in Western Asia, but such problems between two ancient states were of minor importance in comparison to the material and intellectual explosion that followed the arrival of the Greeks, creating a new culture shared by all of the eastern Mediterranean.[25]

However, it seems as if somebody tried to get in control of the Egyptianized Jewish tradition that brought Israel from Egypt to, well, where to? Hecataeus from Abdera, roughly contemporary with Manetho and perhaps also Ezekiel, refers to a Jerusalem, which was founded by Moses.[26] The Hellenistic traditions about the exodus and the 'conquest' display such a variety and such a difference compared to the official biblical tradition that it is meaningful to say that they had no idea about the present editions of these traditions in the Torah, and if they had, they did not feel compelled by these editions.

Where did the control of tradition begin? One way to put the Egyptian exodus into perspective would be to introduce an earlier exodus, which would be the exodus of Abraham to Canaan as a result of the direct intervention of God himself (Gen 12:1–9). Furthermore, this exodus of Abraham from Mesopotamia is put into perspective by his experiences in Egypt showing how potentially treacherous Egypt might be (Gen 12:10–20).[27] In some way we have an exodus (from Mesopotamia) predating the Exodus from Egypt, but also this exodus of Abraham is modified and brought under control by his visit to Egypt.

A better place to see the extent of the controlling factor of another party which took care of the Exodus tradition will be to look at the break in the Exodus narrative which was the main thrust of Gerhard von Rad's famous study of the form history of the Pentateuch, when he argued in favour of a break in the narrative in the Pentateuch at Sinai where the Israelites remained for almost sixty chapters in the biblical story, breaking it up in two separate parts and destroying any dramatic story line which this narrative may have had (von Rad 1938). Although von Rad's theory has been modified several times, he was basically right.

At Sinai, Israel is given the law by God. First we have the Ten Commandments which open with a statement: Israel can have only one God. The rest is mostly of a general character, although the commandment to keep the Sabbath is definitely Jewish. However, no society can accept murder and theft, and ownership is a cornerstone in all ancient Near Eastern societies, as is the relation between the generations. On the other hand, the next part of the legislation at Sinai has its roots in Babylonian academic legal tradition, about which we are informed from the time of the laws of Eshnunna, Lagash, and Hammurabi until neo-Assyrian times and beyond.[28] The first part of the Book of the Covenant (Exod 21:1–22:16) could just as well have been written in Akkadian.[29] The second part is written in the same style and keeps the form of the first part – the classic Mesopotamian law introduced by a protasis stating the case and followed by an apodosis describing the consequences – but its content is unparalleled in Mesopotamian tradition and concerns religious matters. The following many chapters, including rules for most aspects of life, are basically a law for Jewish society although many of these laws, such as the laws that regulate relations within the family, are most likely shared with other societies of Western Asia.

Reading the Pentateuch in this way, the act of control as found in the Sinai legislation exacted on the Egyptian-oriented traditions recalls what happened when in early Islamic history the Umayyads were ousted and substituted by the much more 'Islamistic' Abbasids. Now Judaism should have rules for everything, and the hero of the tales that brought Israel from Egypt to Canaan also had to find his place in the desert to the east of the chosen land. The identification of those who wanted to control the exodus tradition is not too difficult. After all, their hero was Ezra who travelled to Jerusalem from the centre of the Persian Empire in order to settle matters in Jerusalem. Whether he was a historical person or invented for the occasion is, in this context, immaterial.

It will definitely be possible to talk about two conflicting exodus traditions, one from Egypt and another from Mesopotamia and relate both of them to stages in the formation of early Judaism. As a matter of fact, the Pentateuch is, together with other biblical books, a gold mine for such studies when the assumed historical referent is left out of consideration. I have previously often maintained that we have to liberate the Old Testament from history. It now seems to be the case in advanced biblical scholarship. The historical skeleton of Israel's past as described in the biblical books is invented. There should be little doubt about this basic fact. So much more reason for concentrating on the meaning of this history.

But to quote Churchill, we are not at the end, not even at the beginning of the end; we are at the end of the beginning. What is the purpose of creating all these stories about exile and return?

20   *N.P. Lemche*

The clearest expression of a negative interpretation of the Babylonian exile is found in Psalm 137.

> By the rivers of Babylon, there we sat down, yea we wept, when we remembered Zion.
> We hung our harps upon the willows in the midst thereof.
> For there they that had carried us away captive required of us a song.[30]

The major part of Old Testament texts relating to the Babylonian exile is kept in this tone: The exile was like a prison, a punishment from God who gave up his people, his temple, and his land. This accords very well with texts relating to the end of the exile. Take Deutero-Isaiah as an example. From the very beginning, the talk is about a triumphant return to a place that only longs for the return of the people in exile redeemed by God. The reality was that most preferred to stay in Babylon and Egypt. A text like Deutero-Isaiah is best seen as propaganda, with the intent of persuading the people of God that its place is in God's own country. It also created a forum for Judaism, an idea of being united through the same tragic events. Living in exile is a tragedy; however, if you lived in Mesopotamia or in Egypt it was a very tolerable one, as these countries were the richest places in the ancient world, places where you did not need to speculate about food for tomorrow. There hunger was practically unknown, but it was the condition of the Palestinian population who often had to suffer famine and starvation. The motive of the Israelites of the Exodus complaining of having been tricked to leave Egypt for a country that flows with milk and honey clearly reflects the harsh realities of returning to Jerusalem.

Now we have already pointed at a series of reasons for creating a tradition about deportation and return. More are to come. In the Books of Ezra and Nehemiah the plot is governed by ideas about who had the right to inherit God's own country. The Book of Ezra opens with a long list of people who returned and had their papers clear: They were really Jews and descendants of the people who were led into exile. The Book of Nehemiah closes with the purging of non-Jews from Jewish society. Intermarrying with local people could not be tolerated. God's own country was reserved for God's own people. It is easy to see the problem. In the Persian and Hellenistic periods, Palestine may have seen the arrival of foreign people with a new Yahwistic religion – or newly reformulated. According to the propaganda of the new settlers, the country was theirs. However, it was not an empty country as argued by biblical literature; it was populated by people not sharing the religion of the immigrants. As Albrecht Alt wrote in his second essay on the immigration of the Israelites, the first state of this immigration had to do with immigration, rather peaceful and not resented by the former inhabitants of Palestine (Alt 1939). The second stage, however, was different. Now the immigrants were becoming the majority of the country and now they began to expand at the cost of the previous population. It might very well be the case of the return of Jews from Mesopotamia and perhaps Egypt. Few at the beginning, they grew into the strongest political organization in the land and their ideology became the one accepted as the cultural memory of the early Jewish society.

When asked, did the experience of the exile make an impression on the people in exile, the answer may be it did, but only gradually. In order to formulate an exilic identity, local traditions were reformulated. Jews living in Egypt made use of the Hyksos tradition which they turned upside down in their own favour and created the story about a return, however, much earlier than the return from Babylon. The question is: How did this Jewish society emerge? There is no space here for more than a sketch of an answer. The explanation may follow the lines of communication. We have in the Persian and in the early Hellenistic period at least three 'Jewish' societies, i.e. societies whose religion displays a number of mutual traits: One in Egypt, another in central Mesopotamia, and a third in Palestine, alias the future Samarians (Samaritans). In other parts of the Near East a series of satellite Jewish communities undoubtedly arose. These societies were in many ways similar, but at the same time dissimilar, mostly because of their adoption of local traditions. As I already stated, stable political and economic organizations improved communication. It was possible to travel between various centres. It took only a few days to travel from Egypt to Palestine; the distance between the Delta and Palestine is little more than a 100 kilometres. The distance to Mesopotamia is much longer, about 800 kilometres as few people could traverse the desert. Moreover, people belonging to the elite did travel, especially in the Hellenistic period.

Now why an exile? Again if we read the stories about exile and return, including the return of Abraham as well as the return of the tribes under the leadership of Joshua, and the return from Babylon, we may see them as answers to the pollution of the country caused by human beings. This does not so much involve Abraham, who had hardly arrived before he left and went to Egypt where he sold his wife to Pharaoh and became rich. On the other hand, when Jacob leaves Canaan together with his sons (Gen 42–45; 46), it is seen as a response to the pollution of the country which was linked to the way Joseph was handed over to the Egyptians by his brothers (Gen 37:23–36). It was a crime that made the country unclean, and, in order to regain its status as the holy land, the family of Jacob had to leave. It was, however, still their land, because it was a gift from God. Therefore the genocide that followed the return of Jacob's sons in the form of the twelve Israelite tribes was a legitimate one. The Canaanites were foreign to God and for that reason not allowed to live in God's country.[31]

The long history from Joshua to 2 Kings is basically a long complaint about the behaviour of the Israelites after having signed the covenant with Yahweh at Shechem (Joshua 24). This history concentrates on the Israelites and their kings being incapable of keeping even the first commandment. And at the end of their presence in the country they had polluted, the land given

22   N.P. Lemche

to them by God, they were sent away by the very same God in order that the country should be cleansed of their sin. Two things remain: The Israelites are still Israelites, and the land is still theirs *qua* being the gift of God. The fathers polluted the country with their sin, but the sons have no deal in the sins of their fathers (not every biblical writer would agree: the sons got bad teeth because of the sins of their fathers! Jeremiah 31:29). When the Israelites were cleansed from the sins of their fathers, they were invited to return to the land of God – which is essentially the message of Deutero-Isaiah. Now, the land is in other hands, but the local people were not entitled to a part of the land and, in the same way as in the Book of Joshua with its violent message of genocide, these people had to leave, dead or alive. The Book of Joshua allowed for an exception, when the Gibeonites by fraud obtained permission to stay (Joshua 9). In the case of the return from the Babylonian exile, nobody without a proper Jewish passport should be given the chance to live on in the land of God.

The biblical Babylonian exile is simply invented in order to state this point. This does not imply that there were no deportations or exiles. As already said, there were plenty, but the special emphasis in the Old Testament is on the Babylonian exile and not other exiles that may have been operative as a marker that creates boundaries between Jews and local non-Jewish inhabitants of Palestine. So what came first: The idea of the Babylonian exile or the writers who wrote the story of the Babylonian exile? This brings us back to my thesis: The exile did not create a people – we might almost say a 'nation' – living in exile. It was the other way around. The writers involved in the creation of biblical stories about Israel did not belong to a people living in exile. They were definitely Jews, living in the Jewish Diaspora in the Hellenistic Period, and they created the story about the forced exile in order to explain why they and their kinsmen were not living in the holy land of their fathers. But the story also includes a utopian hope for the future, when every Jew has returned to his ancestral home.

The third group here called 'Jews', i.e. the 'Samarians', understood as the people who lived at Gerizim in the early Hellenistic Period, had no part in the myth of the exile. The people living in the territory of the former state of Samaria were – apart from a fraction towards the end of the 8th century and maybe another fraction deported by the Macedonians – never sent into exile. They remained in their country and their worship of the one and only God, Yahweh, was centred on their holy mountain of Gerizim which was the centre of their self-identification as it still was on the two Hellenistic inscriptions in Greek from Delos where 'Israelites' living on Crete stress their allegiance to the sanctuary at Gerizim. Within the emic/etic distinction of ethnicity, it is the only case where we have a definite 'emic' use of the name of Israel.[32] Here we really have reasons for a conflict: On one hand new Jewish immigrants to Palestine seeing Jerusalem as *their* holy place, and on the other 'Israelites', i.e. Samarians or Samaritans, understanding Gerizim as *their* religious home. When we compare the competition between Jerusalem and Samaria, later

Shechem, to the otherwise attested traditional conflict in central Palestine between north and south it is not so difficult to understand why, when Jerusalem or its Hasmonean rulers destroyed the temple at Gerizim, it had, as a result, a mutual disrespect and outlawing, making it clear why the Samaritans in opposition to the Jews were not to be persuaded to join the Jerusalem 'club'.

Not only are the stories of exile and return in the Old Testament invented, they also represent very strong political arguments and were used as such. The interesting thing is that the modern use of the idea of an exile, i.e. by the Zionists who created a story about exile and return, has shown how powerful such stories are. Most of the elements belonging to the biblical story have been repeated in recent times in order to demonstrate that the Jewish immigrants to Palestine are the legitimate heirs of this country, because it is the country of their fathers. If anything, the idea of a return from exile became *the* cultural memory of Jewish civilization but in the hands of the Zionist movement it also became a formidable political tool to achieve the political goals of Zionism. This has nothing to do with whether we like or dislike Zionism; it is simply a very clever strategy for an imagined society. I am quite sure that the Palestinians are aiming at creating their own story of exile and future return.

And hereby we are at the end of the end.

Notes

1 The classic formulation of the thesis was M. Noth 1930. Cf. further M. Noth 1950: 105–30. The impact of the thesis is made clear by its acceptance by the students of W.F. Albright, otherwise a staunch opponent of Noth. Cf. J. Bright 1960: 128–60.

2 Since the days of W.M.L. de Wette more than two hundred years ago. It is revealing to read de Wette's way of dealing with the stories about Abraham, in de Wette 1807: 59–68, and again 1807: 76–116. From here it is only a short step to Wellhausen's famous dictum: *Die Geschichte eines Volkes läßt sich nicht über das Volk selber hinausführen, in einer Zeit, wo dasselbe noch gar nicht vorhanden war.* Wellhausen 1894: 10.

3 Primarily W.F. Albright and his students. Cf. Albright 1957: 236–49, Albright 1963: 1–9; Bright 1960: 60–93.

4 Livy (59 [or 64] BCE–17 CE) belonged to the circle of the imperial family of Augustus. He started writing his history in the beginning of Augustus' reign promoting the new political system.

5 This is definitely not the place to go into a detailed discussion of Jerusalem in the 10th century BCE. The discussion was summarized in Vaughn and Killebrew 2003 by contributions by Jane M. Cahill (Cahill 2003), Israel Finkelstein (Finkelstein 2003), David Ussishkin (Ussishkin 2003), and Margret Steiner (Steiner 2003; cf. also Steiner 2001). Steiner's estimate of the population (c. 1000 inhabitants) would have allowed for less than two hundred grown-up males (allowing for a family size of c. five persons). Steiner talks about a "small fortified town, located on top of a hill, with some public buildings and little room for residential areas" (Steiner 2001: 52). We may prefer not to call it a town but a fortress (*Burg*). Even if Eilat Mazar's findings should end up being dated to the 10th century BCE (Mazar 2006) it will not change Steiner's conclusion.

6 See especially Finkelstein 1988.

24   *N.P. Lemche*

7 Lab'aya is often described as a bandit vis-à-vis his neighbours (thus Finkelstein and Silberman 2006: 51). However, he was probably not very different from other central Palestinian governors in the Amarna period. Thus after Lab'aya's death Šuwardata from Qiltu (Keilah?) or Gath writes "moreover, Lab'aya, who took our cities, has died, but now Abdi-Ḥeba is another Lab'aya who takes our cities" (EA 280:30–35). Abdi-Ḥeba was the governor of Jerusalem.

8 Zedekiah was the vassal of the Babylonian king but broke his oath of loyalty and was duly punished. Samaria had no part in Zedekiah's rebellion. As to evidence 'on the ground', compare for Judah Lipschits 2003, for Benjamin Faust 2012: 209–31, and for Samaria Zertal 2003.

9 Deportations from Samaria 722: Sargons II's annals: ANET 288. The number seems not farfetched, when compared to Sennacherib's inflated numbers in connection with his 701 campaign: 200,150 persons deported (Sennacherib Annals III:24).

10 Assur itself covered at its largest some 70 hectares allowing for a population of perhaps 50,000. Dominique Charpin (1995: 822) refers to the Assyrian habit of concentrating a disproportionate part of the population in its successive capitals as a major reason for the Assyrian collapses.

11 Size of Babylon: c. 9 square kilometres. Any population estimate is of course highly questionable, but can be used in comparisons between different localities. Niniveh at its highest thus embraced c. 7 square kilometres with an estimated population not higher than 150,000 persons.

12 Murashu: Cf. A.T. Clay 1904.

13 Without which a story like Esther would be meaningless, and also the evidence from the Murašu archive tells about their presence c. 400 BCE in central Mesopotamia.

14 Involving more than 120,000 persons during the so-called Operation Ezrah and Nehemiah, 1951–52 (www.jewishvirtuallibrary.org/jsource/Immigration/ezra.html).

15 This is, of course, a hot spot of discussion. Archaeologists from the Hebrew University in Jerusalem normally argue for an interpretation of the archaeological findings that does not contradict the biblical image of the rebuilding of Jerusalem in Nehemiah's time, sometime in the 5th century BCE. Their opponents at Tel Aviv University have quite different ideas, although not completely in agreement. Compare Lipschits 2009 (50 dunams) to Finkelstein 2008 and 2009 (less than a hectare) and Ussishkin 2006 (a small settlement that only began to grow in the 2nd century BCE).

16 Cf. on Samaria in 722 BCE Tappy 2001.

17 In contrast, Zedekiah and his country were punished according to the book having broken his oath of vassalage. His predecessor was removed by the Babylonians and brought to Babylon in 597 BCE, but he evidently did not experience any physical punishment. He was not Nebuchadnezzar's vassal, but the vassal of the Pharaoh.

18 Curtius Rufus, *Historiae Alexandri Magni* [1st century CE], IV, 8–11.

19 Cf. more on this in Lemche 2013.

20 Although Josephus has put a story together about Ptolemy I who, as Alexander's general, conquered Jerusalem, after which he deported the inhabitants together with those living around Gerizim to Egypt and used them to populate the newly founded city of Alexandria (Josephus, *Antiquitates*, 12.1). Whether or not this happened is another matter, as there would not have been much of a Jerusalem to conquer. If it ever happened, it would provide another possibility for understanding how these Alexandrian diaspora Jews (including also former Samarians) created a new ethnic synthesis based on the recollection of common origins. (I am indebted to Ingrid Hjelm for pointing out this Ptolemean environment for the establishment of a common 'Israelite' tradition about the past which is certainly something to be elaborated on in the future.)

21 The fragments from Ezekiel's work are translated by R.G. Robertson in Charlesworth 1985: 803–19.

22 The dissertation of F.A. Nielsen, *The Exodus Story According to Ezekiel the Tragedian and the Exodus Manuscripts from Qumran: A Study of the Early Text History of the Book of Exodus* (unpublished Ph.D. dissertation, the University of Copenhagen, 2000), deals extensively with the status of the fragments of Ezekiel's tragedy.
23 Cf., however, Gmirkin 2006: 170–91 on Manetho and the Hyksos.
24 We may think of the tales of Sinuhe and Wen-Amon. On New Kingdom imagining of the past, cf. C. Manassa 2013.
25 That the competition between the Seleucis and Ptolemaic empires was not only about military supremacy can be seen from the cultural politics of the Ptolemees, creating already in the early 3rd century BCE both the library of Alexandria and the Museion, the centre of intellectual life.
26 Hecataeus as preserved in Diodorus Siculus, Bibliotheca Historica 40.3.
27 On Egypt as a death trap, Lemche 2001.
28 On Babylonian law tradition, Lemche 2008: 244–46.
29 Cf. among others Paul 1970, and several studies by R. Westbrook (Westbrook 2009), although their way of using this material is very different to the views of the present writer.
30 Cf. on this Psalm, my "Psalm 137: Exile as hell!" in this volume.
31 On the role of the Canaanites as the bad guys of a narrative, cf. Lemche 1991.
32 Cf. further on these inscriptions, Lemche 2012.

Bibliography

Albright, W.F. 1957. *From the Stone Age to Christianity: Monotheism and the Historical Process.* 2nd edn. Garden City, New York: Doubleday.
——1963. *The Biblical Period from Abraham to Ezra.* New York: Harper & Row.
Alt, A. 1939. "Erwägungen über die Landnahme der Israeliten in Palästina". Reprinted in A. Alt, *Kleine Schriften zur Geschichte Israels*, I. 1953. München: Beck: 126–75.
Bright, J. 1960. *A History of Israel.* London: SCM Press.
Cahill, J.M. 2003. "Jerusalem at the Time of the United Monarchy: The Archaeological Evidence". In Vaughn and Killebrew 2003: 13–80.
Charlesworth, J.H. 1985. *The Old Testament Pseupepigrapha*, Vol. II. New York: Doubleday.
Charpin, D. 1995. "The History of Ancient Mesopotamia: An Overview". In *Civilizations of the Ancient Near East* II. J. Sasson (ed.). New York: Charles Scribner's Sons.
Clay, A.T. 1904. *Business Documents of Murashû Sons of Nippur Dated in the Reign of Darius II (424–404 B. C.).* Philadelphia: Department of Archaeology and Palaeontology, University of Pennsylvania.
Eissfeldt, O. 1935. "Der geschichtliche Hintergrund der Erzählung von Gibeas Schandtat (Richter 19–21)". Reprinted in *Kleine Schriften* II. Tübingen, 1963: 64–80.
——1975. "The Hebrew Kingdom". In *Cambridge Ancient History* II.2. I.E.S. Edwards, C.J. Gadd, N.G.L. Hammond and E. Sollberger (eds): 537–605.
Faust, A. 2012. *Judah in the Neo-Babylonian Period: The Archaeology of Desolation.* Atlanta: Society of Biblical Literature.
Finkelstein, I. 1988. *The Archaeology of the Israelite Settlement.* Jerusalem: Israel Exploration Society.
——2003. "The Rise of Jerusalem and Judah: The Missing Link". In Vaughn and Killebrew 2003: 81–102.

26   N.P. Lemche

——2008. "The Settlement History of Jerusalem in the Eighth and Seventh Centuries BCE". *RB* 115: 499–515.

——2009. "Persian Period Jerusalem and Jehud: A Rejoinder". *Journal of Hebrew Scriptures* 9: 24, available online at http://jhsonline.org/Articles/article_126.pdf

Finkelstein, I. and N.A. Silberman. 2006. *David and Solomon: In Search of the Bible's Sacred Kings and the Roots of the Western Tradition.* New York: Free Press.

Fohrer, G. 1966. "'Amphiktyonie' und 'Bund'". Reprint in his *Studien zur alttestamentlichen Theologie und Geschichte. BZAW,* 115. Berlin: De Gruyter.

Gmirkin, R.E. 2006. *Berossus and Genesis, Manetho and Exodus. Hellenistic Histories and the Date of the Pentateuch.* New York and London: T&T Clark

Knudtzon, J. A. 1907–1915. *Die el-Amarna-Tafeln.* Leipzig: J.C. Hinrich.

Kuhn, T. 1962. *The Structure of Scientific Revolutions.* Chicago: University Press.

Lawson Younger, Jr., K. 1998. "The Deportations of the Israelites". *JBL* 117: 201–27.

Lemche, N.P. 1972. *Israel i Dommertiden: En oversigt over diskussionen om Martin Noths "Das System der zwölf Stämme Israels."* Copenhagen: G. E. C. Gads Forlag.

——1991. *The Canaanites and their Land. The Idea of Canaan in the Old Testament.* Sheffield: Academic Press.

——2001. "'Fra Ægypten kaldte jeg min søn' (Hosea 11,1) – Exodusmyten i den gammeltestamentlige tradition". In *Traditionen om Ægypten,* vol. 1. E. Christiansen (ed.). Århus: Tidsskriftet Sfinx: 167–76.

——2008. *The Old Testament between Theology and History: A Critical Survey.* Louisville: Westminster John Knox.

——2012. "The Greek Israelites and Gerizim". In *Plogbillar & svärd: En festskrift till Stig Norin.* T. Davidivich (ed.). Uppsala: Molin & Sorgenfrei: 147–54.

——2013. "When the Past Becomes the Present". *SJOT* 27: 98–108.

Lipschits, O. 2003. "Demographic Changes in Judah between the Seventh and the Fifth Centuries B.C.E." In Lipschits and Blenkinsopp 2003: 323–76.

——2009. "Persian Period Finds from Jerusalem: Facts and Interpretations". *Journal of Hebrew Scriptures* 9: 20, available online at http://jhsonline.org/Articles/article_122.pdf

Lipschits, O. and J. Blenkinsopp. 2003. *Judah and the Judeans in the Neo-Babylonian Period.* Winona Lake, IN: Eisenbrauns.

Magen, Y. 2007. "The Dating of the First Phase of the Samaritan Temple on Mount Gerizim". In *Judah and the Judeans in the Fourth Century B.C.E.* O. Lipschits, G.N. Knoppers and R. Albertz (eds). Winona Lake, IN: Eisenbrauns.

Manassa, C. 2013. *Imagining the Past: Historical Fiction in New Kingdom Egypt.* Oxford: Oxford University Press, 2013.

Mazar, E. 2006. "Did I Find King David's Palace?" *Biblical Archaeology Review* Jan/Feb 2006, available online at www.biblicalarchaeology.org/daily/biblical-sites-places/jerusalem/did-i-find-king-davids-palace/

Mowinckel, S. 1958. "'Rahelstämme' und 'Leastämme'". *BZAW* 77. Berlin: De Gruyter: 129–50.

Nielsen, E. 1955. *Shechem: A Traditio-Historical Investigation.* Copenhagen: G.E.C. Gad.

Noth, M. 1930. *Das System der zwölf Stämme Israels.* Stuttgart: W. Kohlhammer.

——1950. *Geschichte Israels.* Göttingen: Vandenhoeck & Ruprecht.

Oded, B. 1979. *Mass Deportations and Deportees in the Neo-Assyrian Empire.* Wiesbaden: Dr. Ludwig Reichert Verlag.

Paul, S. 1970. *Studies in the Book of the Covenant in the Light of Cuneiform and Biblical Law*. Leiden: E.J. Brill.

Pritchard, J.B. (ed.). 1969. *Ancient Near Eastern Texts: Relating to the Old Testament*, 3rd edition. Princeton: Princeton University Press.

Rad G. von, 1938. *Das formgeschichtliche Problem des Hexateuch*. Reprinted in G. von Rad, *Gesammelte Studien zum Alten Testament*. München: Chr. Kaiser: 9–86.

——1944. "Der Anfang der Geschichtsschreibung im alten Israel". Reprinted in G. von Rad, *Gesammelte Studien zum Alten Testament*. München: Beck, 1958: 148–88.

Steiner, M.L. 2001. *Excavations by Kathleen M. Kenyon in Jerusalem 1961–1967, Volume III: The Settlement in the Bronze and Iron Ages*. London: Sheffield Academic Press.

——2003. "The Evidence from Kenyon's Excavations in Jerusalem: A Response Essay". In Vaughn and Killebrew 2003: 347–64.

Tappy, R.E. 2001. *The Archaeology of Israelite Samaria*, 2. Winona Lake, IN: Eisenbrauns, 2001.

Ussishkin, D. 2003. "Solomon's Jerusalem: The Text and the Facts on the Ground". In Vaughn and Killebrew 2003: 103–16.

——2006. "The Borders and de facto Size of Jerusalem in the Persian Period". In Judah and Judeans in the Persian Period. O. Lipschitz and M. Oeming (eds). Winona Lake, IN: Eisenbrauns: 147–66.

Vaughn, A.G. and A.E. Killebrew (eds). 2003. *Jerusalem in Bible and Archaeology: The First Temple Period*. Atlanta: Society of Biblical Literature.

Wellhausen, J. 1894. *Israelitische und jüdische Geschichte*. 9th edn. Berlin: de Gruyter, 1958.

Westbrook, R. 2009. *Law from the Tigris to the Tiber: The Writings of Raymond Westbrook*. Winona Lake, IN: Eisenbrauns.

de Wette, W.M.L. 1807. *Beiträge zur Einleitung in das Alte Testament Band II: Kritik der Israelitischen Geschichte erster Teil*. Halle: bei Schimmelpfennig und Companie.

Zertal, A. 2003. "The Province of Samaria (Assyrian *Samerina*) in the Late Iron Age (Iron Age III)". In Lipschits and Blenkinsopp 2003: 377–412.

2 God leading his people

Exodus' *longue durée*[1]

Fabio Porzia

According to the anthropological approach that regards human culture as a 'symbol system', human beings live in a universe populated by signs (Geertz 1973; Hofstee 1986). Material images are the objects of iconography,[2] while verbal images are the subject of literary analysis,[3] each discipline having its own method. However, in biblical studies, these disciplines suffered a different fate: the former atrophic and the latter hypertrophic.[4] This was not only because of the classic assumption that texts were purer than material culture. In the biblical realm, another element should be considered; namely, that the late biblical programmatic aniconism (and anti-iconism), imposed by Deuteronomy, achieved its goal and conveyed an 'iconoclastic' understanding of ancient Israel rooted in words,[5] which was from time to time disturbed – but not always contradicted – by archaeological finds. Addressing this problem, some scholars tried a new approach: 'iconographic exegesis', although its theoretical and methodological frame has been only recently elaborated (Keel, *ABD* III, 358–74 but especially de Hulster 2009a). The aim is to associate icons – which are as close in time and space as possible – with a biblical passage or expression, so that it might be better understood (see also Klingbeil 1999: 158–65, 268–82; Uehlinger 2000: xv–xxxii; 2006, 2007; Ben-Shlomo 2010: 1–13, 177–90). This chapter attempts an iconographic exegesis patterned after de Hulster (2009a: 148). Our research will proceed as follows: (1) choice of theme; (2) a separate analysis of textual evidence from the Hebrew Bible; (3) an independent study of iconographic evidence from Israel/Palestine; (4) a broader analysis of textual and iconographic evidence from the Ancient Near East;[6] and (5) interrelation of the several, independent conclusions of the foregoing analysis. Historical conclusions will close this chapter, illustrating the ideological network which existed in the East Mediterranean region during the Late Bronze and Iron Ages.

Choice of theme: God leading a people

The Hebrews[7] usually refer to themselves, and are referred to, as the 'chosen people'. If we look at the origin of this choice, we certainly find Abraham. At that time, however, according to the Bible, Israel was nothing more

God leading his people   29

than a promised people: it could have grown only in Egypt, reaching an expansion recognized not as a family or a clan but as a people. Since God's leadership in the exodus is the "most important tradition which prevailed in Israel throughout the biblical period" (Hoffman 1989: 169), this is the theme we choose for our present inquiry.

To be a people with or without a land – and its connected political establishment – makes a difference. The Hebrews had to face this difference several times during their history. They were early forerunners of a world phenomenon that, in recent times, has gained increasing legitimacy, namely 'diasporism'. The paradox of the Hebrew unity existing, both in consciousness and in practice, alongside divisive social and cultural processes was granted by the choice of the myth of allogeny instead of autochthony, finally achieved by the final redaction of the Bible.

This peculiar *forma mentis* has certainly played a role in the phenomenon of diaspora – sometimes voluntary, sometimes compulsory – which characterized the distribution of the Hebrew people since the sixth century BCE, first in a Mediterranean context and then world-wide. The shock of exile elaborated and developed identity, created by a history and tradition which is accorded common categories throughout the whole Near East. The context of migration, creating a unified people, supports an analysis of identity, which increasingly depends on mixed cultural exchanges.

It is obvious that, in the frame of the Persian and Hellenistic Diaspora, concepts of distance from the homeland and of living abroad became important (Ben Zvi and Levin 2010; Rom-Shiloni 2013), as is recently conveyed in the not unproblematic idea of negotiating an identity (Lipschits *et al.* 2011). Certainly, the commonly accepted late redaction of the *Torah* justifies the role of migration in Jewish history. From the Persian period onward, the people actually started to represent its origins in terms of a double migration: first from Mesopotamia (with Abraham) and then from Egypt (with Moses).[8] Of course, the relative chronology of these migrations is based on the biblical narration.[9]

The fortune gained by these narratives also reached classical authors, with the predominance of the exodus traditions over the patriarchal ones.[10] Briefly, the exodus became the ground on which the Hebrews gradually shaped their identity as a people able to survive abroad and in difficult circumstances.

Within the *Torah*, the book of Exodus unquestionably holds a central place, both because the three next books of the *Torah* are developed from it and because Exodus is narratively linked to Genesis (Römer 1990; Schmid 1999; de Pury 2003). One might argue that four fifths of the *Torah* develops a common theme, the exodus, while the remaining fifth constitutes its prequel. As Hendel stated: "The exodus from Egypt is a focal point of ancient Israelite religion. Virtually every kind of religious literature in the Hebrew Bible – prose narrative, liturgical poetry, didactic prose, and prophecy – celebrates the exodus as a foundational event" (2001: 601).

Although the patriarchal traditions and the exodus were independent and disconnected until the exilic period,[11] particular and everlasting traits are

30   F. Porzia

attributed to the divinity in the book of Exodus. The most striking one is that God is the leader; that is, he is the one who liberated, brought out, saved and set his people free.[12] Before it is the argument of a particular book, God's leadership in the exodus from Egypt is the most frequently mentioned theme, motif and tradition in the Hebrew Bible (more than 120 times). While there is no biblical feast to commemorate the creation, the Patriarchs or the conquest of Canaan, the deeds of God linked with the exodus are mentioned in all three annual feasts, as well as the shabbath (Deut 5:12–15).

Textual evidence from the Hebrew Bible

Moving our inquiry to biblical evidence, the following question arises: how does the relevant biblical literature relate to our theme?

While modern languages use a noun (exodus) to refer to that theme, the Hebrew Bible does not. That the noun ἔξοδος, with the sense of exodus from Egypt, is scantly attested even in the *Septuagint* (only Exod 19:1; Num 33:38; 1 Kgs 6:1; Ps 104:38, 113:1), suggests that by the time of its redaction the nominal form had not yet been established. Both in the Hebrew Bible and in the *Septuagint*, exodus is expressed by verbs and thus characterized as an action (God's agency), or better a set of actions, rather than a concept.

Scholars described these verbal expressions used by Hebrew and Greek Bibles in several ways: formula (Humbert 1962; Wijngaards 1963, 1965; Childs 1967; Coats 1967; Spreafico 1985: 21–23), pattern (Daube 1963), stereotyped phrase (Childs 1967) and scheme (Alonso-Schökel 1996: 25–30). Formula is the most common way of address (standard for German writers after Noth 1948, such as Gross 1974 or Rendtorff 1997 to mention only two), where, according to Wijngaards, "we understand by formula, an expression which having been coined in a particular context always conveys a definite, established meaning" (1963: 22, n. 17).

Thus, a first answer to our question can be: the Bible recalls the exodus through 'formulae'. But, as already stressed, since exodus is conceived as a set of actions, its formulaic expression varies according to changes on the paradigmatic (different lexical choices or use of paraphrases) or on the syntagmatic level (different combination of the same constitutive elements). Therefore, the core formula[13] is composed of a *minimum* of two elements (exit from Egypt and entry into Canaan) and a *maximum* of three (when the passage through the desert is recalled). The fact that the desert theme is subordinated and not essential is clear from important texts such as Deut 6:21–23, 26:5–9; Exod 3:8, 17; Judg 2:1, 6:8–9; Ps 80:9–10; Jer 32:20–22.

According to our theme, we need to analyze the first part of this formula – where the divinity is clearly represented as the leader of his people – the *Herausführungsformel* according to Noth (1948: 48–54) or the Exodus-formula according to Wijngaards (1963: 22–27). Its counterpart is the 'Landgiving'-formula, and these two formulae constitute the Exodus-'Landgiving' structure, which, according to Wijngaards, would be originally covenantal (i.e. depending on the juridical value attaching to historical facts in the international vassal-treaties), and have the juridical function, establishing YHWH's right as overlord over Israel, at least within the Deuteronomic tradition (1963: 57–58).

Far from being a fixed formula, God's leadership is modelled by eight different verbal roots. In a total occurrence of 265 times, the verbs are distributed as follows (see the complete survey of the text in which each formula occurs in Wijngaards 1963: 23–25): (1) יצא 83x; (2) עלה 40x; (3) ישע 20x; (4) נצל 13x; (5) פדה 19x; (6) גאל 23x; (7) עשה 37x; (8) קבץ 30x. As it appears, notwithstanding the variety of the exodus formulae, the roots יצא and עלה are the most used,[14] thus creating two expressions with YHWH speaking to his people: 'I *liberated* you from Egypt' or 'I *brought* you *out* of Egypt'.

Accordingly, scholars have concluded that exodus is portrayed in the Bible in a twofold way. Humbert (1962) distinguished two ways to conceptualize exodus: as anabasis and as an exodus itself (see also Boisvert 1975: "*la 'sortie' et la 'montée'*"). It seems possible to go further, distinguishing exodus as anabasis (Exodus-as-anabasis-formula; עלה) and exodus as liberation (Exodus-as-liberation-formula; יצא), on the basis of scholars such as Noth (1948: 48–54), Humbert (1962: 359), Wijngaards (1965: 92–93), Kang (1989: 124), Preuss (*TDOT* 6: 20–49), Dozeman (2000: 61) and Russell (2009: 104–13), who likewise see the *hifil* of יצא as connoting liberation from slavery, not a simple exit.

Several studies have concentrated on the origin of the formula, but without much agreement. Even the basic meaning of the verbal roots is nuanced from time to time, swinging from the mere fact of geographic movement or departure (directions: upward or outward) to a more sophisticated meaning (Boccaccio 1952). For the root יצא we already mentioned the technical meaning of 'going free' or 'being at liberty', but we also have to consider the different connotations of the root עלה (Fuhs, *TDOT* 11: 76–95). One possible connotation is the military one (Humbert 1962: 360), even if it does not really fit the context. Scholars mostly noted the liturgical connotation (e.g. Wijngaards 1965: 99–100), which seems to be at home in the Northern kingdom, and particularly at the sanctuaries of Bethel and Dan. The ascending movement is frequently connected with the cult, since the *qal* can be used for going up both to the city (where the temple lies), and to the במה (the so-called 'high place', where many cults were performed). Moreover, the *hifil* form is used as a *terminus technicus* for offering sacrifices.[15] Nevertheless, even in a cultic context, the basic meaning of 'going up' cannot be ignored. On a general level, this meaning is rather strengthened by the fact that the way back from Canaan to Egypt is consistently expressed in the Hebrew Bible by the verb ירד: the opposite direction, downward. Thus, the opposite movement of the anabasis is the correspondent catabasis (Humbert 1962: 435).

Finally, concerning the dating of these formulae, there is a large consensus among scholars to identify a tendency in some pre-exilic texts (such as Amos 2:10, 3:1, 9:7 and Hos 2:15, 12:13) for an exclusive use of the Exodus-as-anabasis-formula, while exilic and post-exilic authors and redactors are understood as showing a predilection for the Exodus-as-liberation. Paraphrasing Van Seters

32   *F. Porzia*

(1972), we could identify hereby a confessional reformulation in the exilic period.[16] Since the post-exilic redaction of the Bible concerned all texts, it is possible to generally find traces of this later use, יצא, in earlier texts, while later texts adopted the earlier form, עלה, or used both (see Exod 3:8.10; Jer 10, 13; Judg 6:8).[17] It is not insignificant to notice that the later יצא, far from being a mere by-form, replaced the earlier usage.[18] These considerations suggest a preference for a diachronic solution concerning the origins of this formula, rather than a synchronic one. We can therefore conclude that the Exodus-formulae – and *a fortiori* the traditions attached to them – reflect a variety of conceptions with major or minor attention to exodus itself either as anabasis or as liberation.[19] The fact that the account, at its base (Exod 1–15), has no real lexical associations with the formulae that should have arisen from it (or vice versa), is yet another interesting point.

Since the debate on the meaning of this formula is still open, we will now turn to particular iconography that can be helpful in resolving it.

An independent study of pictorial evidence from Israel/Palestine

Can pictorial evidence of divine leadership contribute to our discussion? Amulets and seals, edited by Keel and Uehlinger (1998), generally represent the available local data. This kind of documentation, based on symbolic language, does not convey the same amount of information as in other artistic traditions, e.g. the Egyptian, where extensive pictorial narrations are the privileged form of mythic and historic accounts.

Nevertheless, amulets and seals are scattered abundantly throughout the entire region and provide a particular declension of our theme: Pharaoh's leadership.[20] Moreover, the Amarna correspondence sufficiently attests that the perception of the Pharaoh as divine was widespread and accepted in Canaan, at least in the formal language of diplomacy and ceremonial epithets.[21]

Three key sites will be analyzed to demonstrate the common iconography of the Late Bronze Age to represent the Egyptian king beating his enemies, or leading them captive.[22]

Megiddo

This site provides some important examples of the military actions performed by the Pharaoh, standing in his chariot. The Late Bronze Age marks, in fact, the consecration of the chariot – recently introduced into Hittite and Egyptian military use – as favourite emblem for military depictions. The first datable example of this type is a seal amulet that goes back to the nineteenth dynasty in the thirteenth century BCE (Figure 2.1).

The ivories from Megiddo supply us with even better examples (Matthiae 1997: 136, 146–52). A first collection, dated between 1250 and 1150, contains two unfortunately badly preserved representations of Canaanite rulers in the chariot, without either Egyptian elements or religious symbols (Keel and

Figure 2.1 Seal from Megiddo. Keel and Uehlinger 1998: fig. 60. Reprinted with the permission of Verlag Herder GmbH.

Uehlinger 1998: fig. 63–64). The most famous ivory of Megiddo (Figure 2.2) contains, on the right, the representation of the prince returning from the battle standing in the chariot and leading before him two naked enemies bound to the horse, who are identified as nomadic *Shasu* (Giveon 1971: 201–4; Staubli 1991: 64). In contrast to the previous item, this ivory features the winged solar disk in marking the blessing of the victory by the deity, an extremely popular icon of Ramses III's reign. These ivories attest to the local appropriation of Egyptian themes and symbols, of which the image of the Pharaoh in battle was the most popular (Liebowitz 1980, 1987).

Beth-Shean

The importance of Beth-Shean in the Egyptian administration of Canaan, evidenced by the Egyptian icons, began in the fifteenth century BCE and intensified during the thirteenth century. Egyptian influence is particularly evident on the icons made of precious materials and permeated by Egyptian style owned by the economic and cultural élites.

A cylindrical seal, dating to the period of Ramses II (Figure 2.3), shows the Pharaoh shooting arrows towards a target, in the shape of a copper ingot,[23] which overhangs two Asian prisoners, the real target of the action. On the left, a local god – possibly Reshef or Mekal (Keel *et al.* 1990: 195–204, 302–4) – with elements of goat or gazelle, takes the place of Amon in Egyptian iconography offering Pharaoh the sword of victory.

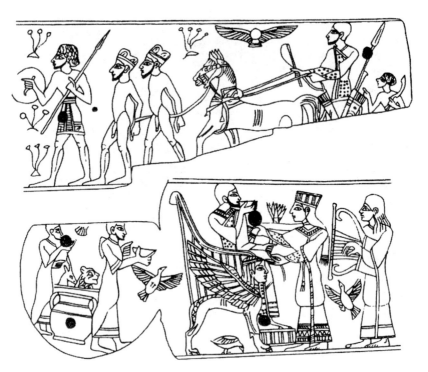

Figure 2.2 Ivory from Megiddo. Keel and Uehlinger 1998: fig. 65. Reprinted with the permission of Verlag Herder GmbH.

Figure 2.3 Cylindrical seal from Beth-Shean. Keel and Uehlinger 1998: fig. 113. Reprinted with the permission of Verlag Herder GmbH.

Figure 2.4 Seal from Beth-Shean. Keel and Uehlinger 1998: fig. 114a. Reprinted with the permission of Verlag Herder GmbH.

A scarab from Beth-Shean (Figure 2.4) and another from Tell el-Ajjul (Keel and Uehlinger 1998: fig. 114b), both dated to the time of Ramses II, show variations on the subject of Pharaoh obtaining the sword of victory from a god and, with this sword, consecrating or simply killing an enemy before the deity.

A stele, imported directly from Egypt, deserves further analysis (ANET, 255). Following the traditional scheme, it shows in the upper register Ramses II holding the bow and receiving the sword from the god Amon, who presents him with the booty of war. In the lower register, instead, eight Asian prisoners – likely nine in origin, given the space and the traditional image of the nine bows – are represented as human torsos surmounting ovals containing names of defeated towns, an iconography that we will discuss in the next paragraph.

Southern Palestine

The influence of ancient Egyptian iconography is especially noticeable in Southern Palestine, and particularly in a site like Lachish. Between the fourteenth and thirteenth centuries BCE, the Pharaoh is the dominating human figure on the seal amulets, where his 'foreign policy' is repeatedly represented. He is usually depicted as sitting victorious on the nine bows, which traditionally indicate the hostile peoples (Keel and Uehlinger 1998: fig. 91), but there are

Figure 2.5 Seal from Southern Palestine. Keel and Uehlinger 1998: fig. 97b. Reprinted with the permission of Verlag Herder GmbH.

many representations as well of the Pharaoh with enemies, especially in the classical pose of beating them (Figure 2.5; see also Keel and Uehlinger 1998: fig. 97a, c) or tying them up and leading them away (Figure 2.6; see also Keel and Uehlinger 1998: fig. 98b).

Another contemporary example, coming from the south (Tell el-Far'ah), shows the Pharaoh on the cart trampling on one of his enemies while two others walk in front of him (Keel and Uehlinger 1998: fig. 61). Depictions of this type – with or without enemies, with or without bow – are found also at Deir el-Balah and Gezer (Wiese 1990: 81–87).

In conclusion, it is worth noting that, around the thirteenth century BCE, the traditional Egyptian motif of kings or gods leading defeated enemies spread throughout the South Levant, generally maintaining the original meaning even in the case of local re-elaboration.

Analysis of textual and pictorial evidence from the Ancient Near East

Obviously, the origin of this iconography is completely Egyptian (see Porzia 2011). Processions of prisoners are widespread on Egyptian temple façades, especially during the New Kingdom, when, starting with the XVIII dynasty, Egyptian foreign politics became more aggressive. A particular iconography, though, needs to be carefully investigated: processions of prisoners represented as human

Figure 2.6 Seal from Southern Palestine. Keel and Uehlinger 1998: fig. 98a. Reprinted with the permission of Verlag Herder GmbH.

torsos[24] surmounting ovals – often crenellated as city walls or perimeter fences – with foreign hieroglyphic toponyms inside, exactly the same as found on the stele from Beth-Shean.[25] These figures are tied to their hips or their elbows, their wrists or their neck, and they are often driven by a divinity – actually or ideally – to a superior divinity or, as it often happens, to a pharaoh. The collection of such images can be found on wall representations, well visible, and often linked to another typical image, i.e. the one of a pharaoh beating the enemy or a group of enemies.

Although this iconography can be dated back to 1900 BCE (Schäfer 1974: 156; Johnson 1992: 94–95) and remained in use until the Ptolemaic period (Shaw 1991: 12), there is no doubt about its popularity during the New Kingdom – in particular, starting with Thutmosis III – nor about the fact that during the New Kingdom the image of a pharaoh beating his enemy on the head was associated with these lists of anthropomorphic foreign toponyms.

Inscriptions related to these processions of anthropomorphic toponyms make clear that the cities and the lands expressed by the toponym are *linguistically and iconographically* treated as prisoners or hostages coming from these places. The physical movement of people – an attested procedure – is thus represented, in terms of material and verbal images, through geographic – not personal – entities.

Actually, the idea that cities or lands move from one place to another is not new in the context of the Late Bronze Age throughout the Near East,

38   *F. Porzia*

especially in the South Levant. And it seems not to be a problem. Some samples of texts from different origins are:

- Rib-Addi (EA 106, 45–49): "Moreover, all the cities I have told you about at the presence of my Lord, he know whether they are back or not [*šumma ta-ru*]: on the day when the troops left from my Lord's field, all of them are hostile";
- Hittite king Shuppiluliuma (HDT 39–40; ANET 318): "I also brought the city of Qatna, together with its belongings and possessions, to Hatti ... I plundered all of those lands in one year and brought them [literally: 'I made them enter'] to Hatti";
- 1 Sam 7:14: "The cities which the Philistines had taken from Israel were restored [*wtšbnh*, literally: 'came back'] to Israel, from Ekron to Gath, and Israel rescued their territory from the hand of the Philistines. There was peace also between Israel and the Amorites".

With rhetorical expressions, one reads about cities and lands that move, alternatively under the leadership of a god or a king. But how could they do so? Many terms can describe a city or a land but surely not any movement. Undoubtedly, the expression is to be considered a metaphor: a city or a land moves politically between different powers and returns when the legitimate governor regains control. The city or the land has never moved from its location but rather its jurisdiction.

This may be an example of what the Italian orientalist Liverani called 'code of movement'. By code of movement, he means verbs of movement applied to entities that cannot move, like cities or lands. In this code, "the political reading is linked to the physical one ... [and] pointing out a hidden political reading implies that ... [the] insistent use of verbs of motion and stasis is not only an unavoidable consequence of the topic, but is also a true expressive code" (Liverani 2004: 135). Moreover, "we should bear in mind that the terminology of 'bringing out' and 'bringing back', 'sending out' and 'sending in', the so-called 'code of movement' ... , had already been applied in the Late Bronze Age texts to indicate a shifting of sovereignty, without implying any physical displacement of the people concerned, but only a shift of the political border. ... Egyptian texts also describe territorial conquest in terms of the capture of its population, even if in fact the submitted people remain in their place. This is an idiomatic use of the code of movement (go in/go out) to describe a change in political dependence" (Liverani 2005: 278).

Discussion

As in everyday life, even academic arguments are susceptible to seasons. For example, recent and passionate, is the discussion about – quoting the titles of just a few recent books on the topic – *How Israel Became a People* (Hawkins 2013), *The Emergence of Israel in Ancient Palestine* (Pfoh 2009), *Israel's*

Ethnogenesis (Faust 2006), or even *Who Were the Early Israelites and Where Did They Come From?* (Dever 2003). As Garbini proposed (2003: 1), a clear distinction needs to be made between the concept of 'beginning' and that of 'origin', the former suiting better historical reconstruction, and the latter mythical narration. In other words, one should be aware of adopting either an etic or an emic perspective. In these terms, the debate about Israel's 'beginnings' is a *mare magnum*. On the other hand, if we put aside the classical authors and the Hellenistic Hebrew writers, the amount of information concerning Israel's 'origins' is limited – if we may say so – to the biblical texts. Our conclusions aim to inquire into one possible 'beginning' for one possible 'origin'.

The collected data are abundant, nonetheless in all of them – both visual and verbal (i.e. seals, reliefs, inscriptions, literary texts) – the subject is always a god, or, in the extrabiblical attestations, a king, that is to say a godly figure if not a god-king as in the case of the Pharaoh. Therefore, the data seem comparable.

This leads us to a preliminay conclusion: the God of the Exodus-formulae is shaped 'in the image and after the likeness' of the Pharaoh,[26] or the Ancient Near Eastern king in general. In one important difference, however, the Pharaoh usually leads enemies to be enslaved in Egypt, while the God of the Exodus leads his people away from enslavement.

It would be a sophism to justify it by maintaining that the Hebrew population in Egypt was indeed in a state of enslavement. But it seems less banal to pay attention to the fact that God's agency resulted in the reversal of the current situation: bringing the people – as is often repeated – from slavery to freedom and divine service. The God of Israel behaves exactly opposite to the Pharaoh, though they both take on a common role as the leader, the supreme ruler, the invincible warrior, a divinity, but the God of Exodus acts for the good of his people, rather than evil.

The code of movement allows another level of analysis. In order to avoid the critics complaining about the late redaction of the biblical evidence, we should turn first to an important acquaintance for biblical scholars: the stele of Mesha. Indeed, here we find a further example of the code of movement (employing the same verb as in 1 Sam 7:14): "Kemosh made it [the land of Madaba] come back [*wyšbh*]".[27] This evidence, (without doubt) dating back to the ninth century BCE, harmonizes well with the later biblical one (1 Sam), and clearly shows that this code persisted in the region during the Iron Age.

One sticking point still has to be addressed. Why interpret the Exodus-formulae as examples of a code of movement? Why can we not accept them as they stand, or look for some other origin? The answer is in the text itself. As always in the historical-critical method, the text – not an exegete's discretion – presents major exegetical problems. We have already stressed that exodus is neither monolithic nor a stable tradition. No one can deny that the biblical exodus never occurred in the manner of its biblical accounts (plural!), not to mention its competition with the patriarchal traditions. In light of the already mentioned research on the beginnings of Israel (whatever Israel means in the period between the Late Bronze and Iron Age),[28] under the sign of an increasing consensus among scholars about the Canaanite background of this phenomenon,[29] the code of movement and its Egyptian echo seems to be a possible explanation for this tradition. After all, the first attestations of the Exodus-as-anabasis-formula, employed in the most ancient textual strata by Amos and Hosea, date only one century after the stele of Mesha: they could still share the same ideological milieu.

Again, compared with the standard usage of the code of movement, we notice the same difference as before: the code of movement usually refers to geographic entities (cities or lands), the Exodus-formulae refer to a people. Such a difference, though, should not weaken the comparison between the code of movement and Exodus-formulae, since the metaphoric level of the former is rendered useless thanks to the substitution of immobile geographic entities with mobile people (Liverani 2005: 277–80). So, the Exodus-formulae are an even better application of the code of movement and, more likely, with everyday experience. The ancient Hebrews, moreover, had real experience of such movement: deportation. This experience possibly affected both the Northern tradition (Exodus-as-anabasis-formula) thanks to Assyrian practice and the Southern one (Exodus-as-liberation-formula) thanks to the Neo-Babylonian practice, which culminated with the exile under Nebuchadnezzar. It has to be noticed, therefore, that not only icons undergo local re-interpretation, but also linguistic expressions.

Exodus as metaphor

The *conditio sine qua non* supporting the confrontation we attempted in this chapter – between different regions, and different expressive forms – is the existence of an ideological *koiné* in the Eastern Mediterranean during the Late Bronze and Iron Age. Therefore, it seems useful to draw a few conclusions about the historical context.

The mainly debated – especially during the 1980s and the 1990s – historical theme for this period is the nature of Egyptian domination in the area. Far from reaching solid conclusions, this debate suggests prudence in treating the topic. Combining textual evidence with the growing amount of information from archaeological finds, what we could call the 'Amarna-centred model'[30] has been increasingly deepened and problematized. In most of the discussion, terms like empire (Weinstein 1981), colonialism (Oren 1984), and imperialism (Morris 2005) are well established.[31] In contrast to these different declensions of an Egyptian direct rule on Canaan, Higginbotham (2000) preferred to recognize a model of elite emulation. Even if former definitions have to be nuanced and elite emulation is a practice in Canaan during this period, nonetheless a direct rule has been reaffirmed on several occasions by archaeological evidence (Martin 2004: 279–80; Burke and Lords 2010: 27–28).

God leading his people 41

Leaving this issue aside, another aspect has to be considered. As recently stated by Sherratt "the first thing that strikes one when contemplating the Late Bronze archaeology of the Levant ... are the obstacles it presents to viewing it contextually as a coherent geographical area" (2013: 497). However, it is astonishing that, notwithstanding this complexity and fragmentation, a high degree of uniformity and continuity is accorded to the Eastern Mediterranean. For example, from a political point of view, the category of a 'regional system' has become established in the literature (Liverani 2014: 278–82). From a diplomatic point of view, one of 'internationalism' (Liverani 1990; Cohen and Westbrook 2000) and from an economic point of view one of 'globalization' (LaBianca and Sham 2006), even a '"world system" network' (lastly Panitz-Cohen 2013: 549–50) has been established. From an artistic point of view, one of 'international style' (Caubet 1998; Feldman 2006) can be used.

In such a network, Ancient Near Eastern populations shared cultural traits as well – as attested by the usage of Akkadian as a *lingua franca* – resulting in an ideological *koiné*. As recently proposed by Van De Mieroop (2005; 2007: 230–34), the best way to explain the establishment of this network[32] – the 'Eastern Mediterranean system' in his terms – seems to be the model of the Peer Polities Interaction, elaborated by Renfrew (1986).[33] Wherever this model is functioning, common features usually are: similar political institutions, common systems of weights and measures, systems of writing, same structure of religious belief (albeit with local variations), same spoken language; in a word – even if controversial – same culture, or better, same ideology.

Quoting Van De Mieroop's statement, we may therefore affirm that "indeed the Eastern Mediterranean of the Late Bronze Age fits the idea perfectly" (2007: 231). Differing from his conclusion – according to which, the same competition that gave birth to this interaction also brought the system to its end – we believe that this ideological *koiné* did not end with the upheaval of the palatial system. Egyptian presence in Canaan was a lasting condition, independent of political and military occupation. After all, the Egyptian political interests in Canaan continued, as further Asian campaigns led by Sheshonq and Necho clearly show. Liverani suggested that "Egyptian rule never ended (at least in principle) and went on until the struggle between Necho and Nebuchadnezzar at the end of the seventh century. ... In principle Egypt never renounced its pretensions, and was never 'thrown away' from Palestine" (Liverani 1997: 113). Therefore, at the beginning of the Iron Age, the Egyptian presence had no longer any political or economic meaning, but the material culture continued to be Egyptinized (Mumford 2007; Ben Dor Evian 2011). The same can be said of ideology.

In this broader context, we propose interpreting the Exodus-formulae as an example of the code of movement, since they both share the same lexicon and ideology: the Pharaoh leading defeated enemies would be at the base of the return journey, with YHWH leading his people out of Egypt. In this sense, YHWH delivers Israel from Egyptian power and gives the Hebrews full

42   *F. Porzia*

autonomy and control of the land, where they already lived, that is without an actual displacement of people. Therefore, the Exodus-formulae seem to be an agreed 'memory' of major political phenomena, which marked the transition from submission to Egypt in the Late Bronze Age to autonomy in the Iron Age. Egypt's control of Syria-Palestine, including Transjordan, and the subsequent withdrawal from the region in the thirteenth and twelfth centuries BCE, may well have been remembered as a movement from a state of oppression to a state of freedom. This newly found freedom might also be attributed to the regional head of the pantheon, YHWH.

In the exilic period, that is to say in a period without land, institutions or cult sites, the Hebrews chose an imaginary captivity as the moment when they were born as a people for the first time.[34] They needed to state that they could continue to exist as a people even in exile. The Egyptian captivity was useful to demonstrate that, already in Hebrew history, enslaved Hebrews became a people when God became their leader. Therefore, in the Bible, before the confession 'God is king', we can see another one: 'God is leader'.[35]

The synergy between text and image, from as broad an ideological network as the Eastern Mediterranean between the Late Bronze and Iron Age, has shown how, within the *longue durée*, collective memory can transform a political linguistic code, first related to geographic entities (cities and lands), into a myth related to human entities and to a whole people, contributing to the definition of an ethnic and 'national' identity. Notwithstanding the relevance of the exilic account of the exodus, we stated that an exodus tradition did exist even in the making of a pre-exilic Israelite collective identity, without requiring a monolithic historical core of the exodus in the Late Bronze Age.

Therefore, among many stories about Israel's 'origins', the Hebrew Bible can be confidently trusted when it states that Israel was born in Egypt. From an historical perspective, of course, it is not necessary to believe the biblical text as it stands. However, in the quest for its 'beginnings', we cannot underestimate three points. The first epigraphic attestation of its name appears in an Egyptian inscription (Merenptah's stele), and the context of its phenomena was Canaan, a region traditionally subjected to Egypt. Finally, the cultural milieu, depending on centuries-old exchanges between Canaan and Egypt, shaped the Hebrews' theological views with long lasting effects.

Notes

1 This chapter originates from the idea that images (both visual and verbal) can survive for long periods and be transformed into something new. From this perspective, the biblical exodus as a motif and a metaphor will be compared with earlier witnesses (from the Late Bronze Age).
2 This is not the place for going into details; it is sufficient to recall that Panofsky's analysis is still widely recognized.
3 For a discussion about what is an image, on the material or the verbal level, see de Hulster (2009b).

4 We can recall here the 'infinite interpretation' of the Bible (Bori 1986): parallel to the continuous actualizing interpretation by believers is the likewise continuous historicizing interpretation by biblical exegetes and historians. To recall another book, this phenomenon is due to the infinite reading of the Bible (Mendonça 2008).

5 For an interesting overall approach to the Hebrew culture and its inner relation with words, see Oz and Oz-Salzberger (2012).

6 I have already dedicated a study to this topic (Porzia 2011).

7 Throughout the chapter, where the Bible is not directly or indirectly quoted, I have chosen the more generic term 'Hebrews', in order to avoid anachronisms or imprecision. We are aware of the lexical warnings expressed for example by Mason 2007 and Miller 2010, 2012. To put it simply, it appears more correct to adopt a more neutral definition as 'Hebrew' for an etic point of view, and 'Israel' for an emic one (mostly the Bible), for geography or for renowned academic debates (Israel's origins, ancient Israel and so on).

8 It is beyond the scope of this chapter to discuss other detached myths of origins, such as de Pury has put forward in several publications (1991, 2001): the idea of two initially competing myths of origins, one being the Jacob cycle and the other the exodus tradition; or the connection suggested by Liverani (1979, 2005: 25) between the mention of the tribe of Raham in a stela of Seti I from Beth-Shean and Abraham, supposing that the members of the tribe called themselves "sons of Raham" (*Banu-Raham) and that their eponymous ancestor was a "father of Raham" (*Abu-Raham), that is, the name of the patriarch Abraham.

9 In narratological terms, it is based on the biblical discourse, where the 'discourse' is the concrete narrative, in its actual shape, that the reader has before his eyes, and the 'story' is an abstract reconstruction in which the reader (re)places the elements of the 'discourse' according to a logical and chronological order and supplies what is missing (Ska 2000: 5–6).

10 Among the possible places of origin: Crete, Lybia, Ethiopia, Assyria and of course Egypt (Catastini 1996, 2013).

11 According to Schmid (1999), the first literary connection of patriarchal and exodus tradition appears in Gen 17 and Exod 6 where the two periods are unequivocally correlated. Gertz (2000, 2002) postulated a literarily independent exodus story linked to the patriarchal tradition only by P. In a similar way, Otto (2000) ascribes the first connection of primeval, patriarchal and Mosaic histories to the priestly narrative. Most recently, Blum supported this position as well, claiming that "on the pre-priestly level a literary connection between Gen and Exod (or between the patriarchal history and the exodus story) cannot be demonstrated" (2002: 152).

12 The role played by Moses should be neither overstated nor understated. The divinity is the main actor, even if in some verses "Dtr [Deuteronomistic] expressions that are elsewhere used to celebrate God's rescue in the exodus are transferred to Moses" (Römer and Brettler 2000: 406, see also Coats 1977). The consequence is, as Rendtorff puts it, that Moses' deeds are almost identified with God's deeds. Moses was more than a prophet, more than any other man, and nearer to God (1997: 517).

13 Many other elements are added: Egypt as house of slavery, God's strong arm, his wonderful deeds, and so on.

14 Even if עשה and קבץ are well attested too, they refer to exodus in a more general way.

15 The most interesting occurrence in this sense is the episode of Jeroboam and the golden calves (1 Kgs 12:25–33), already noticed in previous works but recently extensively analyzed by Russell (2009: 24–55). The verse 28 in particular would set up a parallelism between exodus and cult: "You have *gone up* to Jerusalem long enough. Behold your gods, O Israel, who *brought* you *up* out of the land of Egypt".

44   F. Porzia

16 Here this chronological expression is preferred in order to avoid the attribution to the aleatory Deuteronomic tradition, however one defines it.

17 The example from the book of Judges is particularly interesting. Without doubt we are dealing with a later text since the theological passage 6:7–10 is not present in the fragments of the book found at Qumran. For a discussion on this omission see O'Connell 1996: 147, n. 178.

18 As for the use of יצא *hifil* in pre-exilic texts, there are some interesting data: (1) within Exod 1–15 this form is not well focused and the usage of the root שלח is generally preferred; (2) as for Num 23:22, 24:8, the former seems shaped on the latter, and the latter is within a speech of a non-Israelite, Balaam, professing El as the subject of our verbal form (for a discussion of this see Russell 2009: 78–103).

19 However, as stressed by Russell (2009), attention has to be paid not to oversimplify too much: according to his conclusions, the biblical memories about Egypt and exodus vary by region (distinguishing among Cisjordan Israel, Transjordan Israel, and Judah), and there are plausible historical contexts for differing regional traditions about them. This multiplication of exodus traditions and formulae should not overshadow the general lines traced in this chapter.

20 On the general diffusion of Egyptian style, see Bryan (1996) and, especially, Higginbotham (1996, 2000).

21 We may consider to which extent the Egyptian king was perceived as a god in Canaan. When features of the Egyptian iconographic tradition were employed elsewhere, they could be revised and charged with new or renewed meanings. As time goes by, we see a progressive improvement of the imported model, with different features from the original, depending on the new market. The phenomenon of foreign appropriation presents at least two moments: the acquisition of a model and its serial reproduction. As for the first moment, it is clear that it meant a selection within a wide set of artistic expressions and for the second to which degree was their ideological background comprehensible, shared and communicated. Only partial answers can be given. We should not think of extreme positions of a total interchangeability, between exporting and importing context posing a nominalistic incomprehensibility between them. Intermediate undertones can be recognized according to palatine tastes, i.e. according to the needs of its propaganda, and a growing serial production of stereotyped iconography drawn from local *ateliers* with a sort of emotional disengagement (such an idea is presented by Winter 1976, 1981).

22 For general bibliography see Keel and Uehlinger 1998: 53–94.

23 See the comparison with a relief of Amenhotep II, where the king, riding in a chariot, has just pierced a copper ingot with five arrows. The accompanying text leaves no doubt as to the material of the target (O'Connor 1967). See also Decker 1971: 80–122; 1987: 42–54.

24 The anthropomorphic part of those images is sometimes characterized by typed somatic features of the Egyptian iconography, that make them recognizable: Asians with pointed beards, Libyans or Negros with pulpy lips, earrings and curly hair.

25 For example, the iconography of Amon leading defeated cities away see Schäfer 1974: 157.

26 For the same conclusion, see Staubli (2009: 93–112) and Strawn (2009: 163–211).

27 For this reading (lines 8–9) with the verb *šwb,* and for the one possible of the fragmented line 33, see Jackson (1989: 110) and Niccacci (1994: 228). W.F. Albright (ANET 320) and W. Röllig (KAI 2.168) prefer to recognize the root *yšb*, assuming an error: *wyš[b] bh.* For the discussion about the unsuitability of this emendation, even for space problems, see Miller (1969).

28 Before Davies (1992) questioned the existence or not – and the multiple meanings – of the expression 'ancient Israel', Liverani (1980) had already observed that in the pseudo-problem 'origins of Israel' not only the word 'origins', but also the word

'Israel' should be considered mythical. Which 'Israel's' origins are we looking for? The concept of Israel itself is subject to historical evolution (see also Garbini 1988; 2003: 1–9).

29 Without excluding nomadic components, such as those coming from the eastern desert fringes (Finkelstein and Na'aman 1994), the Canaanite traits remain undeniable.

30 The upper anchor for a comprehension of the real extent of Egyptian domination in Canaan is the Amarna archive. Even if the situation reflected by this archive dates back to the fourteenth century BCE, the implementation of the Egyptian system in Syria-Palestine, including Transjordan, was considered stable for a long period (Helk 1971). The decline of its rule started with Ramses III, and continued at an accelerating pace during the later Ramessides. The reign of Ramses VI seems to be considered as the last one exerting a real Egyptian presence in Palestine.

31 For further discussion and bibliography see Morris 2005: 8–20; Killebrew 2005: 53–55; Hasel 1998: 114–17; Panitz-Cohen 2013: 247–48.

32 The same model has recently been applied to the Hellenistic period by Ma (2003).

33 This model studies the full range of interchange between autonomous socio-political units within a single geographical region (Renfrew 1986: 1). However, it does not explain the growth of 'closely-knit systems' (Van De Mieroop 2007: 231) through classic concepts as domination and subordination, 'primary' and 'secondary' states, nor through the more recent ones of 'core' and 'periphery'. Further, it never considers a socio-political unity as existing in isolation. On the contrary, it shows how it is the interaction itself among autonomous unities – thanks to competition, competitive emulation, warfare, transmission of innovation, symbolic entrainment, ceremonial exchange of valuables, flow of commodities, language and ethnicity (Renfrew and Bahn 2004: 389–91) – to be at the basis of the development of societies sharing a number of common features.

34 On this terminology see Ska (1997: 165–75). He affirms: "Si le terme 'naissance' est préférable, c'est parce qu'il décrit sans doute mieux que d'autre ce qui s'est passé. Israël est 'devenu' un peuple lors du miracle de la mer ; il a cessé d'être une partie du peuple égyptien, sa main d'œuvre servile. Mais tout cela est arrivé somme toute contre son gré (14,10–11). Un peu comme un enfant naît sans qu'on lui demande son avis. Ce récit de 'naissance' se distingue particulièrement des récits d'"alliance' où l'acquiescement du peuple joue un rôle éminent, irremplaçable" (1997: 165).

35 In the accounts related to the exodus, there is only one exceptional occurrence where God is confessed as king (Exod 15:18).

Bibliography

Alonso-Schökel, L. 1996. *Salvezza e Liberazione: L'Esodo*. Bologna: Edizioni Dehoniane.

Beckman, G. 1999. *Hittite Diplomatic Texts*, 2nd edition. Atlanta: Scholars Press.

Ben Dor Evian, S. 2011. "Egypt and the Levant in the Iron Age I-IIA: The Ceramic Evidence". *Tel Aviv* 38: 94–119.

Ben-Shlomo, D. 2010. *Philistine Iconography: A Wealth of Style and Symbolism*. Fribourg: Academic Press/Göttingen: Vandenhoeck & Ruprecht.

Ben Zvi, E. and C. Levin (eds). 2010. *The Concept of Exile in Ancient Israel and its Historical Contexts*. Berlin: De Gruyter.

Blum, E. 2002. "Die literarische Verbindung von Erzvätern und Exodus. Ein Gespräch mit neueren Forschungshypothesen". In *Abschied vom Jahwisten. Die Komposition des Hexateuch in der jüngsten Diskussion*. J.C. Gertz, K. Schmid and M. Witte (eds). Berlin: De Gruyter: 119–56.

Boccaccio, P. 1952. "I termini contrari come espressioni della totalità in ebraico". *Biblica* 33: 173–90.

46   F. Porzia

Boisvert, L. 1975. "Le passage de la mer des Roseaux et la foi d'Israël". *Science et Esprit* 27: 149–59.

Bori, P. C. 1986. *L'interpretazione infinita. L'ermeneutica cristiana antica e le sue trasformazioni*. Bologna: Il Mulino.

Botterweck, G.J. and H. Ringgren (eds). 1986. *Theological Dictionary of the Old Testament*. Grand Rapids, MI: Eerdmans.

Bryan, B. M. 1996. "Art, Empire, and the End of the Late Bronze Age". In *The Study of the Ancient Near East in the Twenty-First Century*. J.S. Cooper and G.M. Schwartz (eds). Winona Lake, IN: Eisenbrauns: 33–79.

Burke, A.A. and K.V. Lords. 2010. "Egyptians in Jaffa: A Portrait of Egyptian Presence in Jaffa during the Late Bronze Age". *NEA* 73(1): 2–30.

Catastini, A. 1996. "Le notizie degli autori classici sulle origini degli Ebrei: considerazioni generali". In *Alle soglie della classicità. Il mediterraneo tra tradizione e innovazione, vol. 1*. E. Acquaro (ed.). Pisa – Roma: Istituti Editoriali e Poligrafici Internazionali: 81–88.

——2013. "La questione delle origini ebraiche". *Quaderni di Vicino Oriente* 4: 71–85.

Caubet, A. 1998. "The International Style: A Point of View from the Levant and Syria". In *Aegean and Orient in the Second Millennium*. E. Cline and D. Harris-Cline (eds). Liège: Université de Liège: 105–11.

Childs, B.S. 1967. "Deuteronomic Formulae of the Exodus Traditions". In *Hebräische Wortforschung*. B. Hartmann (ed.). Leiden: Brill: 30–39.

Coats, G.W. 1967. "The Traditio-Historical Character of the Reed Sea Motif". *VT* 17: 253–65.

——1977. "Legendary Motifs in the Moses Death Reports". *CBQ* 39: 34–44.

Cohen, R. and R. Westbrook (eds). 2000. *Amarna Diplomacy: The 'beginnings' of International Relations*. Baltimore: Johns Hopkins.

Daube, D. 1963. *The Exodus Pattern in the Bible*. London: Faber & Faber.

Davies, P.R. 1992. *In Search of Ancient Israel*. Sheffield: Sheffield Academic Press.

Decker, W. 1971. *Die physische Leistung: Untersuchung zu Heldentum, Jagd und Leibesübungen des ägyptischen Königs*. Köln: Kleikamp.

——1987. *Sport und Spiel im Alten Ägypten*. München: Beck.

Dever, W.G. 2003. *Who Were the Early Israelites and Where Did They Come From?* Grand Rapids, MI: Eerdmans.

Donner, H. and W. Röllig. 1962–1964. *Kanaanäische und aramäische Inschriften*. Wiesbaden: Harrassowitz.

Dozeman, T.B. 2000. "Hosea and the Wilderness Wandering Tradition". In *Rethinking the Foundations: Historiography in the Ancient World and in the Bible*. S. McKenzie and T.C. Römer (eds). Berlin: De Gruyter, 2000: 55–70.

Faust, A. 2006. *Israel's Ethnogenesis: Settlement, Interaction, Expansion and Resistance*. London: Equinox.

Feldman, M.H. 2006. *Diplomacy by Design: Luxury Arts and an "International Style" in the Ancient Near East, 1400–1200 BCE*. Chicago: Chicago University Press.

Finkelstein, I. and N. Na'aman (eds). 1994. *From Nomadism to Monarchy: Archaeological and Historical Aspects of Early Israel*. Jerusalem: Yad Izhak Ben-Zvi – Israel Exploration Society.

Freedman, D.N. (ed.). 1992. *Anchor Bible Dictionary*. New York: Doubleday.

Garbini, G. 1988. *History and Ideology in Ancient Israel*, J. Bowden (trans.). New York: Crossroad. Originally published in Italian as *Storia e ideologia nell'Israele antico*. Brescia: Paideia, 1986.

——2003. *Myth and History in the Bible*, C. Peri (trans.). London: Sheffield Academic Press. Originally published in Italian as *Mito e storia nella Bibbia*. Brescia: Paideia, 2003.

Geertz, C. 1973. *The Interpretation of Cultures. Selected Essays.* New York: Basic Books.

Gertz, J. C. 2000. *Tradition und Redaktion in der Exoduserzählung: Untersuchungen zur Endredaktion des Pentateuch.* Göttingen: Vandenhoeck & Ruprecht.

——2002. "Abraham, Mose und der Exodus: Beobachtungen zur Redaktionsgeschichte von Genesis 15". In *Abschied vom Jahwisten: Die Komposition des Hexateuch in der jüngsten Diskussion*. J.C. Gertz, K. Schmid and M. Witte (eds). Berlin: De Gruyter: 63–81.

Giveon, R. 1971. *Le bédouins Shosou des documents égyptiens.* Leiden: Brill.

Gross, W. 1974. "Die Herausführungsformel: Zum Verhältnis von Formel und Syntax". *ZAW* 86: 425–53.

Hasel, M.G. 1998. *Domination and Resistance: Egyptian Military Activity in the Southern Levant, ca. 1300–1185 B.C.* Leiden: Brill.

Hawkins, R.K. 2013. *How Israel Became a People.* Nashville: Abingdon Press.

Helk, W. 1971. *Die Beziehungen Ägyptens zu Vorderasien im 3. und 2. Jahrtausend v. Chr.*, 2nd edition. Wiesbaden: O. Harrassowitz.

Hendel, R. 2001. "The Exodus in Biblical Memory". *JBL* 120(4): 601–22.

Higginbotham, C.R. 1996. "Elite Emulation and Egyptian Governance in Ramesside Canaan". *Tel Aviv* 23: 154–69.

——2000. *Egyptianization and Elite Emulation in Ramesside Palestine: Governance and Accommodation on the Imperial Periphery.* Leiden: Brill.

Hoffman, Y. 1989. "A North Israelite Typological Myth and a Judean Historical Tradition: The Exodus in Hosea and Amos". *VT* 39: 169–82.

Hofstee, W. 1986. "The Interpretation of Religion. Some Remarks on the Work of Clifford Geertz". In *On Symbolic Representation of Religion*. H.G. Hubbeling and H.G. Kippenberg (eds). Berlin: De Gruyter: 70–83.

Hulster, I. J. de 2009a. "Illuminating Images. A Historical Position and Method for Iconographic Exegesis". In Hulster and Schmitt 2009: 139–62.

——2009b. "What Is an Image? A Basis for Iconographic Exegesis". In Hulster and Schmitt 2009: 225–32.

Hulster, I.J. de and R. Schmitt (eds). 2009. *Iconography and Biblical Studies.* Münster: Ugarit-Verlag.

Humbert, P. 1962. "Dieu fait sortir". *ThZ* 18: 357–61, 433–36.

Jackson, K.P. 1989. "The Language of the Mesha Inscription". In *Studies in the Mesha Inscription and Moab*. A. Dearman (ed.). Atlanta: Scholars Press: 96–130.

Johnson, W.R. 1992. *An Asiatic Battle Scene of Tutankhamun from Thebes: A Late Amarna Antecedent of the Ramesside Battle-Narrative.* Chicago: Chicago University Press.

Kang, S.-M. 1989. *Divine War in the Old Testament and in the Ancient Near East.* Berlin: De Gruyter.

Keel, O. and C. Uehlinger. 1998. *Gods, Goddesses, and Images of God in Ancient Israel*, T.H. Trapp (trans.). Minneapolis: Fortress Press. Originally published in German as *Göttinnen, Götter und Gottessymbole*. Fribourg: Herder.

Keel, O., M. Shuval and C. Uehlinger. 1990. *Studien zu den Stempelsiegeln aus Palästina/Israel*, vol. 1. Fribourg: Academic Press/Göttingen: Vandenhoeck & Ruprecht.

Killebrew, A.E. 2005. *Biblical Peoples and Ethnicity: An Archaeological Study of Egyptians, Canaanites, Philistines, and Early Israel 1300–1100 B.C.E.* Atlanta: Society of Biblical Literature.

48 F. Porzia

Klingbeil, M. 1999. *Yahweh Fighting from Heaven: God as Warrior and as God of Heaven in the Hebrew Psalter and Ancient Near Eastern Iconography.* Fribourg: Academic Press/Göttingen: Vandenhoeck & Ruprecht.

Knudtzon, J. A. 1907–1915. *Die el-Amarna-Tafeln.* Leipzig: J.C. Hinrich.

LaBianca, Ø.S. and S.A. Sham (eds). 2006. *Connectivity in Antiquity: Globalization as Long Term Historical Process.* London: Equinox.

Liebowitz, H.A. 1980. "Military and Feast Scenes on Late Bronze Palestinian Ivories". *IEJ* 30: 162–69.

——1987. "Late Bronze II Ivory Work: Evidence of a Cultural Highpoint". *BASOR* 265: 3–24.

Lipschits, O., G.N. Knoppers and M. Oeming (eds). 2011. *Judah and the Judeans in the Achaemenid Period: Negotiating Identity in an International Context.* Winona Lake, IN: Eisenbrauns.

Liverani, M. 1979. "Un'ipotesi sul nome di Abramo". *Henoch* 1: 9–18.

——1980. "Le 'origini' d'Israele: progetto irrealizzabile di ricerca etnogenetica". *Rivista Biblica Italiana* 28: 9–31.

——1990. *Prestige and Interest: International Relations in the Near East ca. 1600–1100 BC.* Padova: Sargon.

——1997. "Ramesside Egypt in a Changing World: An Institutional Approach". *Quaderni di Vicino Oriente* 1: 101–15.

——2004. *Myth and Politics in Ancient Near Eastern Historiography.* London: Equinox.

——2005. *Israel's History and the History of Israel,* C. Peri and P.R. Davies (trans.). London: Equinox. Originally published in Italian as *Oltre la Bibbia. Storia antica di Israele.* Roma – Bari: Laterza, 2003.

——2014. *The Ancient Near East: History, Society and Economy,* S. Tabatabai (trans.). London – New York: Routledge. Originally published in Italian as *Antico Oriente. Storia, Società, Economia,* 2nd edn. Roma – Bari: Laterza.

Ma, J. 2003. "Peer Polity Interaction in the Hellenistic Age". *Past and Present* 180(1): 9–39.

Martin, M.A.S. 2004. "Egyptian and Egyptianized Pottery in Late Bronze Age Canaan: Typology, Chronology, Ware Fabrics, and Manufacture Techniques. Pots and People?" *Egypt and the Levant* 14: 265–84.

Mason, S. 2007. "Jews, Judeans, Judaizing, Judaism: Problems of Categorization in Ancient History". *JSJ* 38: 457–512.

Matthiae, P. 1997. *La storia dell'arte dell'Oriente Antico,* vol. 1. Milano: Mondadori.

Mendonça, J.T. 2008. *A leitura infinita. Bíblia e interpretação.* Lisboa: Assírio & Alvim.

Miller, D.M. 2010. "The Meaning of *Ioudaios* and its Relationship to Other Group Labels in Ancient 'Judaism'". *CBR* 9(1): 98–126.

——2012. "Ethnicity Comes of Age: An Overview of Twentieth-Century Terms for *Ioudaios*". *CBR* 10(2): 293–311.

Miller, P. 1969. "A Note on the Meša' Inscription". *Or* 38: 461–64.

Morris, E.F. 2005. *The Architecture of Imperialism: Military Bases and the Evolution of Foreign Policy in Egypt's New Kingdom.* Leiden – Boston: Brill.

Mumford, G.D. 2007. "Egypto-Levantine Relations during the Iron Age to Early Persian Periods (Dynasties late 20 to 26)". In *Egyptian Stories.* T. Schneider and K. Szpakowska (eds). Münster: Ugarit-Verlag: 225–88.

Niccacci, A. 1994. "The Stele of Mesha and the Bible: Verbal System and Narrativity". *Or* 63: 226–48.

Noth, M. 1948. *Überlieferungsgeschichte des Pentateuch*. Stuttgart: Kohlhammer.

O'Connell, R.H. 1996. *The Rhetoric of the Book of Judges*. Leiden: Brill.

O'Connor, D. 1967. "Model Ingots in Egyptian Foundation Deposits". In *Cape Gelidonya: A Bronze Age Shipwreck*. G.F. Bass (ed.). Philadelphia: The American Philosophical Society: 172–74.

Oren, E.D. 1984. "'Governors' Residencies' in Canaan under the New Kingdom: A Case Study in Egyptian Administration". *Journal of the Society for the Study of Egyptian Antiquities* 14: 37–56.

Otto, E. 2000. *Das Deuteronomium im Pentateuch und Hexateuch. Studien zur Literaturgeschichte von Pentateuch und Hexateuch im Lichte des Deuteronomiumsrahmen*. Tübingen: Mohr Siebeck.

Oz, A. and F. Oz-Salzberger. 2012. *Jews and Words*. New Haven and London: Yale University Press.

Panitz-Cohen, N. 2013. "The southern Levant (Cisjordan) during the Late Bronze Age". In *The Oxford Handbook of the Archaeology of the Levant c. 8000–332 BCE*. M.L. Steiner and A.E. Killebrew (eds). Oxford: Oxford University Press: 541–60.

Pfoh, E. 2009. *The Emergence of Israel in Ancient Palestine: Historical and Anthropological Perpsectives*. London: Equinox.

Porzia, F. 2011. "Cities Roaming Around, the Code of Movement: A Linguistic and Iconographic Survey". *Studi Epigrafici e Linguistici* 28: 37–53.

Pritchard, J.B. (ed.). 1969. *Ancient Near Eastern Texts : Relating to the Old Testament*, 3rd edition. Princton: Princeton University Press.

Pury, A. de, 1991. "Le cycle de Jacob comme légende autonome des origines d'Israël". In *Congress Volume: Leuven 1989*. J.A. Emerton (ed.). Leiden: Brill: 78–96.

——2001. "Le choix de l'ancêtre". *ThZ* 57: 105–14.

——2003. "Pg as the Absolute Beginning". In *Les dernières rédactions du Pentateuque, de l'Hexateuque et de l'Ennéateuque*. T.C. Römer and K. Schmid (eds). Leuven: Peeters: 99–128.

Rendtorff, R. 1997. "Die Herausführungsformel in ihrem literarischen und theologischen Kontext". In *Deuteronomy and Deuteronomic Literature*. M. Vervenne and J. Lust (eds). Leuven: Peeters: 501–27.

Renfrew, C. 1986. "Introduction: Peer Polity Interaction and Socio-Political Change". In *Peer Polity Interaction and Social Political Change*. C. Renfrew and J.F. Cherry (eds). Cambridge: Cambridge University Press: 1–18.

Renfrew, C. and P. Bahn. 2004. *Archaeology: Theories, Methods and Practice*, 4th edition. London: Thames & Hudson.

Römer, T.C. 1990. *Israels Väter: Untersuchungen zur Väterthematik im Deuteronomium und in der deuteronomistischen Tradition*. Fribourg: Academic Press/Göttingen: Vandenhoeck & Ruprecht.

Römer, T.C. and M.Z. Brettler. 2000. "Deuteronomy 34 and the Case for a Persian Hexateuch". *JBL* 119(3): 401–19.

Rom-Shiloni, D. 2013. *Exclusive Inclusivity: Identity Conflicts between the Exiles and the People who Remained (6th–5th Centuries BCE)*. New York: Bloomsbury.

Russell, S.C. 2009. *Images of Egypt in Early Biblical Literature: Cisjordan-Israelite, Transjordan-Israelite, and Judahite Portrayals*. Berlin: De Gruyter.

Schäfer, H. 1974. *Principles of Egyptian Art*. J. Baines (trans.). Oxford: Clarendon Press. Originally published in German as *Von ägyptischer Kunst: eine Grundlage*. Wiesbaden: O. Harrassowitz, 1963.

50   F. Porzia

Schmid, K. 1999. *Erzväter und Exodus: Untersuchungen zur doppelten Begründung der Ursprünge Israels innerhalb der Geschichtsbücher des Alten Testaments*. Neukirchen-Vluyn: Neukirchener Verlag.

Shaw, I. 1991. *Egyptian Warfare and Weapons*. Haverfordwest: Shire.

Sherratt, E.S. 2013. "Introduction to the Levant during the Late Bronze Age". In *The Oxford Handbook of the Archaeology of the Levant c. 8000–332 BCE*. M.L. Steiner and A.E. Killebrew (eds). Oxford: Oxford University Press: 497–508.

Ska, J.L. 1997, *Le passage de la mer: Étude de la construction, du style et de la symbolique d'Ex 14,1–31*, 2nd edition. Roma: Pontificio Istituto Biblico.

——2000. *"Our Fathers Have Told Us": Introduction to the Analysis of Hebrew Narratives*. Roma: Pontificio Istituto Biblico.

Spreafico, A. 1985. *Esodo: Memoria e Promessa. Interpretazioni profetiche*. Bologna: Edizioni Dehoniane.

Staubli, T. 1991. *Das Image der Nomaden im Alten Israel und in der Ikonographie seiner sesshaften Nachbarn*. Fribourg: Academic Press/Göttingen: Vandenhoeck & Ruprecht.

——2009. "'Den Namen setzen': Namens- und Göttinnenstandarten in der Südlevante während der 18. ägyptischen Dynastie". In Hulster and Schmitt 2009: 93–112.

Strawn, B.A. 2009. "Yahweh's Outstretched Arm Revisited Iconographically". In Hulster and Schmitt 2009: 163–211.

Uehlinger, C. (ed.). 2000. *Images as Media. Sources for the Cultural History of the Near East and the Eastern Mediterranean (Ist Millennium BCE)*. Fribourg: Academic Press/Göttingen: Vandenhoeck & Ruprecht.

——2006. "Visible Religion und die Sichtbarkeit von Religion(en). Voraussetzungen, Anknüpfungsprobleme, Wiederaufnahme eines religionswissenschaftlichen Forschungsprogramms". *Berliner Theologische Zeitschrift* 23(2): 165–84.

——2007. "Neither Eyewitnesses, Nor Windows to the Past, but Valuable Testimony in its Own Right: Remarks on Iconography, Source Criticism and Ancient Data-processing". In *Understanding the History of Ancient Israel*, H.G.M. Williamson (ed.). Oxford: Oxford University Press: 173–228.

Van De Mieroop, M. 2005. "The Eastern Mediterranean in Early Antiquity". In *Rethinking the Mediterranean*. W.V. Harris (ed.). Oxford: Oxford University Press: 117–40.

——2007. *The Eastern Mediterranean in the Age of Ramesses II*. Oxford: Blackwell.

Van Seters, J. 1972. "Confessional Reformulation in the Exilic Period". *VT* 22: 448–59.

Weinstein, J.M. 1981. "The Egyptian Empire in Palestine: A Reassessment". *BASOR* 241: 1–28.

Wiese, A. 1990. *Zum Bild des Königs auf ägyptischen Siegelamuletten*. Fribourg: Academic Press/Göttingen: Vandenhoeck & Ruprecht.

Wijngaards, J.N.M. 1963. *The Formulas of the Deuteronomic Creed (Dt 6/20–23: 26/5–9)*. Tilburg: Drukkerij A. Reijnen.

——1965. "הוציא and העלה A Twofold Approach to the Exodus". *VT* 15: 91–102.

Winter, I.J. 1976. "Phoenician and North Syrian Ivory Carving in Historical Context: Questions of Style and Distribution". *Iraq* 38: 1–22.

——1981. "Is there a South Syrian Style of Ivory Carving in the Early First Millennium BC?". *Iraq* 43: 101–30.

3 Exile and return and the closure of the Samaritan and Jewish canons[1]

Ingrid Hjelm

Concepts of Exile, displacement, replacement and return play considerable roles in ancient Samaritan and Jewish biblical and non-biblical literature. Shared stories of migration appear in both the Samaritan and Masoretic Pentateuch, in which uprooting and creation of identities lie at the core of humanity's first entry on history's scene. So much so, that our first stories end in expulsion from ideal places, such as the Garden of Eden in Genesis 3, the land in which one might have Yahweh's protection in Genesis 4, and the imaginary harmonious centre of the world in Genesis 11. Genesis 6–10 represent a most disturbing variant of this theme in its epitomizing 'retelling' of the Pentateuch's journey through the desert from which only a few survive. When such motives take centre stage in successive stories in which their protagonists are constantly on the move and prevented from, or delayed in, a happy return, one wonders whether biblical narratives advocate or pursue a peaceful and secure life in a close and well defined place. The journey's destination is not the main theme of the narrative and the dramatic result of the Mosaic journey's exchange of one generation for another[2] seems antagonistic to the projected happiness of those embarking on the exodus. As readers, we ask for a continuation that takes the travellers into the land. Such is offered in the canonical Masoretic tradition's Deuteronomistic narratives and our attention easily moves away from being on the road to becoming settlers. The canonical Samaritan tradition does not offer such an assurance of fulfilment, although non-canonical Samaritan parallels to the Masoretic Joshua traditions offer a harmonious continuation. As these are not part of the cultic use of scripture in the Samaritan synagogue, the Pentateuchal journey becomes an ever-reiterated event. Before examining the journey in Pentateuchal literature in Section II, a few remarks on sources of inspiration for the development of themes of travel and exile in biblical tradition will be discussed in Section I. Section III will discuss differences between the closure of the Pentateuchal journey in Samaritan and Jewish traditions.

I

The difficult, the happy and the enlightening journey is a recurrent motif in Greek literature, most often in the form of adventurous sea-journeys, as in

52   *I. Hjelm*

Homer's *Odyssey* and Apollonius of Rhodes' *Argonautica*. One cannot exclude that these and other Greek traditions have influenced and perhaps even determined compositions and themes of biblical narrative.[3] Already in antiquity, Jewish and Christian authors from Aristobolus to Eusebius of Caesarea noticed a striking concord between Plato's *Laws* and the Pentateuch. So much so, that the question of borrowing had to be addressed and readers assured that Plato had been taught by Moses and not the other way around (Wajdenbaum 2011: 58–70). The *Argonautic Epic*, first referred to by Homer and retold by Pindar in his fourth *Pythian Ode* in the 6th century BCE, became vividly dramatized by successive writers, reusing its characters in tragedies and plays (Wajdenbaum 2011: 45). Pindar, Herodotus (*Historiae*, book IV) and Appolonius of Rhodes explicitly linked the *Argonautic Epic* to the foundation of the Greek colony of Cyrene in Libya around 630 BCE. Time passing, the settlers, who had come from the Island of Thera (Santorini) in the Aegean, became acculturated and subjected to Ptolemaic and Roman rule. The city's importance as a cultural and political centre was well established throughout the centuries. Tradition relates Jewish presence in Cyrene and the culturally even more important Alexandria from the third century BCE onwards. According to Josephus' rephrasing of Hecataeus, Ptolemy Lagos settled a Jewish colony there in the late fourth century BCE (Josephus *Against Apion* II, ch. 44). This tradition, however, is disputed, but a Jewish presence in several places in Egypt and Libya is testified in epigraphy and papyri from the mid-third century BCE (Appelbaum 1979: 136). Cyrene is continuously mentioned in early Jewish and Christian sources from the mid-second century onwards[4] implying that it had a Jewish population. Knowledge of Greek traditions, of course, could have come from many other places and circumstances before Alexander's advent. The taste for everything Greek was strong among the Persian elite as early as the fifth century BCE. A striking example from Palestine is the 80% of Hebrew and Aramaic names + 15–20 % Assyrian, Babylonian and Persian names, a few Edomite names, but hardly any Greek names in the Wadi el-Daliyeh Papyri (375–334 BCE). However, the seals attached to these papyri expose a very high influence of Greek iconography in a mixed Greco-Persian style, also known from coins of the same period (Leith 1997: 20–24; Briant 2002: 715). One should not forget the Aegean, Cypriote and Philistine presence in the Levant from the second millennium BCE. The roles played by the Philistines in biblical literature vividly narrate a high degree of cultural interaction in the first millennium BCE. It is the combination of a travel myth with the foundation of a colony or a city that makes the Cyrene tradition interesting for biblical research. However, Greek myths about adventurous travels and settlement in ideal places were as much allegories of the soul as they were meant to dramatize realistic events (Wajdenbaum 2011: 57). The ambiguous possession of the Promised land in Joshua–2 Kings reflects such an idealistic view, when the Patriarchs renounce their claim to that land, and Israel stays in Egypt long after the famine that had caused its exile had ended (Cazeaux 2006). "The true Promised Land is the Law, writes

Cazeaux, a guarantee of the fraternal unity of Jacob's twelve sons", which expressed in "Genesis' happy ending" reflects that "Israel's truth lies in permanent exile rather than in the Promised Land's corrupting tenure" (Cazeaux 2006 quoted in Wajdenbaum 2011: 58).

In Mesopotamian literature it is the fateful passing of streams, deserts and woods which challenge the traveller, whether in regard to the mythic heroes in the tale of Gilgamesh or the description of the advance of neo-Assyrian armies over inaccessible and unknown terrain. Coming from Mesopotamia, these armies not only had to cross dangerous streams, but also deserts and mountains, where "there is no path", "their tops being inaccessible to human passage", "through difficult terrain and remote and inaccessible regions" and "where in none of the kings, his fathers have ever set foot" (Oded 1992: 156; Liverani 1979: 306–9). A constant process of making civilized the unknown and chaotic world eventually brings the Assyrians to fight also the Mediterranean (Hjelm 2004a: 132–33; 2009: 9–10). Ashurnasirpal II and Shalmaneser III "march over the highest mountain regions" to reach the sea of the setting sun and cleanse their weapons in the deep sea of Amurru. Sargon II, however, both traversed the mountains and "crossed many times the depths of the sea" (Lyon 1883: 2; Winckler 1889: 180; Oded 1992: 156). Sennacherib pursued his enemies "like a mountain god (*armu*) in mountainous terrain" and Ashurbanipal traversed "a desert in which no bird flies" (Oded 1992: 156). The biblical Exodus similarly transverses unknown and life threatening terrain, and the military formation of the people on their way to conquer their Promised Land (Hjelm 2004a: 150) is not without allusion to Assyrian war ideology. As the Assyrian armies stand on Anti-Lebanon in anticipation of their subjection of Hatti land to eventually reach an even more fertile region (Egypt) soiled in milk and honey, so the Israelites pause on their way to their Promised Land on Mount Nebo. Biblical authors' familiarity with Assyrian royal propaganda is amply demonstrated in the writings of Isaiah (Hjelm 2004a: 130–42).

Ancient Near Eastern deportation ideology,[5] especially as formulated by the neo-Assyrians, seems also to be part of the canvas which formed the biblical exodus. Rather than admitting that deportation was a loss of one's homeland, culture and identity, it was presented to the deportees in positive terms of survival and contribution to maintaining the world order.

> The zones from which the deportees come gain from the situation, since they shall be re-structured, repopulated and thus gained to cosmos from chaos; the deportees themselves gain from the displacement, since they come closer to the center and so are in the part of the world which works correctly.
>
> (Liverani 1973: 191)

The main purpose, however, was to disperse manpower to cultivate the vast agricultural areas that had come under Assyrian hegemony. Assyrian inscriptions abound with texts that report transference of peoples to unpopulated and

54 I. Hjelm

non-cultivated areas, 'giving' them vineyards, orchards, pasture, livestock, ploughs and draught-horses (Oded 1979: 67–74). We also find an example of such ideology in *Rabshaqeh's* speech to Jerusalem's inhabitants promising them a land flowing with wine, olive and honey if they will abandon their former patron (2 Kgs 18:31–32) and 'be with' the king of Assur (Hjelm 2004a: 43–44). Reflective of Ancient Near Eastern Covenant treaties, such as expressed also in Deuteronomy 28, the Hezekiah narrative is the sole example in the Books of Kings of a fulfilment of the 'my people–your Lord' relationship expressed in Solomon's prayer in Kings' temple inauguration narrative (1 Kgs 8:23–53). Playing with motifs of threat and salvation, the *Rabshaqeh* offers the Judaeans listening on the wall a patronage-solution. His speech contrasts Yahweh's promise to Moses' people: a land flowing with milk and honey, if they had the courage to go in and fight with giants (Num 14:8–9, 24). Just so, the *Rabshaqeh* takes the role of trying to seduce the people into believing that they can have their milk and honey without fighting the Assyrian giant. That they shall live, and not die, in a land "as their own land, a land of grain and wine, of bread and vineyards, of olive trees and honey" (2 Kgs 18:32 par. Isa 36:16, which does not mention 'olive trees and honey'). The rhetoric employed by the *Rabshaqeh* echoes similar rhetoric found in a letter to Tiglath-Pileser III from his officers in Babylon. There they tried to quell Chaldaean sedition by diplomacy rather than warfare arguing that the Babylonians enjoyed special privileges in the empire (Grayson 1995: 961). The Judaeans in Hezekiah's biblical Jerusalem did not fall for the trick and were rewarded by divine salvation (Isa 37:36–37 / 2 Kgs 19:35–36). Real history, however, was not so kind to Hezekiah, who saved his city, but lost most of his kingdom, his population and his riches (Ahlström 1993: 714). The contrast to the biblical Hezekiah's loyal subjects are the Israelites in the desert, all of whom died, but Caleb and Joshua, because they did not have the courage to fight against the giants (which the spies had said lived in the country) but cried, complained, rebelled and died (Num 14:1–12,[6] 21–24, 28–30; 16:12–15; 26.64; Hjelm 2000: 44–45).

II

In biblical literature, the journey is often combined with exile, whether 'voluntary' or forced, limited in time and space, or tied to an unknown future. The traditional causes of exile are drought, hunger and war and the Hebrew Bible most often interprets these as punishment for disobedience (Hjelm 2004a: 239). Following standard phraseology in Ancient Near Eastern treaties,[7] both Leviticus and Deuteronomy threaten with exile as the ultimate consequence of disobedience (Lev 26: 33, 43; Deut 28:64; cf. Neh 1:8; Halvorson-Taylor 2011: 36), and promise blessings and a safe and fruitful life in the country for obedience (Lev 26:3–13; Deut 28:1–14). Both these traditions, P/H and D according to standard source criticism, envision a three-step move: to the land, out of the land, and a return to the land. The first two steps imply an election, a treaty and a covenant whose stipulations are solely decided by the deity. The third step, on the contrary, depends on the people's humble repentance and conversion which brings about the deity's forgiveness and restoration of their lives (Lev 26:40–42; Deut 30:2). The biblical literature of Samaritans and Jews differ in their narrative discourse on these matters, since the Pentateuchal narratives do not explicitly link its journeys with sin, expulsion and forgiveness as does the larger Jewish Bible. The sin occurs during the journey, as in Exodus 32's golden calf episode and Numbers' murmuring narratives, which culminates in a 40 years' return to the wilderness (Num 14:34).

A cursory examination of the vocabulary describing the Patriarchs' and their children's journeys reveals that in Genesis 12–50, the Egyptian exile seems not to be caused by sinful behaviour. None of the thirteen appearances of different forms of חטא/חטאה in Genesis declare that drought, hunger and war or travels to foreign lands are caused by any sin. The lurking sin (רבץ חטאת) lies at the entrance in the Cain story (4:7); the people of Sodom and Gomorrah are evil and sinful (רעים וחטאים; Gen 13:13; cf. 18:20); Yahweh prevents Abimelech from committing a great sin (מחטו לי; 20:6; חטאה גדלה; 20:9); Jacob defends himself against accusations of transgression and sin (מה פשעי ומה חטאתי) when Laban's teraphim are missing (31:36, 39); the Egyptian baker and cupbearer sin against Pharaoh (חטאו; 40:1). The remaining five occurrences of חטא are found in the Joseph narrative (Genesis 37–50). The first appearance is Joseph's rejection of Potiphar's wife, that he should commit this great evil deed (ואיך אעשה הרעה הגדולה) and sin (וחטאתי) against God (אלהים; 39:9). Joseph's utterance functions as a projecting signature: he is a righteous man. It contrasts with the act of his brothers, which Reuben declares was a sin (42:22), when he still thought that they had shed Joseph's blod (37:22). Judah, who took the initiative to sell his brother Joseph to the Ishmaelites (37:26–27), later pledges his own life for Benjamin's return to his father's house (43:8–9; 44:32). The narrative rounds off with Joseph's forgiveness of his brothers' sin (חטאה) and transgression (פשע; 50:17–21), for which they offer to become his slaves. Rather than mastering his brothers, Joseph fathers them by providing for them and comforting them in their misery. The story thus interprets didactically Joseph's dreams (Genesis 37), which had set the plot in motion, contrasting these with the anger and envy these had aroused in the mind of his brothers. The divisiveness caused by Jacob's favouring of Joseph is healed when all of Jacob's family is brought to Egypt and prophesied a return to the land promised to Abraham, Isaac and Jacob (Gen 50:24).

Sin is not mentioned as a cause for the family's exile in Egypt, but it is not difficult to see how the author implies it in a way that alludes to the role it plays in other discourses on exile in the Hebrew Bible.[8] And although punishment is not part of the plot it is implied in the narrative discourse when Reuben fears punishment and Joseph's brothers beg for forgiveness. Repentance and forgiveness, however, are not preceded by punishment and Joseph does not say: "you did evil against me, therefore God sent you into exile" or

56   *I. Hjelm*

"you intended to shed my blood, therefore your blood will come upon you". The logic of retribution so pervasive in the Deuteronomistic literature is replaced by a mercy that allows for evil to be turned into good (Gen 50:20): namely that Joseph was sent to Egypt by God for the purpose of preserving Jacob's family as a remnant in the country (שארית בארץ) and keep them alive by a great deliverance (פליטה גדלה; Gen 45:7). In order to do so, he was made "a father for pharaoh and a master of all of Egypt" (Gen 45:8).[9] Genesis' third hunger and Egypt-tale thus presents Egypt positively as benediction and salvation rather than the negative image expressed in the Abraham and Isaac hunger narratives (Gen 12:10–20; 26:1–11). God even encourages Jacob to go to Egypt and assures him that he will go with him, make him a great people and bring him back (46:3–4). This starkly conflicts with numerous warnings against going to Egypt, the worst of which is found in Jeremiah's diatribe, which promises sword, hunger and pestilence to everyone who goes to Egypt (Jer 42:15–22). The positive image in the Joseph narrative does not invite a permanent stay. 400 years is predicted (Gen 15:13), but in the meantime Joseph and his brothers bring their father Jacob's bones back to Canaan to be buried in Abraham's grave (Gen 50:13), and Joseph makes his brothers promise to bring his bones up from Egypt as well. Reminiscent of the number of years of exile in the Masoretic tradition, Jacob is embalmed for 40 days and mourned for 70 days.

The effects of exile include estrangement, vulnerability and dependency, but do Joseph and his brothers live as strangers (גרים) in Egypt and were they truly at home in their homeland? A recurrent motif in the Patriarchal narratives is Abraham and his descendants position as 'foreigner' or 'sojourner' (גור/גר). One would expect this foreignness to relate to non-Canaanite lands, but Abraham, Isaac and Jacob are repeatedly characterized as foreigners or sojourners in Canaan[10] in spite of their cultic demarcation travels within the land. Their foreignness is so thorough that Jacob upon his arrival in Egypt declares all of his and his forefathers' lifetime as spent in foreignness (מגור; 47:9). The many occurrences of גור/גר in Genesis-Exodus characterize the Patriarchs and their descendants as foreigners or sojourners everywhere, and the narrative cycle of leaving and returning to the Promised Land begins and ends in Egypt (Gen 12:10; 47:4; cf. Exod. 22:26; 23:9). Within this narrative cycle is a cycle of Jacob's sojourn to his family in Haran, where Laban's ill-treatment of him and his wives force them to leave as foreigners (Gen 31:15; 32:5). A border stone marks the boundary between Laban's country and Jacob's country (Gen 31:45–54), and the narrative continuation underscores the separation when Jacob's sons do not establish marital relations with their Aramaean relatives (Schectman 2011).

When Joseph's brothers, in contrast, request that they may live as foreigners in Goshen, Pharaoh gives them permission to settle in the best part of Egypt and Joseph provides for them (Gen 47:1–12). The family prospers and multiplies and they are not characterized as foreigners or slaves, such as are the standard phrases about the Egyptian 'exile' in Exodus-Deuteronomy.[11]

Even the Egyptians mourn Jacob's death. The Egyptians, on the contrary, become slaves of Pharaoh when they sell their land and themselves to Joseph in order to survive from hunger (Gen 47:19, 25). When the Israelites leave Egypt, the biggest threat to a successful 'return' to their homeland is their wish to go back to Egypt to find security, survival, cucumbers and slavery (Exod 14:12; 16:3; Num 11:5; 14:3–4). Their homeland is Egypt and, like Abraham, they leave their homeland to face an insecure future in a foreign land, which – apart from the Judahite Caleb and the Ephraimite Joshua – they forfeit access to on the way. The unification of Israel's sons in Egypt, so central to the narrative plot in the Joseph novella, is lost when Yahweh turns out to be less gracious than Joseph (Num 14:27–38; cf. Gen 50:19). Their status as slaves in Egypt (Exod 1:13; 14:5, 12; 23:9; cf. Gen 15:13) becomes replaced by being slaves or servants (עבד) of God (Exod 10:26; Lev 25:42) and servants of God's land, in which they will be foreigners (גרים) and settlers (תושבים) according to Lev 25:23.[12] Such piety is balanced by numerous utterances (in Exodus-Deuteronomy) about taking care of the foreigners in the land, because of their own experience as foreigners and slaves in Egypt (e.g. Exod 22:20; 23:9; Lev 19:34; Deut 10:19).

III

The closure of Deuteronomy leaves both Samaritans and Jews at the entrance to the Promised Land, but from this point on, their traditions differ in regard to canonization and narrative plot. The Samaritan tradition also includes Hebrew (Gaster 1908) and Arabic (Juynboll 1848; Crane 1890; Stenhouse 1985) versions of a *Book of Joshua* as well as Joshua traditions in larger compilations such as *Sepher ha-Yamim/Chronicle II* (Macdonald 1969; Niessen 2000) and the late medieval Arabic chronicle *Kitāb al Tarīkh* by the Samaritan writer Abu 'l-Fath (Vilmar 1865; Stenhouse 1985). Although their content and scope might suggest that this narrative continuation was intended to form a Hexateuch (Hjelm 2004a: 192), it is not part of the Samaritan canon.[13] From a theological perspective this seems to leave the Samaritans on the road with laws in hand, which prepare them for living in the Promised Land, such as is most often formulated in Deuteronomy's opening phrases about entering the land (e.g. Deut 4:5; 6:1; 8:1; 12:1; 18:9; 26:1). Numerous issues are dealt with in this law book, which seeks to keep the tribes together at a crucial time, when divisiveness threatens. Moving from a well-defined centre in the desert camp to dispersion in the land creates other problems than those dealt with in Exodus-Numbers. Key issues are the appointment of cultic, military and administrative leaders in addition to establishing new centres. A balance between centre and periphery is sought and, depending on a Samaritan or Jewish reading of Deuteronomy 11–12, the replacement of the desert sanctuary may point to either Gerizim or Jerusalem as the chosen place. The verbal forms of בחר in either past or future form have been made the main argument about whether Deuteronomy 12 points to a future (MT)

58   *I. Hjelm*

or a past (SP) choice. Samaritan interpretation ties the utterances in Deuteronomy 12 to Deut 11:29 and 27:4 and thus creates a continuum, rather than the caesura introduced in modern scholarly interpretations based on Martin Noth's source criticism. Harmony is maintained by the ambiguity of the utterance, and conquest and settlement in the land do not destroy that harmony in the Samaritan and Jewish Books of Joshua. Closing the narrative circle, both the Masoretic text of Joshua 24 and Samaritan traditions summon the people in Shechem[14] to a renewal of the covenant (Hjelm 2004a: 195–210). The foreignness, which began with Abraham's first stay in Canaan's Shechem, where Yahweh promised to give the land to his descendants (Gen 12:6–7), has come to an end. This is most explicitly expressed when in Deuteronomy and Joshua the foreigners are always the non-Israelites and Egypt was the land in which the people were foreigners (Deut 26:5). What a success – with relaxed muscles and smiling faces, we did it. We came home. Why doesn't the story end here? Why close it earlier in the Samaritan tradition or much later in the Jewish tradition, in which everything is lost again, and all that is left are memories and longing? The answer might relate to the fact that they did not come home. As I demonstrate in my second chapter in this volume, the desert became their burial place.

Samaritan traditions support a harmonious situation in parallel texts to Joshua 23–24, but, unlike their Masoretic counterpart, they do not open up to expectations of coming disaster or accuse the fathers of having worshipped foreign gods. The people's decision to serve Yahweh is not questioned by Joshua and the covenant is concluded by a sacrifice (on the altar) either on or at the foot of 'the mountain'. The mountain is Gerizim and some traditions name it explicitly. Rather than focusing on the people's patronage relationship with their god Yahweh and abandonment and removal of foreign gods as in MT Joshua 24, some Samaritan traditions stress the fidelity to the 'illustrious', the 'holy' or the 'good' Mountain. According to the main Samaritan Arabic chronicle, Abu 'l-Fath's *Kitāb al Tarīkh* (*AF*), this is the mountain, "God made known to you in his unchangeable Law". The chronicle is compiled from a number of different manuscripts around 1355 (Vilmar 1865; Stenhouse 1985). It offers this small note on Joshua's death:

> As soon as Joshua realized that he was dying, he summoned the assembly of Israel to the Plain of Nablus and he said to them: "I am dying and about to leave you. Do not swerve from the service of the Lord, *neither to the right nor to the left* [cf. Jos 23:6];[15] do not serve foreign gods; *accept no Qibla*[16] *other than the illustrious Mountain which God made known to you in his unchangeable Law, lest the disasters written down on* the scroll of the Law *fall upon you*." They replied and said, "Far be it from us to *do such a thing*, or to follow anybody but our Lord. *We will swerve neither to the right nor to the left*: we will serve our Lord *on this Mountain forever*." *So Joshua then took a young lamb and sacrificed it on the Mountain*,[17]

because of the covenant they had made with him on behalf of themselves and their children.

(AF page 37; transl.: Stenhouse 1985; text in italics is not in the Masoretic Joshua 24)

The Late Samaritan Hebrew *Chronicle II* manuscript JR(G) 1168 (= Ryl. Sam. MS 259; Macdonald's manuscript H2; published by Friedrich Niessen, 2000) specifies that Yahweh's election of Mt. Gerizim is stipulated twice in the Decalogue and several times in the Holy Book. The election is accompanied by a warning against following prophets whom Yahweh has not appointed and elevated ("*die Jahve nicht erwählt und beauftragt hat*"; Niessen, 2000: *Buches Yehošua*, fol. 48b–49a).

Such, however, is not mentioned in the Arabic *Book of Joshua*, the manuscript of which is dated to 1362,[18] but considered to have been copied from earlier manuscripts and thus predating Abu 'l-Fath's *Kitāb al-Tarīkh*. Here we read that

Joshua the son of Nun, reigned forty-five years, and at the approach of his death, he assembled the children of Israel and put them under a covenant and bound them to an obligation that they would carefully keep what the prophet Moses – peace be upon him – had enrolled, and he then offered up for himself and for them the sacrifices and bid them farewell, for he did closely what our master Moses – peace be upon him – did, when he bid them farewell.

(Crane 1890: ch, 49, p. 98; Bowman 1977: 73; Anderson and Giles 2005: 120)

Neither is fidelity to Gerizim mentioned in the genealogical chronicle *Tulidah* from the 12th century CE (Bowman 1954; Florentin 1999) and one might consider it a late addition in *AF* and *Chronicle II* (manuscript JR(G) 1168). But redaction criticism is never that simple in regard to Samaritan manuscripts. John Macdonald's principal manuscript of *Chronicle II* JR(G) 1142, (Ryl. Sam. MS 257) from 1902, which he published in 1969, does not mention fidelity to Gerizim in Joshua's farewell speech. Neither is it mentioned in the Hebrew *Joshua* JR(G) 864 (cod. Gaster 864, 4° [1905]), which was published by Moses Gaster in 1908. The origin and age of *Chronicle II* and the Hebrew *Joshua* are subjects of dispute, but a general consensus dates their manuscripts as at least later than the Arabic Chronicles, which are the *Arabic Book of Joshua* from 1362 and Abu'l Fath's *Kitab al-Tarikh* from 1355.

Joshua's farewell speech and his and Eliezer's deaths do not constitute a stable conclusion of a Samaritan canon. The deaths of both demarcate periods of favour and disfavour as found also in the Masoretic tradition's disastrous period of Judges. In the Samaritan tradition, however, the 260 years of favour (*Raḍwān/Riḍwān*) begins with Joshua and ends with the death of Samson. Joshua is the first of thirteen kings of that period, and his and Phinehas' roles

60   *I. Hjelm*

as foundational fathers are concluded by a much more stable tradition which stresses the significance of the Law.

All the Samaritan chronicles, apart from the Arabic Book of Joshua, conclude the *Raḍwān* by a reference to the testimony of Abisha that he has written out (copied?) the Holy Book ("Book of Holiness") in the 13th year of dominion of the Israelites over the land of Canaan. The *tashqil* they quote begins at Deuteronomy 6.4 (10):

> I, Abisha, son of Phinehas, son of Eliezer, son of Aaron the priest upon whom be the Raḍwān of the Lord and his Glory: I wrote out[19] the Book of the Holiness at the entrance to the Tent of Meeting on Mount Gerizim in the thirteenth year of the dominion of the sons of Israel over the land of Canaan, to its borders around it. I give praise to the Lord.
>
> (*AF* 38–39; Stenhouse 1985: 45)

AF 38 states that the Holy Book "is now to be found in Nablus". This is testified also in a marginal note in the *Tulida* (747AH / 1346), which, lacking in the autograph (1149 CE; Bowman 1977: 59 n. 86), adds that this scroll is kept in custody in the High Priest's house in Shechem (Crown, Tal and Pummer 1993: 5; Bowman 1977: 45; Florentin 1999: 69). Such is mentioned also in Mss. of *Chronicle II* (JR(G) 1142 and JR(G) 1168); fol. 52a: "in the synagogue in Shechem".

The Abisha reference usually follows the chronology of the narrative, that it was written in the 13th year after the entrance into the land, but in *AF* page 38.5–39.8 it is placed as a conclusion of the 260 years of the Raḍwān[20] and before the Eli controversy. Manuscripts of *Chronicle II* place the reference after the story about Joshua's successor, Nethaniel (MT Otniel; Judg 3:7–11), Caleb's nephew from the tribe of Judah. He is presented as paying homage to Gerizim and the High Priest, whom he must obey. In both these traditions the placement of the reference seems significant in regard to Samaritan–Jewish controversies over cult place, tradition and authority. Whether the Abisha tradition is a late medieval addition,[21] one must ask if it was intended to be the canonical closure of the Samaritan journey. If not, there seems to be a religious and psychological tension between having a canonical tradition – which in Deuteronomy 34 leaves the Samaritans at the utopian entrance of their Promised Land – and living in the place to which they arrived extra-canonically. In these extra-canonical traditions, they established their holy places around a central shrine, so that at the end of Joshua's and Eleazer's leadership a temple, an altar and the twelve stones have been erected on the summit of Gerizim. Enemies have been conquered or pacified, the land has been allotted to the tribes and Israel lives in harmony. Administration, festivals and covenants have been re-instituted. The Patriarchal sites Shechem, Bethel, Moriah, Elon Moreh, (Gilgal), and the altars and burial places of the Patriarchs, leaders and High Priests all have become closely associated with Gerizim. What a contrast to the insecure future which closes

Deuteronomy. However, the continuation from Deuteronomy's closure on the doorstep of a future not yet realized moves the narrative in both the Samaritan and Masoretic tradition from cult to history. That move might not have been desirable, as it eventually takes the audience from grace to fall. The corruption that follows the periods of favour in both traditions, whether told in the Jewish Judges tradition or the Samaritan Eli and David traditions, hardly invites spiritual imitation. However, both traditions create a cultic continuum by closing the narrative cycle of exile, exodus and settlement with an admonition to keep the Law (ספר תורת משה in MT Jos 23:6; תוראת אלהים ספר in MT Jos 24:26 and the *Holy Book* in *AF* 38–39).

Notes

1 This article is a reworked and much enlarged version of Hjelm (forthcoming).
2 See also my second chapter in this volume.
3 For recent comparative analyses of Hellenistic and biblical literature, see Wajdenbaum 2011; Gmirkin 2006; Thompson and Wajdenbaum 2014.
4 E.g. 1 Macc 15:23; 2 Macc 2:23; Matt 27:32; Mk 15:21; Luke 25:26; Acts 2:10; 6:9 and 11:20; Josephus *Antiquities* 14.114–16, 118; 16.169.
5 Large-scale deportations of subdued civilians were practised by Egyptian, Hittite and Mesopotamian rulers from as early as the third millennium BCE.
6 Slain by Yahweh with plague (נכה בדבר), as were the Israelites in Exod 32.35 (נגף) and the Assyrians in 2 Kgs 19.35 par. Isa. 37.36 (נכה). Whether the last mentioned involves a plague or something else (cf. the discussion in various commentaries) seems to have been without interest to the author, who stresses the fact that the Assyrians were slain by Yahweh.
7 Mendenhall 1955; MacCarthy 1963; Frankena 1965; Grayson 1987; Parpola and Watanabe 1988; Weinfeld 1991 and 2005; Halvorson-Taylor 2011; Altman 2012.
8 *The Book of Jubilees* 34.18–19 institutes the Day of Atonement as a commemoration of Jacob's grief when he sees Joseph's bloodstained coat and asserts that a wild animal has devoured him; cf. Carmichael 2000.
9 Echoes of such narrative discourse are found in 2 Samuel's narrative about Absalom's rebellion. In David's answer to Shime'i, who is the first of Joseph's house to return to David and ask for forgiveness (2 Sam 19:21–24; cf. 16:5–13) after David's 'victory' over Absalom, David, King of Israel, graciously refuses to punish him. The divisiveness caused by Absalom's uproar, however, only finds its closure when Yahweh punishes David in 2 Samuel 24's census story. Intertextually, this narrative confirms David's eponymic role in its concordance with the Aqeda narrative in Genesis 22 (cf. Hjelm 2004a: 239–44).
10 E.g. Gen 17:8; 23:4; 36:7; 37:1; 47:9; Exod 6:4; 18:3.
11 E.g. Exod 22:20; 23:9; Lev 19:34; Deut 10:19; 23:8; 24:8; 26:5.
12 Cf. Abraham's words to the Hittites in Gen 23:4: גר ותושב אנכי עמכם
13 For general introductions to the Samaritan literature, see e.g. Montgomery 1907; repr. 1968; Gaster 1925; repr. 1976/80; Coggins 1975; Bowman 1977; Stenhouse 1989; Hjelm 2004b; Anderson and Giles 2005.
14 In the LXX the event takes place in Shiloh with the purpose of creating a literary continuity from the sanctuary in Shiloh to Solomon's temple in Jerusalem (Hjelm 2004a: 197–98)
15 The command not to swerve to the right or to the left is reminiscent of Deut 5:32 and 28:14, and in both Masoretic and Samaritan Joshua traditions, it frames

62   *I. Hjelm*

Joshua's period as leader (Jos 1:7 and 23:6). The metaphor alludes to Exodus' waters, which stood as a wall to the right and the left of them, when the Israelites went through on dry ground (Exod 14:22, 29).

16 An Arabic term referring to the direction towards which one must pray. For the Samaritans, Mount Gerizim is the Qibla, the 'Chosen Place'; cf. Stenhouse, *AF*, i, n. 3.

17 The sacrifice appears in all editions. In the manuscripts published by Gaster 1908, Macdonald 1969 and Niessen 2000, Joshua builds an altar at the foot of Mount Gerizim, next to the stone of witness. In Samuel Rylands MS 863, 864 and 269, Shechem is called holy; cf. also The Shechem Poem of Theodotion (Eusebius, *Praeparatio evangelica* 9.22), discussed in Hjelm 2000: 138–46.

18 The manuscript was first published by Juynboll 1848 and translated into English by Crane 1890; see also Bowman 1977 and Anderson and Giles 2005.

19 Hebrew: כתב√

20 AF Page 39: "This illustrious Book represents the Raḍwān" (Stenhouse 1985: 45); idem n. 159: " يقوم مقام الرضان: i.e. makes present, discloses the time of the Raḍwān".

21 A scribal note dates the scroll presented as the Abisha Scroll to 1065 CE, but modern scholars argue that it stems from the middle of the 12th century CE (1149) and has been patched with later additions due to corruption of the original manuscript; cf. Pérez-Castro 1959 and Crown 1975. Its rediscovery has been associated with the Samaritan High Priest Abisha ben Phinehas, who is also known as 'the Master of Poems', from the 14th century CE. The Samaritan tradition about the original scroll's disappearance, of which was left only Num 35:2–Deut 34:10, can be read in Bowman 1977: 47–48.

Bibliography

Ahlström, Gösta W. 1993. *The History of Ancient Palestine from the Palaeolithic Period to Alexander's Conquest.* Sheffield: JSOT Press.

Altman, Amnon, 2012. *Tracing the Earliest Recorded Concepts of International Law: The Ancient Near East (2500–330 BCE).* Leiden: Brill.

Anderson, Robert T. and Terry Giles. 2005. *Tradition Kept. The Literature of the Samaritans.* Peabody, MA: Hendrickson.

Appelbaum, S. 1979. *Jews and Greeks in Ancient Cyrene.* Leiden: Brill.

Bowman, John. 1954. *Transcript of the Original Text of the Samaritan Chronicle Tolidah.* Leeds: University of Leeds.

——1977. *Samaritan Documents Relating to Their History, Religion and Life.* Pittsburgh: Pickwick Press.

Briant, P. 2002. *From Cyrus to Alexander. A History of the Persian Empire.* Winona Lake, IN: Eisenbrauns.

Carmichael, Calum. 2000. "The Origin of the Scapegoat Ritual". *Vetus Testamentum*, L, 2: 167–82.

Cazeaux, Jacques. 2006. *Le partage de minuit, essai sur la Genèse.* Paris: Cerf.

Coggins, R.J. 1975. *Samaritans and Jews: The Origins of Samaritanism Reconsidered.* Oxford: Basil Blackwell.

Crane, Oliver T. 1890. *The Samaritan Chronicle, or the Book of Joshua the Son of Nun.* New York: John B. Alden.

Crown, Alan D. 1975. "The Abisha Scroll of the Samaritans". *Bulletin of John Ryland's Library,* 58: 36–55.

Crown, Alan. D., Abraham Tal and Reinhard Pummer (eds). 1993. *A Companion to Samaritan Studies.* Tübingen: J.B.C. Mohr (Paul Siebeck).

Florentin, Moshe. 1999. *The Tulidah: A Samaritan Chronicle. Text, Translation and Commentary*. Jerusalem: Yad Izhak Ben-Zvi. In Hebrew.

Frankena, Rintje. 1965. "The Vassal Treaties of Esarhaddon and the Dating of Deuteronomy". *OTS* 14:122–54.

Gaster, Moses. 1908. "Das Buch Josua in hebräisch samaritanischer Rezension. Entdeckt und zum ersten Male herausgegeben". *ZDMG* 62: 209–79, 494–549.

——1925. *The Samaritans, Their History, Doctrines and Literature*. London: Oxford University Press; repr. 1976 and 1980.

Gmirkin, Russel E. 2006. *Berossus and Genesis, Manetho and Exodus. Hellenistic Histories and the Date of the Pentateuch*. New York and London: T&T Clark.

Grayson, A.K. 1987. "Akkadian Treaties of the Seventh Century B.C.". *JCS* 39: 127–60.

——1995 "Assyrian Rule of Conquered Territory in Ancient Western Asia". In *Civilizations of the Ancient Near East*. II. J.M. Sasson (ed.). New York: Scribner's Sons: 959–68.

Halvorson-Taylor, Martien A. 2011. *Enduring Exile. The Metaphorization of Exile in the Hebrew Bible*. Leiden: Brill.

Hjelm, Ingrid. 2000. *The Samaritans and Early Judaism: A Literary Analysis*. Sheffield: Sheffield Academic Press.

——2004a. *Jerusalem's Rise to Sovereignty in Ancient Tradition and History: Zion and Gerizim in Competition*. London and New York: Continuum and T&T Clark International.

——2004b: "What do Samaritans and Jews Have in Common? Recent Trends in Samaritan Studies". *Currents in Biblical Research* 3.1: 9–62.

——2009. "The Assyrian Evidence. A Reply to Salibi's Questions Regarding Assyrian Sources for their Campaigns in Palestine and the Existence of a Bît Humria in Palestine in the Iron II". In *SJOT. Studies in Honour of Thomas L. Thompson*, N.P. Lemche (ed.) 23/1: 7–22.

——Forthcoming. "Concepts of Exile and Return in Samaritan and Jewish Literature". In *Studies on Samaritan Traditions: Papers of the 8th Congress of the Société d'Etudes Samaritaines*. Stefan Schorch (ed.). Berlin and Boston: de Gruyter.

Juynboll, Theodore W.J. 1848. *Chronicon samaritanum, arabice conscriptum, cui titulus est Liber Josuae*. Leiden: S. & J. Luchtmans. Engish translation by Oliver T. Crane. *The Samaritan Chronicle, or the Book of Joshua the Son of Nun*. New York: John B. Alden, 1890.

Leith, M.J.W. 1997. *Wadi Daliyeh I. The Wadi Daliyeh Seal Impressions*. Oxford: Clarendon Press.

Liverani, M. 1973. "Memorandum on the Approach to Historiographic Texts". In *Approaches to the Study of the Ancient Near East: A Volume of Studies Offered to Ignace Jay Gelb on the Occasion of His 65th Birthday*. G. Buccellati (ed.), 178–94. Rome: Pontifical Biblical Institute/Los Angeles: Undena.

——1979. "The Ideology of the Assyrian Empire". In *Power and Propaganda: A Symposium on Ancient Empires*. M.T. Larsen (ed.). Mesopotamia, Copenhagen Studies in Assyriology 7; Copenhagen: Akademisk Forlag: 297–317.

Lyon, D. G. 1883. *Keilschrifttext Sargons, König von Assyrien (722–705 v. Chr.)*. Leipzig.

MacCarthy, Dennis J. 1963. *Treaty and Covenant. A Study in Form in the Ancient Oriental Documents and in the OT*. Rome: Pontifical Biblical Institute.

Macdonald, John. 1969. *The Samaritan Chronicle no. II (or: Sepher Ha-Yamim). From Joshua to Nebuchadnezzar*. Berlin: W. de Gruyter.

64 *I. Hjelm*

Mendenhall, George E. 1955. *Law and Covenant in Israel and in the Ancient Near East*. Pittsburg: Biblical Colloquium.

Montgomery, J.A. 1907. *The Samaritans: The Earliest Jewish Sect: Their History, Theology and Literature*. Philadelphia: The John C. Winston Co. Reproduction, New York: Ktav, 1968.

Niessen, Friedrich. 2000. *Eine Samaritanische Version des Buches Yehošua und die Šobak-Erzählung: Die Samaritanische Chronik Nr. II, Handschrift 2: JR(G) 11 68 = Ryl. Sam. MS 259, Folio 8b-53a*. Hildesheim: Georg Olms.

Oded, B. 1979. *Mass Deportations and Deportees in the Neo-Asyrian Empire*. Wiesbaden: Reichert.

——1992. *War, Peace and Empire: Justifications for War in Assyrian Royal Inscriptions*. Wiesbaden: Reichert Verlag.

Parpola, Simo and Kazuko Watanabe. 1988. *Neo-Assyrian Treaties and Loyalty Oats*. Helsinki: Helsinki University Press.

Pérez-Castro, F. 1959. *Sefer Abisa, edicion del fragment antique*. Madrid: CSIC.

Schectman, Sarah. 2011. "Rachel, Leah and the Composition of Genesis". In *The Pentateuch. International Perspectives on Current Research*. Thomas B. Dozeman, Konrad Schmid and Baruch J. Schwartz (eds). Tübingen: Mohr Siebeck: 207–22.

Stenhouse, P. 1985. *The Kitāb al Tarīkh of Abu'l-Fath. Translated into English with Notes*. Sydney: The Mandelbaum Trust, University of Sydney.

——1989. "Samaritan Chronicles". In *The Samaritans*. A.D. Crown (ed.). Tübingen: Mohr Siebeck: 218–65.

Thompson, Thomas L. and Philippe Wajdenbaum (eds). 2014. *The Bible and Hellenism. Greek Influence on Jewish and Early Christian Literature*. Durham: Acumen.

Vilmar, E. 1865. *Abulfathi Annales Samaritani*. Gothae: F.A. Perthes. English transation by P. Stenhouse. *The Kitāb al Tarīkh of Abu'l-Fath. Translated into English with Notes*. Sydney: The Mandelbaum Trust, University of Sydney, 1985.

Wajdenbaum, Philippe. 2011. *Argonauts of the Desert. Structural Analysis of the Hebrew Bible*. London and Oakville: Equinox (CIS).

Weinfeld, Moshe. 1991. "The Covenant of Grant in the Old Testament and in the Ancient Near East". In *Essential Papers on Israel and the Ancient Near East*. Frederick E. Greenspan (ed.). New York: New York University Press: 69–102.

——2005. *The Loyalty Oath in The Ancient Near East*. In his *Normative and Sectarian Judaism in the Second Temple Period*. London and New York: T&T Clark: 2–44.

Winckler, H. 1889. *Die Keilschrifttexte Sargons*. Leipzig: Eduard Pfeiffer.

4 Constructions of exile in the Persian period

Cian Power

This chapter is an effort to discern distinctive perspectives on exile within the Hebrew Bible. Specifically, I shall trace varying assessments of the meaning and significance of the mass deportations from Jerusalem and Judah carried out by the Neo-Babylonians in 597 and 587 BCE. The texts I shall analyze are those written after the fall of Babylon to Cyrus, during the period of Achaemenid Persian hegemony in the Near East (ca. 539–331 BCE). I shall ask questions of these texts such as: How long did the exile last? Who went into exile? How significant was this event for Judah? The goal is to discover, in this formative period, the variety of attitudes towards the exile that were current when the meaning of the events had not yet achieved fixity.

Daniel L. Smith-Christopher (1997: 7–11) has described the wide range of assessments scholars have made of the significance of the Babylonian exile in biblical history. This range of opinions is partly due to the paucity of evidence for the centuries following the deportations, but should also be attributed to the range of "ways the Bible constructs its ideology of exile", as Adele Berlin (2010: 342) puts it. Rainer Albertz (2003: 3–44), Robert P. Carroll (1997) and others have attempted to elicit some of this diversity in several aspects, and this chapter intends to further the discussion by focusing specifically on works from the Persian period.

While greater attention has been paid in recent years to the Persian period Yehud and to the situation of Judaeans inside and outside the province, our knowledge is still limited.[1] Likewise, the confidence with which we can date biblical texts within this period is not strong.[2] Thus it will not be possible to construct a diachronic picture of conceptions of the exile in this literature, or to explain them with reference to historical situations. This chapter is therefore structured in order to allow comparison between the ideas found in the texts. I shall begin with the prophetic books, in which broadly two attitudes towards exile can be discerned. I shall then move to the writings, examining the similar attitudes in Ezra, Nehemiah and 1 & 2 Chronicles, finally considering Esther, which displays a distinctive perspective.

Prophets

Exile plays a major role in Ezekiel and Jeremiah, texts which purport to have been written in the midst of the Babylonian deportations and in their

66   *C. Power*

immediate wake.[3] The place of exile in later prophetic literature, however, is less clear.

Isaiah 56–66

The material in Isa 56–66 ('Third Isaiah') is commonly dated to the Persian period, since it is considered distinct from and later than the prophecies of Isa 40–55 ('Second Isaiah'), which reflect the historical situation of the last years of the Neo-Babylonian period. These chapters several times mention Israelites living among the nations, always in a context of ingathering. For instance, Yahweh is the one "who gathers the outcasts of Israel [מקבץ נדחי ישׂראל]" (56:8), and he promises Zion that, when foreigners come in the future to honour Jerusalem, they will "bring your children from far away" (60:9, recalling 49:22; cf. 60:4 and 66:20).[4]

Based on these and other passages, Bradley C. Gregory (2007: 475) has argued that Third Isaiah "provides one of the earliest attestation [sic] of the idea of a theological exile that extends beyond the temporal and geographical bounds of the Babylonian captivity". Such an enduring exile is a recognized theme in the book of Daniel (see esp. ch. 9), where Jeremiah's prophecy of seventy years of desolation for Jerusalem (Jer 25:12; 29:10) is transformed into a prediction of seventy 'weeks' of years. Gregory (2007: 481–88) claims that language of ongoing captivity in Third Isaiah attests to the presence of this theme in the work: "Yahweh ... has sent me ... to proclaim liberty to captives [לשׁבוים], and release to prisoners" (Isa 61:1).[5]

It is certainly true, as Gregory notes, that Third Isaiah portrays Judah's current state of affairs negatively, in need of Yahweh's intervention; these chapters talk of restoration and ingathering as future realities, not as past ones. But to connect this so closely with the *Babylonian* deportations specifically, and thus to dub this negative state of affairs 'exile' is unjustified. Babylon is not mentioned in Isaiah 56–66, and the root גלה, the standard biblical Hebrew word for 'exile' or 'deportation', is absent in reference to exile; in addition, the closely associated root שׁבה, 'to take captive', only occurs once, in 61:1, quoted above, where the location of the captives is not specified. Rather, the vague language of captivity reflects a general reality: the forecasted ingathering will bring Israelites to Jerusalem from *all* the nations where they have been scattered throughout history, and they will come with "foreigners who join themselves to Yahweh" (58:6). Following the usage of Third Isaiah, 'desolation' would be a more apposite name than 'exile' for this state of affairs. Third Isaiah should not, therefore, be considered to display the very specific notion attested in Daniel that an exile, which began with the Babylonian deportations, extends well into the Persian period.

Joel

In general, Joel makes few references to Israel's historical traditions as it elaborates upon its chief concern: agricultural scarcity as a result of a swarm of locusts. Although the roots גלה and שבה are absent, the book suggestively evokes the threat associated especially with the Babylonians when it calls the swarm "the northerner" [הצפוני] (2:20; cf. Jer 1:14–15, Ezek 39:1–2).[6] However, no clear conception of exile is discernible in the book. In one oracle (4:1–3), Yahweh promises to judge "all the nations" for having scattered [פזרו] Israel "among the nations". Thus the book shows general awareness that throughout history, Israelites have fled and been deported. But no specific destination is given, nor is any particular aggressor nation named. According to Carroll (1997: 68), "[t]his scroll does not really belong to a survey of diaspora discourses in the prophetic literature".

Haggai and the remnant

The intended historical setting of the book of Haggai is made clear by date formulae, which assign the oracles to the second year of Darius's reign.[7] Carroll (1997: 71) rightly claims that "[t]he Haggai scroll has nothing to say about deportation or restoration", insofar as it does not speak of scattering or dispersal, or of a return of people from abroad. The roots גלה and שבה are not used, and although the book predicts that the nations will bring their treasures to Jerusalem (Hag 2:6–7), this is not associated with the return of Israel's dispersed.

However, the effects of exile can be discerned in Haggai. The phrase העם שארית, 'remnant of the people', is used three times in the book. One of Haggai's oracles is addressed to Zerubbabel, Joshua and "the remnant of the people" (2:2) and, in the narrative sections of the book, the same 'remnant' listens to the prophet's injunction (1:12) and is inspired by Yahweh to rebuild the temple (1:14). The prophet does not specify who makes up this remnant. In other books שאר is applied as well to those left behind in the land after the deportations (2 Kgs 25:12) as to those who were removed (Ezek 11:13). Indeed, since Haggai's community seems to contain 'returnees' such as Zerubbabel and Joshua (see Ezra 2:1–2), Bustenay Oded (2003: 62) is probably correct to claim that "[i]n the book of Haggai there is no distinction between those who returned from Babylonia and those who had remained in the land".

In using this term, Haggai displays an understanding of the effects of the Babylonian depopulations that is also found in Jeremiah (e.g. 24:8), Ezekiel (11:13), and Nehemiah (1:2–3). In this understanding, these events changed the nature of the nation: the people is no longer whole; Judah is truncated and stunted, a remnant of its former self. In this prophet's work, then, the exile played a significant role.

Zechariah

It is common to divide the book of Zechariah into two broad sections. The oracles and visions of chs. 1–8, the so-called 'First Zechariah', address the situation of Judaeans in the early years of the Persian-period restoration of

68   *C. Power*

Jerusalem. The origin and authorship of the often difficult chs. 9–14 ('Second Zechariah') are unclear. If, as Carol L. and Eric M. Meyers (1993: 15–28) argue, the work was composed in response to the situation of the fifth century, then, like chs. 1–8, it represents a piece of Persian period literature. It is worth considering the meaning and significance of exile in these two sections separately.

The 'seventy years' in First Zechariah

The duration of the exile is an interesting point of divergence in texts from the Persian period. In particular, First Zechariah's temporal understanding differs from that found in Chronicles and Ezra. All three works seem to rely on prophecies from Jeremiah that use a figure of seventy years to describe the duration of Babylonian dominion (Jer 25:12; 29:10).[8] In Chronicles and Ezra, the fulfilment of Jeremiah's prophecy is associated with Cyrus's decree permitting Judaeans to return to Judah (2 Chr 36:20–22; Ezra 1:12).[9] Thus the end of Yahweh's punishment of Judah is signalled by the liberation of the captive Judaeans, the end of the exile. This decree is dated, in Chronicles and Ezra, to the first year of Cyrus's reign (over Babylonia), that is, 538 BCE.

In Zech 1–8, however, the extent of the 'seventy years' is different. The figure occurs twice in these chapters (without explicit reference to Jeremiah). In an oracle dated to the second year of Darius I's reign, 519 BCE (Zech 1:7), Zechariah's angelic guide asks, "O Yahweh of hosts, how long will you withhold mercy from Jerusalem and the cities of Judah, with which you have been angry these seventy years [זה שבעים שנה]?" (Zech 1:12). In another oracle, dated to Darius's fourth year, 517 BCE (7:1), Yahweh denounces insincere religious observance: "When you fasted and lamented in the fifth month and in the seventh for these seventy years [וזה שבעים שנה], was it for me that you fasted?" (Zech 7:5).

Zechariah's seventy-year period therefore extends two decades further than the Chronicler's and Ezra's, and its end is not marked by the same thing. Since Zech 6:10 speaks of "the exiles ... who have arrived from Babylon [מבבל הגולה ... אשר באו]", the prophet is clearly aware that a return of some kind has taken place, which included the high-profile figures Zerubbabel and Joshua.[10] This return, however, does not mark the end of the seventy years of Yahweh's disfavour; rather, the restoration of the cities of Judah and Jerusalem, and the rebuilding of the temple, which hover in the near future, appear to play this role instead (Zech 1:14–17).[11]

Zechariah's difference from Ezra and Nehemiah in the book's neglect of 'exile' in defining this period is extremely important historiographically. It shows how differently these books divide Israelite history into eras. According to the periodization in Ezra and Chronicles, it would be meaningful to divide Judaean history into pre-exilic, exilic and postexilic periods. For Zechariah, however, while exile is certainly one sign of divine wrath, it does not in itself characterize the period following the conquest of Jerusalem. Thus 'pre-exilic',

'exilic', and 'postexilic' would not appropriately describe Zechariah's interpretation of Judaean history, reflecting a significant difference in understandings of the impact of exile in the life of Judah.

Second Zechariah

Second Zechariah has little to say about exile and exiles, but in one passage in particular the return of the dispersed is meditated upon at length (10:6–12). Yahweh says: "Though I sowed them among the nations, yet in far countries they shall remember me, and they shall rear their children and return. I will bring them home from the land of Egypt, and gather them from Assyria" (10:9–10).[12]

This passage gives no indication of the means by which Yahweh brought about the scattering of his people. It is clear, however, that the dispersed of the northern kingdom (the "house of Joseph", v. 6) as well as of Judah are in view, so no particular act of deportation in the history of Israel, nor any specific group of deportees is recalled.

Summary

In the texts so far considered, variations are found in the significance of the Babylonian exile in the minds of these prophets. Joel, Second Zechariah and Third Isaiah, have in common that they consider Israel's current existence to be marked by dispersion. Israelites live among the nations, outside the land, and these texts emphasize a return from these places to a greater or lesser extent. But the Babylonian deportations are not awarded a special place. No distinction is made between the general Israelite diaspora that has resulted from successive deportations and migrations, and a specific deportation of Judah to Babylon. Nor has the exile come to constitute the identity of Israel in these books. Hence we should regard the Babylonian exile as at least marginal in the thought of these prophets.

The situation is different in Haggai and First Zechariah. In Haggai's eyes, the people have been reduced to a 'remnant' as a result of Babylonian destruction and deportation. Zechariah sees in those events the beginning of a period of desolation, soon to end, in which exile figures largely, though not exclusively. Exile can thus be seen to have had a significant impact on the thought of these texts.

Ezra and Nehemiah: defining a community through exile

The books of Ezra and Nehemiah depict efforts to rebuild a Judaean community around Jerusalem in the Persian period. Without addressing the complex compositional issues surrounding these books,[13] I will treat Ezra and Nehemiah separately, which seems to be justified on canon-critical and source-critical grounds, and will prove fruitful in this investigation of exile.

70   *C. Power*

Ezra

As Bob Becking writes, "the narratives in Ezra function as a self-definition of one stream of Judaism in the final decades of the Persian period" (Becking 1998: 53). Specifically, for the author of Ezra, the experience of exile is centrally important in the identity of Judah in the Persian period. This is revealed by Ezra's unique use of הגולה. Already in Ezekiel, הגולה is used to refer to a specific group of Judaeans – namely, those currently in a state of exile – who form Ezekiel's audience (Ezek 11:25). Relatedly, הגולה is used in Zechariah to refer to those who once were exiles, but who have since returned to Jerusalem: Yahweh commands Zechariah to "collect silver and gold from the exiles [מאת הגולה] – from Heldai, Tobijah and Jedaiah – who have arrived from Babylon" (Zech 6:10). Here the term picks out a very limited group among the restoration community, a few wealthy returned exiles.

In Ezra, הגולה is very common, particularly in collocations such as בני הגולה, "the children of the exiles", (10:7), and קהל הגולה, "the assembly of the exiles" (10:8).[14] But in contrast to prior usage, in Ezra the term has a very broad application: it designates the entire restoration community, and seems to be used interchangeably with 'Judah' and 'Israel' (compare 9:1 with 9:4, and 10:9 with 10:16).[15] This usage is clearly a development from the use of הגולה in Ezekiel and Zechariah, but it has significant implications. For Ezra, returned exiles make up such a significant part of Israel that they *are* Israel, and exile is an experience that they can all be considered to have gone through. Exile is now a definitive event in the people's history.

This is not simply a rhetorical device, but has concrete relevance for the restoration community. The punishment imposed in 10:8 on those who fail to dissolve their mixed marriages is exclusion from "the assembly of the exiles". Thus, for the author of the work, it is membership of Judah *qua* exilic community which is of chief importance. Likewise, the group prohibited from making mixed unions with (עמ(י) הארצ(ות "the people(s) of the land(s)", is "the exiles" (10:7) and "the children of the exile" (10:16). By limiting legitimate marriages, and therefore legitimate offspring, to members of this group Ezra and the leaders of the people ensure that all future generations of Judaeans will be descended from the exiles.

It is widely assumed that behind the conflicts that in Ezra are presented as occurring between the exilic restoration community on the one hand, and the 'people(s) of the land(s)', on the other, lie real social divisions of a different nature. Hugh G. M. Williamson (1985: 131–32) observes that the label 'the people(s) of the land(s)' is probably a polemical device for categorizing groups from whom the author of Ezra wishes to distance himself. Others have sought to discover the make-up of these groups, and one strong candidate is those left behind in Judah after the deportations (see Carroll 1992: 84). Hostility between those exiled and those left behind arose early after the deportations (see Ezek 11:14–25; Jer 24:1–10). Indeed, the existence of a group left behind is never explicitly acknowledged in Ezra, and in that sense they are denied a part in Ezra's vision of the restoration community, a community forged by exile. The situation is different, however, in Nehemiah.

Nehemiah

Although many of the concerns of Ezra are shared by Nehemiah, such as reconstruction of the Judaean community in Judah, in Nehemiah they receive a slightly different emphasis and expression. In particular, exile in the book of Nehemiah is less constitutive for Judaean identity than in Ezra.

Firstly, in Nehemiah 'the Judaeans' (היהודים) is the standard way of referring to the restoration community (see e.g. Neh 1:2; 5:1–13), in contrast to 'the exiles' of Ezra.[16] This contrast is clear in Nehemiah's own mixed-marriage crisis (13:23–27), which is described as the union of 'Judaeans' with 'Ashdodite, Ammonite, and Moabite women', without reference to 'the exiles' or 'the peoples of the lands'. Nehemiah's terminology does not therefore stress the essentially exilic character of Persian-period Judah.

In addition, unlike Ezra, Nehemiah seems willing to acknowledge that the restoration community consists, at least in part, of Judaeans who remained in the land after the deportations. When he asks some Judaeans visiting Susa about the welfare of his Judaean kin, he asks "about the Judaeans that survived [היהודים הפליטה], those left [הנשארים] from the captivity" (1:2).[17] The travellers respond that "those left [הנשארים] there in the province who are left [אשר נשארו] from the captivity are in great trouble and shame" (Neh 1:3).[18] Although ambiguous, these references are most naturally interpreted as referring to those left in the land after the destruction.

Thus, in contrast to Ezra, there is little sense in Nehemiah that Judah's future belongs solely to the descendants of returned exiles. Although it certainly shaped Judah, the exile for Nehemiah is not definitive of Judaean identity.

The extent of the exile in 1 & 2 Chronicles

The books of Chronicles have traditionally been regarded as containing the clearest expression of the 'myth of the empty land'.[19] Albertz, for instance, describes the Chronicler's presentation of the exile thus:

> first ... during this period the land lay totally fallow and uninhabited (cf. Lev 26:43). Second, even more totally than in Kings, the entire surviving population of Judah (and Benjamin) was deported (2 Chr 36:20). ... Third, continuity between pre-exilic and postexilic Israel could be established only through the Babylonian golah.
>
> (Albertz 2003: 14)

If this were so, the significance of the exile according to the Chronicler would be great indeed. It would have ended five centuries or more of Judaean

72   C. Power

settlement in Judah, and, being a bottleneck through which the entire community had passed, would have become deeply imprinted on the collective memory and identity of Israel.

The significance of the exile in Chronicles is in question, however, in light of Sara Japhet's (2009) arguments about the theme of 'uninterrupted settlement' in the work. According to Japhet, the Chronicler presents Israel as continuously settled in its land throughout its history: "Foreign armies come and go but the people's presence in the land continues uninterrupted" (Japhet 2009: 339). Naturally this is incompatible with the 'myth of the empty land'.

In support of her thesis, Japhet observes that Chronicles does not narrate the deportation by the Assyrians of the majority of the inhabitants of the northern kingdom (cf. 2 Kgs 17), but only of the Transjordanian tribes (1 Chr 5:26); and furthermore that Hezekiah's letters to 'Ephraim and Manasseh' assume a populated north. Regarding the Babylonian deportations, Japhet points out that, whereas two deportations are narrated in 2 Kgs 24–25, only one is found in 2 Chronicles (36:19–20). Moreover, she argues that this deportation is presented as restricted to the city of Jerusalem, since this is the only location mentioned in these verses; Judaeans in surrounding areas were not removed.

In these differences between events narrated in the books of Kings, Japhet sees a sustained attempt by the Chronicler to downplay the significance of deportations in Israel's history. These deportations never fundamentally disturbed Israel's presence: "'All Israel', in the true meaning of this term for the Chronicler, had never been exiled and never left the land!" (Japhet 2009: 339). The Babylonian deportations, then, could not acquire the significance in Chronicles that they have in Ezra, as experiences definitive of the entire community.

However, Japhet's theory is open to several objections which undermine the relevance of her arguments in assessing the significance of exile in Chronicles. Her argument requires that if the Chronicler does not narrate an event, like a mass deportation, then, according to him, it did not happen. But the Chronicler's repeated, explicit citation of external sources makes it clear that his history of Israel is not intended to be exhaustive. That the Chronicler does not narrate deportations from Israel, then, is not reason to believe that, according to him, they did not happen.[20] Regarding the deportations from Judah, William Johnstone (1996: 250) has noted that there are in fact indications in Chronicles that the Babylonian exile was not limited to Jerusalem: he claims that 2 Chr 36:19–20 is ambiguous, not clearly restricting the exile to Jerusalem; moreover, other verses in the work suggest an exile of broader scope, e.g. 1 Chr 5:41, "Yahweh sent Judah and Jerusalem into exile by the hand of Nebuchadnezzar" (cf. 9:1).

Thus, Japhet does not present a convincing case that the Babylonian exile of Judah was not, for the Chronicler, total. In fact, the universality of the exile from Judah has an important function for the Chronicler: allowing the fulfilment of the requirement in Lev 25:2–7, that the land should 'keep Sabbath', that is, lie fallow, one year in seven. By remaining unworked for the seventy years of the exile, the land makes up for its previously unobserved sabbatical years (2 Chr 36:21). It is hard to see how this could be accomplished if the Chronicler imagined that a population remained in the land all that time.

The Chronicler's perspective of exile, then, is close to Ezra's: it is a communal experience shared by Judah, and constitutive of its future identity. This similarity should not be surprising given the clear (redactional?) link between these works, created by the inclusion of the decree of Cyrus in both (2 Chr 36:22–23; Ezra 1:1–4). In fact, we may say that Chronicles is even more explicit in denying reality to Judaean survivors in the land than is Ezra. As Carroll (1992: 83) and Becking (1998: 53) have noted, denying reality to this group may have served to marginalize their significance in the Persian-period restoration community.

Esther

The tale of Esther is set in the Persian period, probably during the reign of Xerxes I (486–465 BCE), and likely composed a century or so later (see Berlin 2001: xli) As readers we are aware that the setting of the action in the book of Esther depends upon the deportations and flights from Jerusalem of the early sixth century. These saw Judaeans spread across the Near East, from Babylonia to Egypt. But the explicit role that exile plays in the work is small, being limited to one verse:

> [5]Now there was a Judaean in the citadel of Susa whose name was Mordecai son of Jair son of Shimei son of Kish, a Benjaminite,[6] who had been exiled [הָגְלָה] from Jerusalem among the exiles who were exiled [עִם־הַגֹּלָה אֲשֶׁר הָגְלְתָה] with King Jeconiah of Judah, whom King Nebuchadnezzar of Babylon had exiled [הָגְלָה].[21]

> (Esth 2:5–6)

Whether we are supposed to believe that it was Mordecai who was exiled or rather one of his ancestors (see Jon D. Levenson 1997: 26), the function of this verse is to explain the presence of a Judaean in Susa, one of the Persian capitals.[22] Here, Mordecai is granted "a developed … exilic identity" (Halvorson-Taylor 2012: 477 n. 35). Thus the book of Esther acknowledges that its action takes place in a world shaped by Babylonian deportation, a significant acknowledgement, given that the book is silent about other formative events and figures in Israelite history. In particular, the fourfold use of the root גלה in the short verse 2:6 emphasizes the particular historical moment of Jeconiah's exile from Jerusalem.

But if the Babylonian exile was significant to the author of Esther, no further reference to it is made in the book. The root גלה does not occur elsewhere in the book with reference to exile.[23] In this respect, and in that the verse contains the book's only references to Judah, Jerusalem, Jeconiah, Babylon

74   *C. Power*

and Nebuchadnezzar, it is anomalous. In fact, there are text-critical reasons to think that this verse is not original. Halvorson-Taylor (2012: 477) has pointed out that 2:6 is missing from the Greek Alpha Text (AT) of Esther, in contrast to MT and LXX. While the debate over the text-critical value of AT is unresolved,[24] it may in places bear witness to an earlier version of Esther than MT, in which this verse was absent. If this verse were secondary, the book of Esther would contain no reference to exile,[25] and Mordecai's characterization would lack the exilic element (Halvorson-Taylor 2012: 477 n. 35).

Apart from this disputed verse, then, Esther lacks explicit reference to the Babylonian exile, but one other verse clearly alludes to the effects of exile. When Haman submits his genocidal request to the king, he describes the situation of the Judaeans as diaspora: "There is a certain people scattered and separated [מפזר ומפרד] among the peoples in all the provinces of your kingdom" (Esth 3:8). Haman's words here recall the trope, common in curses, prophecies and psalms, according to which Yahweh scatters the peoples as an act of war or retribution (e.g. Deut 4:27; Ps 92:10 [√פרד]; Joel 4:2 [√פזר]). Through this, the author of Esther appears to display awareness of the standard biblical interpretation of the exile as a deliberate punishment inflicted on Israel. However, by putting this on Haman's lips, the author distances himself from this view and leaves his own perspective ambiguous.

Since these two verses, 2:6 and 3:8, exhaust clear references to exile in the book, other observations concerning Esther's understanding of exile will primarily be negative ones, noting absences. For instance, starkly absent from Esther is a sense that the period of living in exile is over, or that any restoration has taken place. Neither the narrator nor the characters seem aware that Judah, as a place, is anything more than a memory, and Jerusalem is not mentioned as a living city.[26] A specific, distinctive community of Judaeans living in the Persian province of Yehud is not singled out from the general diaspora of "Judaeans ... in all the provinces of the king" (8:5). What is more, no 'return' is envisaged or enjoined, in contrast to Ezra, Nehemiah, 2 Chronicles, Haggai and Zechariah.

Since exile is not presented as completed in Esther, we might assume that the author thinks of it as ongoing. But the idea of an ongoing exile, as is found in Daniel, is also absent from Esther. The exile is presented in the book as a historical event (2:6), not a present reality. Similarly absent are negative descriptions of the Judaeans' life outside of Judah as שׁבי, 'captivity' (e.g. Ezra 2:1; Neh 1:3) from which they must 'escape' (Zech 2:7). Instead, in Esther, although life in Xerxes' kingdom is certainly full of grave risks, it also affords great possibilities to Judaeans: Esther becomes queen of the realm and Mordecai grand vizier. The book has often been interpreted as laying out a lifestyle for diaspora, accepting the condition of living away from Judah.[27]

Exile in Esther is therefore a complicated topic. The author introduces the historical event emphatically, but downplays the topic thereafter. Exile does not appear to be the category by which the author understands current

Constructions of exile in the Persian period   75

Judaean existence, and he distances himself from certain understandings in which exile is a dominant mode.

Conclusions

This investigation has revealed a significant amount of diversity in biblical literature of the Persian period with regard to perspectives on the Babylonian exile. One important divergence was the understanding in these texts of the duration of the exile. First Zechariah set the end point of this period around twenty years later than Ezra and 2 Chronicles; in Third Isaiah there were indications that a state of captivity characterized the condition of Israelites into the Persian period.

Another major disagreement was the existence and status of those left behind in Judah after the deportations. First Zechariah, Haggai and Nehemiah had no problem admitting that the restoration community consisted of such a remnant as well as of returnees, while Ezra and 2 Chronicles seemed to deny the reality of those left behind, and thus granted them no part in the new Judah.

A final major point of divergence among these texts was how central they imagine the story of the exile to be to the future of Israel. For Ezra, the exiles who returned from Babylonia constituted the future of Israel, to such an extent that 'the exiles' was coterminous with 'Judah' and 'Israel'. In Esther, the exile seemed to be strictly an event in the past, and was not seen as defining the future of the Judaeans. For Joel, Third Isaiah and Second Zechariah the Babylonian exile was not awarded any special place among the various deportations Israel suffered throughout its history.

In this way it has been fruitful to try to detect divergent voices in these biblical texts. Such detection can be a difficult task, because of the harmonizing and homogenizing action of "canonic processes", as Carroll (1997: 73) has observed. The juxtaposition of Nehemiah with Ezra, for instance, tends to obscure the differences in their perspectives, as does the process of supplementation and redaction in, for instance, the book of Zechariah.

Discerning these divergent perspectives is justified as a means of reconstructing a more accurate historical picture of the society that produced the Hebrew Bible. It shows that the meaning of the exile for Israel was not formulated at once. In the Persian period, various possible understandings of it were available. In addition, detecting the various viewpoints provides lessons that we modern scholars should bear in mind in retellings and analyses of biblical texts. For instance, since the relevant books disagree as to when, if at all, the exile ended, we should be hesitant to use 'exilic' and 'postexilic' to describe historical periods. To use these terms without qualification is to accept one particular narrative of Israel's history, in preference to several others that show through in these texts. Similarly, we should recognize that being in exile was not an experience that belonged to the entire Persian-period Judaean community. It was the experience of a specific group whose

76 *C. Power*

narrative nevertheless came to occupy a prominent role in that community's life. Without denying the enormity of the Babylonian destruction and deportations, we should therefore be careful not to treat the exile, in our biblical histories, as an event that 'Judah' *simpliciter* underwent. It is hoped that these results and reflections demonstrate the importance of detecting and understanding the various constructions of exile present in biblical texts from the Persian period.

Notes

1 Lipschits, with others, has gathered many studies that illuminate this dark age in various respects; see Lipschits & Oeming 2006; Lipschits, Knoppers & Albertz 2007; Lipschits, Knoppers & Oeming 2011. Other works (e.g. Briant 2002) have greatly increased our understanding of the Persian empire at large. In this chapter, 'Judah' and 'Judaean' translate יהודה and יהודי respectively. Admittedly these English words involve some anachronisms, but they usefully capture the ambiguity of the Hebrew terms, which convey various types of identity.

2 The texts I examine are those whose composition is generally dated to the Persian period, and which clearly address the situation of that period (for dates, I refer the reader to the standard modern commentaries).

3 In fact, it is most probable that Ezekiel and Jeremiah contain much material from later periods. In the case of Jeremiah, text-critical issues indicate that MT contains major expansions, of unknown date, in comparison with LXX; see Tov 2001: 319–26. Later additions to Ezekiel have been detected by most commentators, e.g. Zimmerli 1979: 397; Eichrodt 1970: 256–58. In this article, however, I do not examine these books, both because there is significant disagreement in how to date them, and because the role of exile in Ezekiel and Jeremiah has already been studied in depth (see e.g. Albertz 2003: 302–75).

4 Unless otherwise noted, translations follow NRSV. I change NRSV's 'LORD' to 'Yahweh' throughout.

5 NRSV, modified.

6 Joel 4:1 contains the phrase, common in Jeremiah and Ezekiel, אשיב את שבות יהודה, usually translated "restore the fortunes of Judah". The context may suggest a connection with שבה, 'to take captive' (cf. BDB), though the root does not occur elsewhere in the book.

7 I.e. 520 BCE, if this Darius is to be identified with Darius I, as is most often assumed to be the case in Haggai and Zechariah (e.g. Meyers & Meyers 1987: 11–19; Merrill 1994: 12–14).

8 For a discussion of this theme in Jeremiah, including its complicated textual history, see Halvorson-Taylor 2011: 154–64.

9 The figure of seventy years is not mentioned in Ezra.

10 In Zechariah 1–8, as in 9–14, שבה is not used to describe this or any other exile.

11 Halvorson-Taylor 2011: 165–80 detects redactional activity in this passage, which attempts to delay the declaration of the end of the 'seventy years' by making the signs of the end more and more specific. This may be an indication of growing disappointment with the progress of the restoration.

12 NRSV, modified.

13 On these, see, among others, Williamson 1985: xxxv–xxxvi.

14 On קהל הגולה, see Weinfeld 2005.

15 When Ezra specifies the condition of living *outside* of Judah as an exile, the word שבי, 'captivity', is used (2:1; 3:8; 8:35; 9:7). The word is found in the same use throughout Nehemiah (e.g. 1:2; 7:6; 8:17).

16 Unusually in these books, the community is described as עבדים, 'slaves', in Neh 9:36, a term which stresses the perceived status of the community as subjugated, if not its exilic nature.
17 NRSV, modified.
18 NRSV, modified.
19 See Carroll 1992 and Barstad 1996. The prevalence of this 'myth' in other biblical texts has been questioned by Oded 2003.
20 Cf. 2 Chr 30:9.
21 NRSV, modified. The event is the deportation in 597 BCE, as the reference to Jeconiah (Jehoiachin) makes clear.
22 The reader assumes that Kish's family migrated the three hundred or so miles from Babylon to Susa in the century following their deportation.
23 שבה is entirely absent
24 See Halvorson-Taylor 2012: 469–75 for an assessment of the text-critical value of AT.
25 AT does contain reference to Jeconiah's exile (Addition A, v. 2). Like LXX, AT contains the six 'Additions' to Esther, which are widely regarded as secondary.
26 The 'other place' from which help for the Judaeans may come (4:14), is very mysterious indeed, perhaps referring to Judah or Jerusalem, or to Yahweh. See Levenson 1997: 81.
27 See esp. Humphreys 1973.

Bibliography

Albertz, R. 2003. *Israel in Exile: The History and Literature of the Sixth Century B.C.E.*, D. Green (trans.). Atlanta: Society of Biblical Literature.
Barstad, H. M. 1996. *The Myth of the Empty Land*. Oslo: Scandinavian University Press.
Becking, B. 1998. "Ezra's Re-enactment of the Exile". In *Leading Captivity Captive*. L.L. Grabbe (ed.). Sheffield: Sheffield Academic Press: 40–61.
Berlin, A. 2001. *Esther*. Philadelphia: Jewish Publication Society.
——2010. "The Exile: Biblical Ideology and its Postmodern Ideological Interpretation". In *Literary Construction of Identity in the Ancient World*. H. Liss and M. Oeming (eds). Winona Lake, IN: Eisenbrauns: 341–56.
Briant, P. 2002. *From Cyrus to Alexander: A History of the Persian Empire*, P.T. Daniels (trans.). Winona Lake, IN: Eisenbrauns.
Carroll, R.P. 1992. "The Myth of the Empty Land". *Semeia* 59: 79–93.
——1997. "Deportation and Diasporic Discourses in the Prophetic Literature". In *Exile: Old Testament, Jewish, and Christian Concepts*. J.M. Scott (ed.). Leiden: Brill: 63–85.
Eichrodt, W. 1970. *Ezekiel, a Commentary*, C. Quin (trans.). London: SCM.
Gregory, B.C. 2007. "The Postexilic Exile in Third Isaiah: Isaiah 61:1–3 in Light of Second Temple Hermeneutics". *Journal of Biblical Literature* 126: 475–96.
Halvorson-Taylor, M.A. 2011. *Enduring Exile: The Metaphorization of Exile in the Hebrew Bible*. Leiden: Brill.
——2012. "Secrets and Lies: Secrecy Notices (Esther 2:10, 20) and Diasporic Identity in the Book of Esther". *Journal of Biblical Literature* 131: 467–85.
Humphreys, W.L. 1973. "A Life-Style for Diaspora: A Study of the Tales of Esther and Daniel". *Journal of Biblical Literature* 92: 211–33.
Japhet, S. 2009. *The Ideology of the Book of Chronicles and Its Place in Biblical Thought*. Winona Lake, IN: Eisenbrauns.

78   C. Power

Johnstone, W. 1996. "The Use of Leviticus in Chronicles". In *Reading Leviticus: A Conversation with Mary Douglas*. J.F.A. Sawyer (ed.). Sheffield: Sheffield Academic Press: 243–55.

Levenson, J.D. 1997. *Esther*. Louisville, KY: Westminster John Knox Press.

Lipschits, O. and M. Oeming. 2006. *Judah and the Judeans in the Persian Period*. Winona Lake, IN: Eisenbrauns.

Lipschits, O., G.N. Knoppers and R. Albertz. 2007. *Judah and the Judeans in the Fourth Century B.C.E.* Winona Lake, IN: Eisenbrauns.

Lipschits, O., G.N. Knoppers and M. Oeming. 2011. *Judah and the Judeans in the Achaemenid Period*. Winona Lake, IN: Eisenbrauns.

Merrill, E.H. 1994. *Haggai, Zechariah, Malachi: An Exegetical Commentary*. Chicago: Moody.

Meyers, C.L. and E.M. Meyers. 1987. *Haggai, Zechariah 1–8*. New York: Doubleday.

——1993. *Zechariah 9–14*. New York: Doubleday.

Oded, B. 2003. "Where is the 'Myth of the Empty Land' to be Found? History versus Myth". In *Judah and the Judaeans in the Neo-Babylonian Period*. O. Lipschits and J. Blenkinsopp (eds). Winona Lake, IN: Eisenbrauns: 55–74.

Smith-Christopher, D.L. 1997. "Reassessing the Historical and Sociological Impact of the Babylonian Exile (597/587–539 bce)". In *Exile: Old Testament, Jewish, and Christian Concepts*. J.M. Scott (ed.). Leiden: Brill: 7–36.

Tov, E. 2001. *Textual Criticism of the Hebrew Bible*, 2nd edn. Minneapolis: Fortress.

Weinfeld, M. 2005. "The Crystallization of the 'Congregation of the Exile' (קהל הגולה) and the Sectarian Nature of Post-Exilic Judaism". In his *Normative and Sectarian Judaism in the Second Temple Period*. London: T & T Clark International: 232–38.

Williamson, H.G.M. 1985. *Ezra, Nehemiah*. Waco, TX: World Books.

Zimmerli, W. 1979. *Ezekiel*, vol. 1, R.E. Clements (trans.). Philadelphia: Fortress.

5 Exile as pilgrimage?

Ingrid Hjelm

My other chapter in this volume demonstrated that the Israelites of the Pentateuch were more at home in Egypt than in Canaan, where their foreignness had been so thorough that Jacob, on his arrival in Egypt, declared all of his and his forefathers' previous lifetime as spent in foreignness (מגור; Gen 47:9). The settlement of Jacob's family in Egypt does resemble a refugee's humble and vulnerable dependency on the good will of their lords and neighbours. But their fate is quite good. When Joseph's brothers request that they may live as foreigners in Goshen, Pharaoh gives them permission to settle in the best part of Egypt and Joseph provides for them (Gen 47:1–12). The family prospers and multiplies and they are not characterized as foreigners or slaves, such as are standard phrases about the Egyptian 'exile' in Exodus-Deuteronomy.[1] The level of their integration is such that even the Egyptians mourn Jacob's death. The Egyptians, in contrast, become slaves of Pharaoh when they sell their land and themselves to Joseph in order to survive from hunger (47:19, 25). This narrative is in stark contrast to Yahweh's prediction to Abraham of his descendants' four hundred years of foreignness and slavery in Egypt in Gen 15:13. In fact, Exod 1:8–11 narrates that slavery only occurred in the last phase of their settlement in Egypt. The four hundred years' stay in Egypt makes it their homeland and, when they leave Egypt, the biggest threat to a successful 'return' to an imaginary homeland is their wish to go back to Egypt to find security, survival, cucumbers and slavery (Exod 14:12; 16:3; Num 11:5; 14:3–4). During the wandering in the desert and the extinction of the generation that had left Egypt, this orientation changes, so that in Deuteronomy and Joshua, the foreigners are always the non-Israelites and Egypt is the land in which the people were foreigners (Deut 26:5). One may say that the people came home. Standing across Jericho on the plains of Moab rejoicing seems a proper reaction: "we did it". But, in fact, they didn't make it. Their fathers, brothers, husbands and leaders, all men from twenty years of age, had died on the way (Num 26:64; 32:11–13) and what remained is a fatherless and widowed homeless people. Of the 600,000 men who had left Egypt, only Moses, Joshua and Caleb remain. Soon the people will have to mourn Moses' departure also, when his time has run out at the ideal age of 120 years of Gen 6:3, which only Moses fulfils in the entire Hebrew Bible.

80   I. Hjelm

That's the end of the story in the canonical tradition of the Samaritans, which is rehearsed year by year, leaving the Israelites on the brink of their Promised Land in Deuteronomy 34. Their entrance and settlement in the land happens extra-canonically in the Joshua traditions, which diverge from those in the Masoretic tradition.[2] In the canonical Jewish tradition in Genesis to 2 Kings, disaster and a failed future are projected and nobody remains in the Promised Land. One must ask, "Was the land meant to be entered after all?" But perhaps we should rather ask, "What is the difference between the desert and the land?"

Bittersweet is Moses' farewell address with its prediction of defection and apostasy in its allusion to the postponed punishment of the golden calf episode:

> I know that after my death, you will surely become corrupted and depart from the way, which I have commanded you, and evil will befall you in the latter days (באחרית הימים), because you will do evil in the sight of Yahweh and provoke him to anger by the work of your hands.
>
> (Deut 31:29; cf. Exod 32:34)

There is, however, an apparent tension between Yahweh's last words to Moses, which forbid him to enter the land because of his and Aaron's unfaithfulness (Deut 32:50–52; 34:4; cf. Num 20:11; 27:12–14), and Moses' perpetual presence in the land as mediator of Yahweh's words in written form (Deut 31:24–26). Albeit used as instruction, these words are intended to be a witness against the people (Deut 31:26); a measuring line for a people whom he never praises for any steadfastness or good deeds:

> Take this book of the Torah and place it beside the ark of the covenant of Yahweh your god that it must be there as a witness against you. For I know your rebellion and your stiff neck. When you rebel against Yahweh while I'm still alive with you today, how much more (will you rebel) after my death.
>
> (Deut 31:26–27)

One may say that the outcome is known and that Moses plays the role of the first prophet to warn the people against their desire to decide for themselves. Disaster was or has already been there, literature came afterwards. *Vaticinia ex eventu* is the term we use for such texts, and they probably are. But when we compare this utterance from Deuteronomy 31 and similar utterances in Leviticus 26 and Deuteronomy 28 with Ancient Near Eastern Vassal treaties, the *vaticinium* also takes the form of *pro eventu* as predicted curses for violating the covenant (Weeks 2004). Although Yahweh reminds Moses of his promise of the land to Abraham, Isaac and Jacob (Deut 34:4), the covenant, which Moses leaves for the Israelites to submit to, is not a covenant of grant, but of obligation and submission. It protects the rights of the master rather

Exile as pilgrimage? 81

than the servant (Weinfeld 1970: 184–203), and threatens death and destruction in every possible form for violating the covenant (Halvorson-Taylor 2011: 23; Balzer 1971: 15). Take it or leave it, the land is yours already, but whether you will take possession of it and stay there is your decision, seems to be the implied argument.

There is nothing romantic about the Israelites' arrival in the Promised Land when preceded by the conquests of Transjordan and the Midianites. Their killing of the Midianites, especially, is a story of unheard cruelty (Numbers 31), which seems to be an implicit test of Moses' loyalty and criticism of his marriage with a Midianite woman. The story is linked to another narrative about a marriage between an Israelite man and a Midianite woman, called Kozbi, in Numbers 25. Rather than attacking the Moabites and Midianites, the Israelites fornicate with their women, worship their gods and eat of the meat offered to Ba'al-Peor (Num 25:2–3). Of course, Yahweh becomes outraged. Loyalty and unfaithfulness are, after all, the main themes of the Pentateuch. He orders the killing of the leaders of the people and anyone else participating in the excesses and 24,000 die. It only stops when Phinehas, son of Eleazar, son of Aaron, overturns Yahweh's jealousy by killing the Israelite groom and his Midianite bride (v. 7–8). Forming a thematic loop with Exodus 32, Eleazar is rewarded with the everlasting priesthood, because of this deed (v. 11–13). In Numbers 31, Yahweh's frenzied rage has turned against the Midianites and he orders Moses and Eleazar to fulfil his vengeance with a genocide, which leaves alive only 32,000 virgins "unmarked by the contagious Other" (Niditch 2007: 157). These might be taken as wives after a period of transformation and mourning according to Deut 21:10–14. All the tribes participate in the slaughter and nobody protests the deed. When afterwards the tribes of Reuben, Gad and Manasseh settle in Transjordan, they are reminded of their oath of loyalty, as they might be suspected of not wanting to participate in the conquest of the Land. The reprimand warns them against repeating the failure of their ancestors, who were not fully with Yahweh, thereby causing the extinction of a whole generation. A repetition of that sin will cause an even longer stay in the desert and the utter destruction of the people (Num 32:10–15). The contrast is the death of those 600,000 men from 20 years up who had left Egypt (Exod 12:37). At the end of their journey they have been replaced by 601,730 men, none of whom had been mustered by Moses and Aaron in the desert of Sinai in the second year after their departure from Egypt (Num 26:51, 64; cf. 1:46: 603,550 men).

In spite of Deuteronomy's claim that Yahweh had taken care of his people in the desert (Deut 2:7), one might conclude that Numbers' desert is the realm of death, much as the usual depiction of the desert in the Semitic world (Fensham 1963). Exodus-Numbers seemingly bring a people from one place to another, but they are certainly not brought home. The risk of losing one's life and god on the way is as much a part of these books' theology as it is the standard curse in Ancient Near Eastern treaties. As concluded by Halvorson-Taylor in *Enduring Exile* from 2011, p. 37: "The comparison of ancient Near

82   I. Hjelm

Eastern and biblical texts on exile further shows that both shared the notion that exile was one facet, and a very powerful one, of divine annihilating wrath. Exile may have been expressed as a denial of futurity, a deprivation of the benefits of the land, or as a disintegration of the body politic, but at its heart, exile was lethal because it was the result of the inescapable anger of YHWH." What began as liberation from an Egyptian oppression, in fact, took the form of a devastating exile. However, Yahweh's continual presence during the exilic desert, for good and for bad, describes an exile that differs from traditional depictions of exile in Ancient Near Eastern texts. When a people is deported from its land, its gods do not accompany it in exile (Halvorson-Taylor 2011: 24), and especially the desert is usually conceived as a godless place, where demons reign. One such demon god, known from Leviticus 16, is Azazel, contractor of all sins sent to him on the head of a goat on the Day of Atonement. In passing, we must notice that the ritual obviously didn't work for the Israelites in the desert or they forgot to perform it. And this, of course, opens up a most disturbing wonder about the usefulness of all the performative rituals the Israelites have been told to observe, when, in fact, no story evidences that a sacrificial ritual affects Yahweh's will or turns away his wrath in the Pentateuch. He rather responds to apotropaic intercession, supplication and submission (Rochberg 2003; Broida 2013). The pedagogy seems to be almost unlimited punishment before there can be atonement and reconciliation as in Numbers 16's story about Datan's and Abiram's challenge of Moses' and Aaron's authority.

The homeless god, Yahweh (2 Sam 7:6), was as much a nomadic god as was the people he chose to adopt (Flight 1923; Budde 1895: 724ff.). His epithet, El Shadday, may best be translated as the "god of the wilderness" as argued by Axel Knauf (1995), rather than the "god of the mountain" as suggested by Albright (1968: 94) and Cross (1973: 52–60) on the basis of Delitzsch's *Assyrisches Handwörterbuch* from 1896.[3] Yahweh's fight for becoming a national god with a people and a land is as much part of the biblical narrative as is the people's transforming detachment from human slavery to divine submission. "Throughout the story of the sojourns at Sinai and Kadesh the people feel that Yahweh is to be feared because of the vengeance that He will inflict upon the slightest violation of His holiness" (Flight 1923: 200).

The above-mentioned narratives about the Midianites and the Transjordanian tribes are given as examples of the required loyalty of the new generation and they point forward to what it takes to conquer the land. Patterned after an imaginary holy precinct, the border areas create a buffer zone, the outer court rooms so to speak, between the outer world with all its temptations and the Holy Land as the inner court room. In the centre of the land is the temple with its holy of holies. In Numbers, complete submission is required of the Israelites who will enter the land, cleanse it of all its foreignness and settle there as a holy people. Concepts of centre and periphery prevalent in Neo-Assyrian ideology (Liverani 1979 and 1990) also apply to designs for the desert camp

Exile as pilgrimage? 83

and the visions of the Land in the Pentateuch. Holiness radiates from centre to periphery, and beyond its borders reign chaos, wilderness and rebellion. It is "a failed cosmos, not yet realized" (Liverani 1979: 306; Oded 1992: 111). Such a view also permeates the Book of Kings' description of Solomon's kingdom and Ezekiel 40–48's vision of a rebuilt Jerusalem (Galambush 1992: 152–53).

The Assyrians, however, did not simply slaughter their subjected peoples; they assimilated and incorporated them, moved them around and exploited them. Neither did they segregate their populations; this habit was the policy of the Persians in regard to the general population. The eradication of subjected enemies as expressed in the biblical concept of ban (חרם) might not be without parallels in the ancient world (Stern 1991), at least if one considers literary texts, but the Mesha inscription is the only attestation of it (Kang 1989: 81; cf. Brekelmans 1959). In both the Bible and the Mesha inscription, the ban has a sacrificial character as offered to either Yahweh or Chemosh respectively, in spite of a condemnation of human sacrifice in Deut 12:31 and 18:10 (Collins 2003: 7). Susan Niditch's claim that the enemy deemed worthy of being offered to God carries a sign of respect (Niditch 1993: 50) is hard to swallow. Collins (2003: 6) strongly protests the interpretation: "One hopes that the Canaanites appreciated the honor. Rather than respect for human life, the practice bespeaks a totalistic attitude, which is common in armies and warfare." Following Niditch's further consideration that "The ban as sacrifice requires a wider view of a God who appreciates human sacrifice" (1993: 50), biblical literature condones rather than contests such practice. A mitigation of the חרם is found in Deuteronomy 20's stipulation of a distinction between "far away" towns – of which the enemy may surrender and accept enslavement – while in towns that are nearer to the centre and inhabited by Israelites (Deut 20:10–15), a complete ban (חרם) results in a "wholesale killing of men, women, and children" (Niditch 2007: 150). The distinction, however, does not apply to border areas in Joshua's and Judges' narratives about the conquests (Gottwald 1964). Contamination by the abhorrent religious practices of the foreigners and their gods is what must be avoided (20.18). The remedy is a removal of temptation and a segregation of the Israelites from the dangerous 'Other'. Only Abraham's family of nations from Edom, Moab and Ammon are freed from total eradication in Deuteronomy's retelling of the past.

In an allegorical reading, the conquests and genocide can be interpreted as fighting one's own temptations and threatening alienation from the divinity. In such a reading, the wandering in the desert may be construed as a pilgrimage, which brings people through several trials on their way to perfection. Martin Noth (1940) argued that the itinerary in Numbers 33 was based on a pilgrim-route, which he traced to North Arabia. The use of the terms *hag* and *hagag* in Exod. 5:1 and 10:9, common in texts which describe the annual festivals supported his thesis. M.S. Smith (1997) suggested that the entire Book of Exodus is construed as a double pilgrimage in chapters 1:1– 15:21 and 15:22–40:38 with Mount Sinai, the giving of the Law and the

84   *I. Hjelm*

sanctification of the people as the journey's goal. The narrative pattern was modelled after the annual festivals and pilgrimages to the temple in Jerusalem, with its "sense of temporarily re-capturing the primordial peaceful and abundant relationship with God. The temple experience also anticipated how wonderful life would be when God comes to save Israel in the future" (Smith 1989: 45; 1997: 109). "The total result of the Priestly materials and redaction in Exodus is not simple information for the Israelites about the priesthood, but a reformulation of Israel's primary identity: thanks to their sacred institutions, Israel is to be transformed into a fundamentally special and sacred, even priestly people (Exod 19:5–6), which belongs no longer to Pharaoh but to Yahweh" (Smith 1997: 283). Apparent obstacles to such a reading, however, are that the Exodus story continues beyond the Book of Exodus with an envisioned Promised Land as its goal (Davies 1999: 150). This continuation does not narrate a blissful relationship between god and man, when Yahweh's patience with Israel's lack of trust and obedience ends with the tenth provocation, which causes an almost complete annihilation of the 'pilgrims' (Num 14:22). Although pilgrims may "express their ultimate loyalty to their God by giving away or relativizing all other needs" (McConville 2004: 27), such a catastrophic outcome is not to be expected. The Israelites went out to worship their god in the desert and they went with Yahweh, but they did not reach their goal. This predominately negative perspective on the wilderness in the Pentateuch, however, is ambiguously countered with a positive image of the wilderness as an intimate meeting place between God and man (Feldt 2012) – a place where man is taught the will of the deity and exposed to the deity's grace. When this grace, however, takes on phantasmatic proportions as in the manna, the quail and the spy narratives, the people react with disobedience, doubt, rebellion and a strong desire for normativity and everyday life (Feldt 2012). Contrary to what one might expect, the demonstration of divine power creates fear and leads to Israel's rejection of Yahweh rather than to love and supplication. As man also reacts ambiguously to the experience of Yahweh's marvels, the wilderness is presented in "an irreducible ambiguity". It "oscillates between a benign and a malign, a real and a phantasmatic presentation, between terror and nostalgia, past and present, between Yahweh's bounty chamber and utter deprivation, between treat and promise, rescue and punishment" (Feldt 2012: 82). Feldt's examination of the wilderness narratives in the Hebrew Bible leads her to conclude that the wilderness experience is not about an election of a people or a possession of a Promised Land, which in any case remains fragile. It is about personal and communal religious transformation. As the narratives disclose a discrepancy between the ideal Israel (devout, law-abiding and remembering Yahweh) and the "real" Israel (apostate, disobedient and forgetful), they function as "a call to transformation" and "communicate an invitation to regard religious identity as unfinished" (p. 86). Although she does not suggest such a reading, Feldt's conclusion naturally leads to an allegorical interpretation of the Pentateuch's journey.

Exile as pilgrimage? 85

Such an interpretation has been prevalent in Christian theology – interpreting the journey through the wilderness towards the Promised Land as a paradigm of the Christian journey through a fallen world towards the heavenly homeland (Dyas 1998). Antecedents of such interpretation had already been presented in book 2 of Philo's *De Vita Mosis*, which interpreted Moses' death as a virtue and an ἀποικία, i.e. a migration from earth to heaven (2.288). As Finn Damgaard concluded in his analysis of Philo in *Recasting Moses* (2010: 87): "When the direct company of the hero Moses is about to cease and the whole nation is shocked and in grief, the community is left with his laws and wisdom, which actually enable them to repeat his ἀποικία." Philo, in fact, interprets the conquest of Moab in Numbers 21 allegorically, as overcoming one's desire and disturbance caused by being subjected to false opinions, sophism and the deceptive impression of the senses (Philo, *Legum Allegoria liber* iii: 224–35).

In Samaritan literature, Book V of Memar/Tibat Marqeh from the Byzantine period tells two stories about Moses' death on Mt. Nebo in terms of sanctification (MM: V§3–4; TM: ב258–70; Hjelm, forthcoming b).[4] In the first story, Moses entered the cave to which the great Glory (כבודה רבה; that is God) had led him.

> Great was that moment when the mighty prophet Moses lowered his head and entered the cave. He turned his face toward Mt. Gerizim, lay down on the ground, looking straight ahead of him. God made sleep fall upon him[5] and his soul departed without difficulty, without him knowing.
> (MM: V 126.23–26)

The second story compares the deaths of Jacob, Aaron and Moses creating an ontological difference: "Aaron was buried by men; Moses was buried by the Divine one". The author's summary of biblical narrative has Jacob buried by Joseph, the king; Aaron by his son Eleazar and Moses; and Moses by God (cf. Deut 34:6). In Marqeh's story, Moses was met by 600,000 men and all the angels at his ascent to Mt. Nebo and "when he reached the top of the mountain, the cloud came down and lifted him up from the sight of all the congregation of Israel. He was buried there by God." (cf. Deut 34:6; MM: V 128.1–2). In an ascending line of divinization, the congregation mourns Moses' departure in a hymnic praise of his deeds as he disappears in the cloud. Each of the fourteen stanzas is initiated by the phrase (חסלך), which may be translated as the congregation's interjection of protest: "Far be it from you", as in Macdonald's translation (MM, vol. 2, p. 203). Ben-Hayyim's translation into Hebrew: חלילה לך (TM, p. 320) retains this possibility. Other translations, however, are possible as the Aramaic verb חסל also means to fulfill, complete, finish or ripen. Given the content of the hymn it seems possible to interpret the phrase in light of the messianic fulfilment uttered by Jesus on the cross in the Gospel of John 19.30. A legitimate translation would thus be: "It is fulfilled for you" or "It has come to an end for you".

86 *I. Hjelm*

It is fulfilled for you, O crown of the Righteous
It is fulfilled for you, O deliverer of the Hebrews
It is fulfilled for you, O establisher of the Favour
It is fulfilled for you, O revealer of the Wonders
It is fulfilled for you, O receiver of the Tablets
It is fulfilled for you, O faithful one of God's House
It is fulfilled for you, O you who tore the veil
It is fulfilled for you, O you who trod into the fire
It is fulfilled for you, O man of God
It is fulfilled for you, O you who were called a god
It is fulfilled for you, O you with whom God spoke mouth to mouth
It is fulfilled for you, O you whose face radiated light
It is fulfilled for you, O you whose voice was heard with the voice of God
It is fulfilled for you, O you who brought life to the generations for ever
(MM: V, p. 124; Eng. transl. vol 2, p. 203; TM: 320–21 [ב2261];
my translation in Hjelm, forthcoming b).

The hymn closes in four stanzas, each initiated by "who will after you … pray for us?", " … make atonement for our sins?", " … have compassion on us?" and, " … extinguish the fire of wrath from upon us?"

In light of these examples, Numbers' new generation may signify an ultimate transformation rather than a disastrous ending for those who embarked on the journey. What died in the desert were their apostasy, disobedience and forgetfulness. The transformation may thus be interpreted within the tripartite model of Gennep's *rites de passage* (van Gennep 1960; cf. Cohn 1981), or it may represent a continuous negotiation of religious identity and relationship between deity and human (Feldt 2012).

Notes

1 E.g. Exod 22:20; 23:9; Lev 19:34; Deut 10:19; 23:8; 24:8; 26:5.
2 On this see also my other chapter in this volume.
3 For etymological considerations, see Weippert 1976: 873–81.
4 The only extant English translation of *Memar Marqeh* (MM) is the pioneering edition by John Macdonald (1963). An annotated Hebrew edition with introduction and a Hebrew translation has been published by Ben-Hayyim (1988), who also suggested changing its title to *Tibåt Mårqe* (TM) from Arabic *safinat*, meaning chest or box corresponding with the ark [תבה] of Noah and Moses in the HB. Introductions to the work can be found in these editions and in Broadie (1981); Tal (1989: 462–65); Anderson and Giles (2005: 256–79); Hjelm (forthcoming a).
5 Moses in the image of a second Adam is frequently found in Samaritan literature (Macdonald 1964: 221), and Marqah 'opens' the doors of Eden for Moses (Tsedaka 2008: 215).

Bibliography

Albright, W.F. 1968. *Yahweh and the Gods of Canaan. A Historical Analysis of Two Contrasting Faiths*. London: Athlone Press.

Anderson, R.T. and T. Giles. 2005. *Tradition Kept. The Literature of the Samaritans.* Peabody, MA: Hendrickson.

Balzer, K. 1971. *The Covenant Formulary in Old Testament, Jewish and Early Christian Writings*, D.E. Green (trans.). Philadelphia: Fortress Press.

Ben-Hayyim, Z. 1988. *Tibåt Mårqe. A Collection of Samaritan Midrashim.* Edited, translated and annotated. Jerusalem: The Israel Academy of Sciences and Humanities. In Hebrew.

Brekelmans, C.H.W. 1959. *De Ḥerem in het Oude Testament.* Nijmegen: Centrale Drukkerij.

Broadie, A. 1981. *A Samaritan Philosophy. A Study of the Hellenistic Cultural Ethos of Memar Marqah.* Leiden: E.J. Brill.

Broida, M. 2013. "Apotropaic Intersession in the Hebrew Bible and the Ancient Near East". In *Studies on Magic and Divination in the Biblical World.* H.R. Jacobus, A.K. De Hemmer Gudme and P. Guillaume (eds). Piscataway, NJ: Gorgias Press: 19–38.

Budde, K. 1895. "The Nomadic Ideal in the Old Testament". *The New World* 4: 726–45.

Cohn, R.L. 1981. *The Shape of Sacred Space. Four Biblical Studies.* Chico, CA: Scholars Press.

Collins, J.J. 2003. "The Zeal of Phinehas: The Bible and the Legitimation of Violence". *Journal of Biblical Literature* 122/1: 3–21.

Cross, F.M. 1973. *Canaanite Myth and Hebrew Epic. Essays in the History of the Religion of Israel.* Cambridge, MA: Harvard University Press.

Damgaard, F. 2010. *Recasting Moses. The Memory of Moses in Biographical and Autobiographical Narratives in Ancient Judaism and 4th Century Christianity.* Ph.D. Thesis. Copenhagen: Det Teologiske Fakultet. 2nd rev. edn. Idem, *Recasting Moses: The Memory of Moses in Biographical and Autobiographical Narratives in Ancient Judaism and 4th-Century Christianity.* Frankfurt: Peter Lang, 2012.

Davies, G. 1999. "The Theology of Exodus". In *In Search of True Wisdom: Essays in the Old Testament in Honour of Ronald E. Clements.* E. Ball (ed.). Sheffield: Sheffield Academic Press: 137–52.

Delitzsch, F. 1896. *Assyrisches Handwörterbuch.* Leipzig.

Dyas, D. 1998. *Pilgrims Were They All? Aspects of Pilgrimage and their Influence on Old and Middle English Literature.* PhD thesis, University of Nottingham.

Feldt, L. 2012. "Wilderness and the Hebrew Bible Religion – Fertility, Apostasy and Religious Transformation in the Pentateuch". In *Wilderness in Mythology and Religion. Approaching Religious Spatialities, Cosmologies, and Ideas of Wild Nature.* L. Feldt (ed.). Berlin: W. de Gruyter: 55–94.

Fensham, F.C. 1963. "Common Trends in Curses of the Near Eastern Treaties and Kudurru-Inscriptions Compared with Maledictions of Amos and Isaiah". *Zeitschrift für Altestamentliche Wissenschaft* 75: 155–75.

Flight, J.W. 1923. "The Nomadic Idea and Ideal in the Old Testament". *Journal of Biblical Literature* 42, No. 3/4: 158–226.

Galambush, J. 1992. *Jerusalem in the Book of Ezekiel: The City as Yahweh's Wife.* SBL130. Atlanta: Scholars Press.

Gennep, Arnold van. 1960. *The Rites of Passage*, Monika B. Vizedom and Gabrielle L. Caffee (trans.). Chicago: Chicago University Press.

Gottwald, N. 1964. "'Holy War' in Deuteronomy: Analysis and Critique". *Review and Expositor* 61: 297–310.

Halvorson-Taylor, M.A. 2011. *Enduring Exile. The Metaphorization of Exile in the Hebrew Bible.* Leiden: E.J. Brill.

88   I. Hjelm

Hjelm, I. Forthcoming a. "Samaritan Literature in the Roman Period". In *Oxford Companion to the Literatures of the Roman Period*. D. L. Selden and P. Vasunia (eds). Oxford: Oxford University Press.

——Forthcoming b. "Portraits of Moses in the Samaritan Pentateuch (SP) and the Fourth Century Samaritan Midrash Memar (M.M.) or Tibat Marqah (T.M.)". In *Portraits of Moses*. G.J. Steyn and Peter Nagel (eds). London and New York: T&T Clark.

Kang, S.-M. 1989. *Divine War in the Old Testament and in the Ancient Near East*. Berlin: De Gruyter.

Knauf, A. 1995. "Shadday". In *Dictionary of Deities and Demons in the Bible*. K. van der Toorn, B. Becking and P.W. van der Horst (eds). Leiden: E.J. Brill: 1416–23.

Macdonald, J. 1963. *Memar Marqah. The Teaching of Marqah* (2 vols). Beihefte zur Zeitschrift für die Alttestamentliche Wissenschaft 84. Berlin: Töpelman.

——1964. *The Theology of the Samaritans*. New Testament Library. London: SCM Press.

McConville, G. 2004. "Pilgrimage and 'Place' in the Old Testament". In *Explorations in a Christian Theology of Pilgrimage*. C.G. Bartholomew and F. Hughes (eds). Burlington: Ashgate Publishing: 17–28.

Niditch, S. 1993. *War in the Hebrew Bible. Study in the Ethics of Violence*. Oxford: Oxford University Press.

——2007. "War and Reconciliation in the Traditions of Ancient Israel: Historical, Literary, and Ideological Considerations". In *War and Peace in the Ancient World*. K.A. Raaflaub (ed.). Malden, MA/Oxford/Victoria, AU: Blackwell: 141–60.

Liverani, M. 1979. "The Ideology of the Assyrian Empire". In *Power and Propaganda: A Symposium on Ancient Empires*. M.T. Larsen (ed.). Mesopotamia, Copenhagen Studies in Assyriology, 7; Copenhagen: Akademisk Forlag: 297–317.

——1990. *Prestige and Interest: International Relations in the Near East ca. 1600–1100 B.C.* HANE/S, 1. Padova: Sargon srl.

Noth, M. 1940. "Der Wallfahrtsweg zum Sinai (4. Mose 33)". *Palästina Jahrbuch* 36: 5–28.

Oded, B. 1992. *War, Peace and Empire: Justifications for War in Assyrian Royal Inscriptions*. Wiesbaden: Reichert Verlag.

Rochberg, F. 2003. "Heaven and Earth. Divine-human Relations in Mesopotamian Celestial Divination". In *Prayer, Magic and the Stars in the Ancient and Late Antique World*. S. Noegel, J. Walker and B. Wheeler (eds). Pennsylvania: Pennsylvania State University: 169–87.

Smith, M.S. 1989. *Psalms. The Divine Journey*. New York: Mahvah.

——1997. *The Pilgrimage Pattern in Exodus*. Sheffield: Sheffield Academic Press.

Stern, P.D. 1991. *The Biblical Ḥerem: A Window on Israel's Religious Experience*. BJS 211. Atlanta: Scholars Press.

Weeks, M. 2004. *Admonition and Curse: The Ancient Near Eastern Treaty/Covenant Form as a Problem in Inter-Cultural Relationships*. JSOTS 407. London: T&T Clark.

Weinfeld, M. 1970. "The Covenant of Grant in the Old Testament and in the Ancient Near East". *Journal of the American Oriental Society* 90/2: 184–203.

Weippert, M. 1976. "Šaddaj (Gottesname)". *Theologisches Handwörterbuch zum Alten Testament* II: 873–81.

Tal, A. 1989. "Samaritan Literature". In *The Samaritans*. A.D. Crown (ed.). Tübingen: Mohr Siebeck: 413–67.

Tsedaka, B. 2008. *Marqeh to Every Reader. Observations in Tibat Marqeh*. Collection of Israelite = Samaritan Homiletic Commentaries on the Pentateuch. Holon: A.B.-Institute of Samaritan Studies Press. In Hebrew.

6 Psalm 137

Exile as hell!

Niels Peter Lemche

Bringing into mind the chorus from Verdi's *Nabucco* "Va, pensiero sull'ali dorate" ("Fly, thought, on wings of gold") the memory of the Babylonian exile was always one of imagining Babylon as a prison. Psalm 137 is without doubt the strongest example of this experience but the preaching of Deutero-Isaiah also rests on this idea of Babylon as a prison from which the God of Israel is going to rescue his people and bring it to the land of promise. Reality was very different. As a matter of fact, not much indicates that the people carried away by Nebuchadnezzar in 597/587/582 BCE were really interested in returning, as nothing points to a migration from Mesopotamia (or for that matter any other place) to Judah at the end of the 6th century BCE. We clearly have a conflict between an imagined identity and the realities of the Jewish presence in Mesopotamia, building up the idea that Babylon was hell, while the extended Jewish community there was to survive for almost 2500 years.

Exile is always a hell, even the golden ones.

Nowhere is the Babylonian exile as clearly described as hell on earth as in Ps 137:

> v.1: By the rivers of Babylon, there we sat down, yea, we wept, when we remembered Zion.[1]

The perspective is clearly the past, 'we sat there', we do not sit there anymore. It is, so to speak, a remembrance of the exile of the past, subtly introducing another memory, that of Zion. First step into hell: The remembrance of the place of origin of the person in exile. Second step: Exile means prison – we sat there, and did nothing except remember Zion. So exile is also lack of purpose, and the feeling of uselessness. A code word in this verse is זכר 'to remember'.

זכר is also the code word for the rest of the psalm, reappearing in vv. 6 and 7 with a dynamic change from our remembrance to the Lord's remembrance, when the remembrance is turned from the remembrance of Zion to the Lord's remembrance of the enemy, in this case the Edomites. However, the motif of memory does not stop here but is extended by a negative reversal of זכר in the form of v. 6 אם־לא אזכרכי 'if I do not remember you', and in this way is still

90   *N.P. Lemche*

used in the sense of 'remembering'. So the first step into hell is definitely the remembrance of the place which you left to travel into exile.

> v. 2: We hung our harps upon the willows in the midst thereof.

Here the second step into hell is extended: We had nothing to do there. Our music was laid aside. The exile is not a place of joy, it is hell.

The mocking constitutes the third step into hell. When we have given up singing, the oppressors, the ones who dragged us into hell, demand the opposite:

> v. 3: For there they that carried us away captive required of us a song; and they that wasted us required of us mirth, saying, sing us one of the songs of Zion.

Mocking the defeated enemy is a fixed trope, not only in ancient times but even today, although of course not sponsored by the authorities and the reason for a public outcry when it is shown on television. But as Brennus said: "Vae victis!" "Woe to the defeated!" (Livy, *Ab Urbe Condita*, Book 5 Sections 34–49).

> v. 4: How shall we sing the Lord's song in a strange land.

So hell is to be in a foreign place remembering the place from where you came, being idle and being mocked by those who carried you away into exile. The rest of the psalm is about remembering not the exile but the past, commencing with a warning against forgetting Jerusalem:

> v. 5 If I forget thee, O Jerusalem, let my right hand forget her cunning[2]

followed by two instances of 'remember' זכר:

> v. 6: If I do not remember thee, let my tongue cleave to the roof of my mouth; if I prefer not Jerusalem above my chief joy.

and

> v. 7: Remember, Oh Lord, the children of Edom in the day of Jerusalem; who said, Erase it, raze it, even to the foundation thereof.

Here the fourth part of hell is revealed: Hatred. The people in exile are consumed by the hatred of their foes; first Edom, who for some reason is singled out as especially active in the destruction of Jerusalem, something not remembered either by 2 Kings or 2 Chronicles, and then Babylon itself in what are probably the nastiest verses of the entire Bible:

Psalm 137: Exile as hell! 91

vv. 8–9: O daughter of Babylon, who art to be destroyed; happy shall he be, that rewardeth thee as thou has served us.

Happy shall he be, that taketh and dasheth thy little ones against the stones.

There is no excuse for these verses, especially not v. 9, except that the psalmist has nothing in mind except revenge, although when this psalm was put into writing the revenge might already have taken place: 'who art to be destroyed'. Hebrew השדודה REB has 'the destroyer' reading as proposed by BHS השודה. Here the unvocalized pre-Masoretic text might have the advantage of *double entendre* – an expression often seen in connection with the interpretation of the Song of Songs – that a text may at one and the same time have more than one meaning. Read as vocalized in the Masoretic text, the psalmist is stating what may in his time already be a fact: Babylon is no more. As is well-known, Babylon was in full existence in 323 BCE when Alexander died there; however, a century later it was no more but was replaced by the capital of the Seleucid Empire, Seleucia. But read as proposed by the BHS on the basis of the Septuagint's ἡ λῃστίς 'the robber', 'the pirate', the perspective is kept in the future, and is about what is to happen to Babylon.

It might be an indication that Babylon is in this psalm not so much any longer the historical Babylon but a metaphor of some immanent enemy of the psalmist in his own time, linking up with the curse against Edom, which has really nothing to do with the destruction of Jerusalem as recorded in other parts of the Old Testament, apart from appearing in a similar context in Lamentations 4:21 – "Rejoice and be glad, O daughter of Edom, that dwellest in the land of Uz; the cup also shall pass through unto thee: thou shall be drunken, and shalt make thyself naked." In v. 22, the attention is turned to Jerusalem: "The punishment of thine iniquity is accomplished, O daughter of Zion; he will no more carry thee away into captivity: he will visit thine iniquity, O daughter of Edom; he will discover thy sins." Still, Lamentations does not say that Edom or Edomites were active in the destruction of Jerusalem in 587 BCE. But in the period that followed, down to Hasmonean times, Edom became the direct neighbour of Judah and Jerusalem with a border situated at Beth Zur only c. thirty kilometres from Jerusalem, and north of the traditional Judean town of Hebron.[3]

So in this way Ps 137 may draw on the recollection of the destruction of Jerusalem as found in the historiography of the Old Testament, but its real aim is a plea to Yahweh to assist the psalmist and his people against their present enemies, which could be the Seleucids and the Edomites, Babylon representing the Seleucid Empire very much in the same way as it in later literature becomes a pseudonym for Rome.

But let us return to the main theme, the exile as hell, and now also as punishment, a theme totally absent in Ps 137 but very much alive in other biblical literature with a few exceptions like, e.g. Psalm 89, with its accusation against Yahweh for having deserted his Messiah without any known reason, a

92   *N.P. Lemche*

theme also known from Psalm 79 and 80, both of them otherwise similar in content to Lamentations and including a series of motifs also found in Lamentations. The lack of understanding of what happened to them is also dominant in Ps 137. There is nothing about the people of God being in exile because of its sins against its God.

Punishment as the reason for exile is a main theme in Lamentations, and the natural place to be if you have sinned is – also today – in prison. Hell and prison are synonyms, and still are in most places not accustomed to the relative comfort of Scandinavian prisons. However, when it comes to the description of this prison, the Old Testament is definitely not very particular. This could be the fourth step into the hell of Ps 137 – being in prison without knowing why. Nothing indicates any sense of guilt when it comes to Ps 137 (which was also the case in the aforementioned three other psalms), and nothing is probably worse than being in prison although still innocent of the accusations which may have been levelled against you.

But in other parts of the Old Testament this feeling of guilt is dominant, in the historiography as well as in Prophets. We could use the Book of Jeremiah as our example. However, the links between Jeremiah and the historiography of the Deuteronomistic History (disregarding this time the present discussion about the existence of this history) are too obvious; definitely a case of one coin with two sides.[4] The Book of Ezekiel is difficult in this context with its focus on the situation before 587 – Ezekiel is supposed to be one of those who were carried away from Jerusalem in 597 BCE – although his book in some passages comes close to, say Lamentations, in his description of the punishment of the two unfaithful sisters, Ohola and Oholiba (Ezekiel 23, cf. already Ezekiel 16). But the Book of Isaiah is perfect in the sense that it includes as well the reason for the punishment (the first part, chapters 1–39) as the effects of the sins of the people having been exonerated in the prison of exile (the second part, chapters 40–55).[5]

Officially both parts belong to the message of Isaiah, a prophet said to have lived around 700 BCE, although we 'know' better, having found Cyrus of Persia mentioned as the new Messiah in the second part (Isaiah 41 most likely; 44:28; 45:1–4). Normally biblical scholars speak about the first and the second Isaiah, or Proto-Isaiah and Deutero-Isaiah, but as the book is preserved, some of the latest parts of the Book of Isaiah are found in the first Isaiah, notably 'the little apocalypse' in Isaiah 24–27, making the usual separation between the two Isaiah's rather questionable. The return is described as liberation from prison and terminology is used of the same kind as present in the Exodus-mythology in the Old Testament. Moreover the perspective is linked to the idea of liberation and return from Exile in the final verses of Chronicles (2 Chron 36:22–23), and in Ezra and Nehemiah, although neither Ezra nor Nehemiah argues that the Exile included every Jew living in Mesopotamia. However, the return from the Exile is massive, and signifying the end of the tribulations of Israel because of its sins.

Simultaneous with the return of God's chosen people, the Book of Isaiah includes a lengthy passage about the fate of the daughter of Babylon, seen as

Psalm 137: Exile as hell! 93

a prophecy of her reduction to obscurity. The wording 'the daughter of Babylon' בת־בבל is the same as found in Ps 137:8 with the extension 'the virgin' בתולת. The theology here is the same as in Isaiah 10:5–11: "Oh Assyrian, the rod of my anger". Babylon is the tool of punishment used by Yahweh, but has extended its 'duty' for its own pleasure and will accordingly be punished by Yahweh. It is more or less the same theme that comes up in Ps 137:3 when the oppressors ask the people in exile to sing.

Isaiah was wrong. Cyrus did not destroy Babylon or reduce it into an inferior status. Babylon remained very much the centre of the world, and especially the religious centre of the Ancient Near East, supported by no other than Cyrus himself. This is at least what he is telling us in the 'Cyrus-cylinder', stressing his benevolence towards Babylon and its inhabitants and vice versa the loyalty of the Babylonians towards himself.[6] As I already mentioned, more than 200 years later Babylon was still in existence as one of the major centres of the world, although that was not going to last. The prophesies about Babylon in Isaiah, and the hatred in Ps 137, were not about something that happened in the real world, but rather something which provokes an open question about what is going on in the biblical texts.

In light of what has been said about the 'memory' of the exile in the Old Testament as hell, and about the exile in general, it has to be stressed that from a historical point of view a Babylonian exile of the character found in biblical sources never was. Although Chronicles, in contrast to 2 Kings puts stress on the assertion that everybody was sent into exile (2 Chron 36:11–21) where they lived as slaves until the Persians took over (in contrast 2 Kings 25:11–12 argues that only the very poor were left behind to till the land and keep the vineyards; however, these poor people probably constituted up to 90% of the population), the number of people exiled to Mesopotamia was less than 10,000, far less than the 27,290 persons whom the Assyrians brought out of Samaria in 722 BCE (ANET 285). The idea of Chronicles 36:21 that the exile was to last for seventy years (thus also Jeremiah 25:11) would not have allowed, not even 10,000 people, within this short span of years to have grown into the multitude said in Ezra and Nehemiah to have returned from the exile, 42,360 men. Especially as this number only covers those who returned, and not the people (without number) who stayed in Mesopotamia and Persia, and especially if it was true that the people in exile were treated as slaves. It is evident that the traditional number of years allotted in historical-critical scholarship to this exile, 587–538 BCE, less than fifty years in all, would be even more problematic.

So the *biblical* exile in Babylon is a literary construction. This does not mean that there was no exile. As it has been stressed several times, not least by Thomas Thompson,[7] there were many exiles. I have already mentioned the deportation from Samaria. It was, as a matter of fact, an often-used device to break up traditional patronage societies by removing the patrons and thereby destroying their networks, substituting them with new networks set up by the new masters. Therefore it is hardly a coincidence that we later find a governor of Samaria of the name of Sanballat, a localized version of the Assyrian royal name of Sinuballit.

According to 2 Kings, the Assyrians removed the population of the former kingdom of Israel to other places in the Assyrian Empire and settled people from many places in Samaria in exchange (2 Kings 17). Of course scholars have read this as it stands and interpreted the passage according to their own standards as a total deportation. It should rather be read in line with the description of the deportation from Jerusalem a little more than a hundred years later, which was far from total, as an exchange of the group of patrons. Maybe it was not very different from Alexander's later politics of mixing up the many ethnic groups of his new empire.[8]

It squares well with this that the Assyrians may not in their external propaganda have described the deportations as abductions into a forced and cruel exile. This is not the impression they wanted to inscribe in the mind of visitors to the royal palace of Khorsabad where they showed Assyrian soldiers playing with children from Lachish. Rather the famous relief wants to tell a different story about those who surrendered and therefore had earned a better life in a better place chosen for them by their new Assyrian lords, in contrast to the hard-core opponents of Assyria who were skinned and impaled.[9]

In line with the different kind of exile which we speak about here is also the conclusion that there never was a massive return from Mesopotamia to Judea and Jerusalem. Somehow the return as described in Ezra and Nehemiah is no more historical than the conquest of the land by Joshua, and just as invisible. As I once concluded a lecture about the return, "Where are the Babylonian cooking pots?" Would women travelling from Mesopotamia into the unknown new home of the Jewish people leave their utensils behind? Maybe academic males would believe so, or not have a thought about it, but is it really likely? So far no hoard of shards in the Babylonian style has been found in Jerusalem and in other places where people returning from Mesopotamia settled. They are invisible, but most likely they never were (Lemche 2001).

All things taken into consideration, life in Mesopotamia was, in antiquity, much easier and much more secure than the life in the barren mountains of Palestine. Mesopotamia was, together with Egypt, the bread basket of ancient times. The present, partly desolate landscape in Iraq is the outcome of the Mongolian conquest in the Middle Ages that destroyed the ancient system of irrigation. No wonder that paradise is supposed to be in the east! Food was abundant, whereas in Palestine starvation was always a threat when rain was failing. Therefore we also had huge population concentrations in Mesopotamian cities of the time, measured in square miles and counting hundreds of thousands of people. One big Mesopotamian city counted more people than all of Palestine. The size of these cities is remembered in the Old Testament, especially in the description of Nineveh in the Book of Jonah.

When it came to making a living, conditions in Mesopotamia were definitely much better than in Palestine, especially if you lived in the mountains of central Palestine. Mesopotamia was simply the centre of the Ancient Near East, the hub of all interregional trade. The opportunities for making a decent living and becoming wealthy were so much better than was the case in Palestine. As a matter of fact, there was only one reason for leaving Mesopotamia and travelling to Palestine: Memory, including religion.

In this way, remembering Jerusalem is the correlate of remembering Mesopotamia. While Babylon should be remembered as the hell it never was in the real world, Jerusalem, in remembrance, became paradise. It really became the *Jerushalaim shel zahav*, the golden Jerusalem, a remembrance that works even today. So after having degraded the place of 'exile', now in brackets, while at the same time elevating Jerusalem and the land of Israel, the ideology of 'return' became the primary objective of those who wrote the books of the Old Testament. They invented the exile as a place of desolation, and at the same time invented the land of Israel as the land flowing with milk and honey. It is not difficult to see how it was done; the principal means was an extended use of the principles of 'places to be remembered' (in the sense of Paul Nora, *lieu des mémoires* – cf. Nora 2007; Schwarz 2010; and the first part of Erll and Nünning 2010). Jerusalem was, of course, at the centre of this construction, and golden Jerusalem was moulded as the place where God lived, with a splendid temple and a godly people. But other places became places of memory – for example, Hebron, the place where Abraham stayed, now also lost as it was deep in Edomite territory.

I will end the discussion at this point. Now we only have to decide when this 'idea about return' had a background in real life, i.e., when did it become operative?

The debate about Jerusalem between Nebuchadnezzar's destruction of the city and its growing to a major regional centre in the early Hasmonean period has been hot – even ill-tempered. This is not the place to review the discussion. Allow me, however, to present some of the main positions:

1. The biblical position: A massive return c. 538 BCE from Babylon to Jerusalem and Judea. This never happened, except in literature. The reasons have already been presented here.
2. A major rebuilding of the city, perhaps including its temple (Edelman: 2005), sometime in the 5th century BCE, and its walls (Nehemiah).
3. This position is challenged by some Israeli historians and archaeologists like O. Lipschits, I. Finkelstein, and D. Ussishkin, the latter arguing in favour of a Jerusalem that after 587 BCE was hardly a city before Hasmonean times, and beginning to grow in earnest in the first part of the 2nd century BCE (Ussishkin 2006).

The problem with the second position, which will mostly be found among archaeologists originating at the Hebrew University, is the lack of remains from the wall of Nehemiah (Finkelstein 2009; Lipschits 2009), or, as a matter of fact, the very scanty remains of occupation in Jerusalem in the Persian

96 *N.P. Lemche*

Period. This will always be a challenge to scholarship as we still have the Elephantine letter, Cowley No. 30 (l. 18) mentioning the *rab cohanin*, Johannan, in Jerusalem, saying that, c. 400 BCE, there was a religious establishment in Jerusalem and a priest related to it. Moreover we also have the answer to this letter (Cowley 1923: No. 130–32). However, a temple is not a city and the presence of priest at a sanctuary in Jerusalem does not prove that there was a major settlement around this sanctuary.

The facts seem to be that Jerusalem after 200 BCE grew into a major regional Hellenistic centre, which accords with another fact that Hellenization came late to the central highlands. At the same time it grew into a regional religious centre with plenty of religious and political aspirations. One consequence of this was the destruction by John Hyrcanus I of the competing Israelite (Samaritan) sanctuary and city at Gerizim. The idea of being the true 'Israel' that was carried into exile, but returned and accordingly was the true possessor of all the land of Israel may not have originated at the same time, but it was definitely developed as a religio-political programme in those days.

> Va, pensiero sull'ali dorate:
> Fly, thought, on wings of gold;
> go settle upon the slopes and the hills,
> where, soft and mild, the sweet airs
> of our native land smell fragrant!

The image of return lived on, and became a memory of all returns: Verdi's line from the libretto of *Temistocle Solera* to *Nabucco* was as much minted in Italy as among the ancient Jews. Like the Exodus myth, the myth of the Babylonian exile never lost its meaning as liberation theology.

Notes

1 KJV: "Sat down", Hebrew has יָשַׁבְנוּ (perfect) which should perhaps here better translated as "sat", "at the rivers of Babylon we sat".

2 So KJV: REB "may my right hand wither away" Hebrew: תִשְׁכַּח יְמִינִי, the qal form normally substituted with niph'al תִשְׁכַח "be forgotten", but here rather *שׁכח II or III either "whither" or "sink down" DCH VII.

3 Cf. for a recent development of the borders of Judah, Lipschits 2005, Chapter 3, "Changes in the Borders of Judah between the End of the Iron Age and the Persian Period", and compare the maps, *ibid.* p. 145 (time of Josiah) and p. 183 (Persian Period).

4 The relationship between Jeremiah and the Deuteronomistic History can be seen as the works by two authors (in the sense used by John Van Seters about the Yahwist, e.g. in Van Seters 2013) writing in mutual support: Jeremiah predicts the destruction of Jerusalem, and the Deuteronomistic History tells the story of its destruction. The aim is to show that Jerusalem brought the punishment upon itself by not listening to the prophets, and the Deuteronomistic History shows that the prophets were right in predicting the fate of unfaithful Jerusalem.

5 Cf. on the motive of redemption in Isaiah 43 and elsewhere, and especially the motif of Yahweh having paid for the release of his people (Isa 43:1, 3–4.14; 52:3).
6 Translation in Lemche 2008:158, following Berger 1975. It is interesting to see how Sennacherib and Xerxes were remembered in later tradition. Sennacherib destroyed Babylon in 689 and was killed by his sons (the first thing his successor, Asarhaddon, did was to commission its rebuilding), and Xerxes brought considerable destruction to the city in 482 and was killed by the commander of his bodyguard (in 465).
7 See thus Thompson 1999: 217–25.
8 Sennacherib boasts in his annals of having deported 200,150 persons from Hezekiah's kingdom (III:24). This would probably have made more than twice the size of the population of Judah in his time. The number of deported from Samaria twenty years before as 27,290 persons (ANET 288) gives a better expression of what was logistically possible in those days. For a recent overview, cf. Hjelm 2005.
9 Cf. on these reliefs, Ussishkin 1982.

Bibliography

Berger, P.-R. 1975. "Der Kyros Zylinder mit Zusatzfragmenten BIN II Nr. 32, und die akkadischen Personennamen in Danielbuch". *Zeitschrift für Assyriologie* 64: 192–234.

Clines, D.J.A. (ed.). 1993. *Dictionary of Classical Hebrew.* Sheffield: Sheffield Academic Press.

Cowley, A.E. 1923. *Aramaic Papyri of the Fifth Century B.C.* Oxford: Clarendon Press.

Edelman, D. 2005. *The Origins of the "Second Temple": Persian Imperial Policy and the Rebuilding of Jerusalem.* London: Equinox.

Erll, A. and A. Nünning. 2010. *A Companion to Cultural Memory Studies.* Berlin: de Gruyter.

Finkelstein, I. 2009. "Persian Period Jerusalem and Jehud: A Rejoinder". *Journal of Hebrew Scriptures* 9: 24, available online at http://jhsonline.org/Articles/article_126.pdf

Hjelm, I. 2005. "Changing Paradigms: Judaean and Samarian Histories in Light of Recent Research". In *Historie og Konstruktion. Festskrift til Niels Peter Lemche i anledning af 60 års fødselsdagen den 6. september 2005*. M. Müller and T.L. Thompson (eds). Copenhagen: Museum Tusculanum: 161–79.

Lemche, N.P. 2001. "Jordan in the biblical tradition. An overview of the tradition with special reference to the importance of the biblical literature for the reconstruction of the history of the ancient territories of the state of Jordan". *Studies in the History and Archaeology of Jordan* VII: 347–51.

——2008. *The Old Testament Between Theology and History.* Louisville: Westminster John Knox Press.

Lipschits, O. 2005. The Fall and Rise of Jerusalem: Judah under Babylonian Rule. Winona Lake: Eisenbrauns

Lipschits, O. 2009. "Persian Period Finds from Jerusalem: Facts and Interpretations". *Journal of Hebrew Scriptures* 9: 20, available online at http://jhsonline.org/Articles/article_122.pdf

Nora, P. 2007. "From Between Memory and History: Les Lieux de Mémoire". In *Theories of Memory: A Reader.* M. Rossington and A. Whitehead (eds). Baltimore: The Johns Hopkins Press: 144–49.

Pritchard, J.B. (ed.). 1969. *Ancient Near Eastern Texts: Relating to the Old Testament*, 3rd edition. Princeton: Princeton University Press.

Schwarz, B. 2010. "Memory, Temporality, Modernity: Les lieux de mémoire". In *Memory: Histories, Theories, Debate.* S. Radstone and B. Schwarz (eds). New York: Fordham University Press: 41–58.

98   *N.P. Lemche*

Thompson, T.L. 1999. *The Bible in History: How Writers Create a Past*. London: Jonathan Cape.

Ussishkin, D. 1982. *The Conquest of Lachish by Sennacherib*. Tel Aviv: Institute of Archaeology, Tel Aviv University.

——2006. "The Borders and de facto Size of Jerusalem in the Persian Period". In *Judah and Judeans in the Persian Period*. O. Lipschitz and M. Oeming (eds). Winona Lake, IN: Eisenbrauns: 147–66.

Van Seters, J. 2013. *The Yahwist: A Historian of Israelite Origins*. Winona Lake, IN: Eisenbrauns.

Part II
Motifs of exile and return

7 Sheep without a shepherd

Genesis' discourse on justice and reconciliation as exile's *raison d'être*

Thomas L. Thompson

Exile and return, justice and reconciliation

In a previous article, I argued that the story of Cain's murder of Abel in Genesis 4 introduces a series of narrative themes, which are particularly rich in their potential for the development of Samaritan-Jewish allegories, which reflect utopian elements of the myths of exile and return. The story's reiterations maintain and feed a number of central plotlines of the Pentateuch (Thompson 2011a). In this article, I identified the opening of four thematic developments from Genesis 4.

1. The leitmotif of the cursed land bringing exile and estrangement is found in a narrative thread, which begins first in the curse of Adam in Genesis 3:17–19. This motif is reiterated and thematically expanded in Gen 3:23; 4:10–14; 5:29; 6:7, 11–12; 8:21–22; 9:25–27 and 12:1–4.
2. The theme of 'brothers fighting brothers' (Hjelm 2003) linked closely to the stereotypical motif of the younger supplanting the elder, first brought forward in the prophetic allegorical conflict of Jacob and Esau's birth narrative (Gen 25:19–34).
3. The thematic opposition of ever-intensifying revenge and ever-elusive reconciliation is a theme which dominates ancient Near Eastern discourse on blood-guilt.
4. The dark side of the great ancient Near Eastern theme of the king as shepherd of his people explores the fate of such sheep when they have lost their shepherd (Thompson 1999: 293–374; 2013a: 163–82 and 205–35; Wyatt 1996; 2001; 2005: 38–71; Pfoh 2009; 2012).

Central to the Abraham stories is the pivotal and wide-ranging discourse on the ethical righteousness of Yahweh in his royal role as judge of this world (Gen 18:25), a discourse which ultimately succeeds in giving both a critical and comprehensive closure to Genesis as a coherent literary whole. Key to this discourse on justice are three variations of a story, which begin in exile and the motif of abuse of the generous host and close in the reconciliation of shepherds quarrelling. While this discourse is furthered by tales of conflict,

102   *T.L. Thompson*

injustice and reconciliation through the Jacob narratives (Thompson 2013a: 55–66), three narratives, centering on women and sexuality, effect a transvaluation of ethics, which is first illustrated in the story of Lot's daughters in Genesis 19:30–38, but becomes systemic in three bridge narratives, which bind the Jacob narratives to Genesis' resolution in the Joseph story. These stories – namely, the Dinah story, the story of Tamar and that of Potiphar's wife – ultimately succeed in giving both a critical and comprehensive closure.

Exile and chaos as a fundamental motif of biblical narrative

The polarity in the creation hymn of the divine spirit (רוח אלהים), ordering the waters of the deep (תהום) in Genesis 1:2, stands in contrast to the complex reversal of creation and return to chaos, ever implied in the desert-oriented motif of chaos and emptiness (תהו ובהו; *tohu wa bohu*) and some dozen of its variations such as we find in the use of the word-pair, בקק ובולקה, a wasteland and a desert of Isaiah 24:1, and the similar trope expressing chaotic destructiveness, captured by the 'nonsense' reiteration of desolation and reproach (שממה ומשמה) in Ezekiel 6:14 (Thompson 2013a: 174–78). I have been able to show that such literary techniques mark a structural polarity imbedded in the symbol-system that is so ubiquitously apparent throughout biblical literature (Thompson 2013a: 133–46). The richness of the motif of *tohu wa bohu* and its variants exposes an intriguing compositional technique, which is employed in countless scenes of divine destruction, not least those related to themes and motifs of exile in both narrative and prophetic literature. The entrenched ideological association of this motif with themes of chaos and creation is marked by an ideological stress in the presentation of such dramatic cameo figures of Jerusalem destroyed as the city of emptiness (קרית תהו) in Isaiah 24:10 and elsewhere, as well as in the Bible's only full reiteration of *tohu wa bohu*, which we find in Genesis 1's referential echo in Jeremiah's vision of the coming Jerusalem's barren emptiness (Jer 4:23; Thompson 2013a: 169–74). This allegorical portrayal of Jerusalem's destruction and exile is filled with the rich imagery of desert, most notable in the prophet Jeremiah's failed search through Jerusalem's streets for but a single one who is righteous and seeks truth. Whether small or great he might serve as hostage in support of a plea for the city in Yahweh's forgiveness (Jer. 5:1–5), a plea that finds a parallel reiteration in Abraham's plea on behalf of the righteous of Sodom in Genesis 18, which challenges the assumption of the justice of Yahweh himself.

Such engagement of the creation hymn in Isaiah and Jeremiah, and particularly in Jeremiah's search for mercy for Jerusalem as doomed to destruction and exile, finds its culmination within the complex, double reiteration, having deep roots in both the Pentateuch and in ancient Near Eastern literature, which we find in the closure of 2 Samuel, where David asks Yahweh to forgive the city for his crime of having carried out the forbidden census, a crime which he had been enticed by Yahweh to commit (2 Sam 24:1–25; cf. 1 Chron 21:1–30). This story's reiteration in Chronicles 21 is kinder, if perhaps more shallowly oriented, to both Yahweh and David, marking, as it does, the temptation to take a census as having come from Satan. David is not only portrayed in a better light by paying for the threshing floor in gold rather than silver, his ordering of the census in Chronicles is also met by a mitigating element of resistance and even disobedience from the people, not least from the tribes of Levi and Benjamin. In both variations of the narrative, David is presented by Yahweh with a three-fold choice of punishment: three years famine, three months flight from his enemies or three days of plague. David, who ever illustrates a heroic piety, chooses to depend on Yahweh's mercy rather than the mercy of men and so chooses three days of plague for his punishment. As this plague rages against Israel, the story turns to a closure centred in a – for Chronicles – somewhat problematic reiteration of repentance: first by Yahweh and then by David, when the plague had killed 70,000. As the angel stretched his hand against Jerusalem, Yahweh repented the evil he had brought over Israel and halted the plague (2 Sam 24:16–17; 1 Chron 21:15–17: an echo of Num 16:22!). Both variations of the Jerusalem story are united in celebrating an etiology for the function of Jerusalem's sacrificial-cult in bringing mercy to the people. David's repentance and the argument he raises in response in both 2 Samuel and 1 Chronicles, most significantly, also engage Genesis 18's question regarding the righteousness of Yahweh's judgment in its reiteration of the thrice doubled episode in Exodus-Numbers, in which Moses – like David – begs Yahweh to punish him rather than his people (Ex 32:7–14; Num 11:10–15 and Num 14:13–19; see Thompson 2011a: 14–20 and below).

Divine irascibility

In the David story, both the folktale motif of a choice between three punishments and David's closing admission of guilt and responsibility are grounded in the ancient principle of justice, known since the flood story. This trope is captured eloquently by Ea's rebuke of Enlil for sending the flood in the Gilgamesh version of that myth (Speiser 1969: 95), a rebuke which calls for limits to even a god's wrath:

> How could you, unreasoning, bring on the deluge?
> On the sinner impose his sin; on the transgressor impose his transgression!
> Yet be lenient, lest he be cut off; be patient, lest he be dislodged!
> Instead of your bringing on the deluge, would that a lion had risen up to diminish mankind!
> Instead of your bringing on the deluge, would that a wolf had risen up to diminish mankind!
> Instead of your bringing on the deluge, would that a famine had risen up to l[ay low] mankind!
> Instead of your bringing on the deluge, would that a plague had risen up to smite mankind!

104   *T.L. Thompson*

The story of David in 2 Samuel 24 joins this discourse with its closure in an etiological narrative for the sacrificial cult of the Jerusalem temple. Not only is the reiteration of the motif of mercy presented in the description of the 'gods smelling the sweet savour' of a burnt offering in the flood story tempering both their and Yahweh's anger (Gen 8:21; Lev 1:13; Speiser 1969: 95; tablet 11: 160), but also the function of this scene as a narrative bridge to 1 King's story of Solomon's construction of the temple, a story which also closes in a prayer for mercy in 1 Kings 8, is confirmed. This closure in the Kings' narrative establishes an ideological basis for the opening of 1 Chronicles' narrative about David, with variations on both David's accession to the throne and his conquest of Jerusalem (1 Chron 11:1–9). It also supports Chronicles' revisionary reiteration of an episode in 2 Samuel 6:12–16, in which David brings the ark to Jerusalem (1 Chron 13; 15), introducing David's appointment of Levite ministers to the ark. After reiterating David's burnt offerings and peace offerings (2 Sam 6:17–19; cf. 1 Chron 16:1–3), the Chronicler has his Levites sing a song (1 Chron 16:8–36), which echoes David's prayer in the census story. The song is given in three segments (reiterating Ps 105:1–15; 96:1–13 and 106:1.48, respectively), creating a thanksgiving song in celebration of Yahweh's covenant and the fulfilment of his promises to Israel. The song is dedicated to Yahweh, who – in a reference to Abraham's Yahweh of Genesis 18 – is defined as Judge of the Earth (1 Chron 16:33)! This strikingly celebratory theme, reflecting the role given to David throughout Chronicles, finds an ideological variation in 1 King 8's reiteration of David's prayer and placed in the mouth of Solomon at the dedication of the temple: a prayer which determines the ultimate narrative trajectory of 1–2 Kings. Solomon's prayer admonishes his people to hold to Yahweh with the whole of their hearts (1 Kings 8:54–61) and closes in a scene, grandly reiterating the David story's burnt offerings: 22,000 oxen and 120,000 sheep over a doubled seven days festival (1 Kings 8:62–66; cf. 2 Sam 24:18–25)!

Rather than closing the story of the dedication of the temple with Chronicles in thanksgiving, Solomon's prayer (1 Kings 8:22–53) determines destiny by sketching the people's distant future, far beyond the closure of Kings' narrative. Continuing to build on its reiteration of the David story from 2 Samuel 6, Solomon's prayer to Yahweh moves the presentation of the figure of Yahweh as judge to centre stage.

> Hear and forgive! If someone sins against his neighbor and must take an oath and comes and swears this oath before your altar in this house, then, in heaven, hear and act and judge your servants, condemning the guilty by bringing his conduct upon his own head.
>
> (1 Kings 8:30–32)

When defeat in war and when drought, famine, plague or sickness come, shall Yahweh forgive his people their sin (1 Kings 8:33–40)? And, reaching out to the future exile

If they (your people) sin against you – *for there is no man who does not sin* – and you are angry and you give them to an enemy, so that they are carried away captive. ... If they repent with all their mind and with all their heart in the land of their enemies ... then hear their prayer and supplication ... forgive your people ... and grant them compassion.

(1 Kings 8:46–53)

Jeremiah's search of Jerusalem's streets for a single just man also evokes images of siege against an unpardoned Jerusalem by describing – in an echo of the ancient Near Eastern flood story's wolf and lion – an attack of wild beasts from forest and desert, as the coming disaster of destruction and exile overwhelm Jerusalem in its allegorical role as Yahweh's garden – using a metaphor of gleaners in a vineyard, who collect their small remnant from not-entirely-stripped vines (Jer. 5:6–10; cf. Isa 5:1–7). In Jeremiah's commentary, the empty spirit of Jerusalem's prophets is likened to shouting into the wind (or, variously, "a feeding on the wind": Eccl 1:17; Hos 12:1). Yahweh's word in Jeremiah comes, Janus-faced, ever with a Pentateuch's devouring fire (Jer. 5:11–17; see Lundager Jensen 2000).

The cluster of thematic elements in Jeremiah 4–5 is striking in its support of similarly interrelated motifs reiterated throughout Genesis. This marks not merely a thematic polarity of a desert's emptiness over against the rich ambivalence of Genesis 1's creative and destructive divine spirit hovering above the waters of chaos, but also the expansive compositional techniques which project a considerable variety of analogies related to themes of exile and return throughout Genesis. The function of such dominating motifs of Genesis as 'holy war' (Gen 9:2) and 'stranger in the land' (Gen 12:3), overcoming the violence of revenge through reconciliation and peace-making, encourage me to attempt a sketch of the broad compositional coherence of Genesis, which is exposed by the reiteration and implicit interaction of the clustering of such thematic elements of separation and exile, reconciliation and return, together with a number of expansive variations, which bear an intrinsic thematic dissonance between tropes set in polarity, such as 'creation and destruction' and 'alienation and reconciliation'. My effort is to sketch an implicit discourse, which defines Genesis as an interpretive and allegorical introduction to both the Samaritan *Torah* and the Masoretic *Tanak* (Thompson 2013b).

The *toledoth* structure of Genesis

While most commentaries organize the narratives of Genesis in four major blocks – a primeval story, which is followed by the three patriarchal chain-narratives centred in the figures of Abraham, Jacob and Joseph – they do so by implicitly subordinating the Isaac narratives to the Abraham story in a search for coherence and balance in a projected history of composition. The chain narratives created by the segmented structure of what is presented in a generational order under Genesis 5:1's titular *Book of the Toledoth of Adam*,

106 *T.L. Thompson*

develops both a chronological subordination in a ten-fold expanding *toledoth* (Tengström 1981; Thompson 1987: 61–132), presenting the primary progenitors within a coherent structure of generations and introduces the names and stories of their descendents in order. However, it also creates a double narrative plotline – first within the limits of relatively short tales, such as we find in the episodic narratives of the garden story in Genesis 2:4–3:24, the Cain and Abel story of 4:1–24 and then in the Tower of Babel story of Genesis 11:1–9. The *toledoth* structure then presents a series of often typologically distinctive genealogical narrations, each of which bears its own theme and plotline. So the '*toledoth* of Adam' of Genesis 5:1–32 brings the reader from the first man, Adam, through ten dynastic representatives to the next segment of the greater *toledoth* framework; namely, the *toledoth* of Noah with his three sons, the ancestors of post-diluvian mankind (Gen 6:9; 10:1). It creates thereby not only a plotline, which fills the world with sons and daughters, but also gives the reader an expansive room to include a Hebrew version of the flood story and a new link in the chain of narratives, which had begun in the opening poem of creation in Genesis 1. The *toledoth* maintains its plotline and thematic coherence until the close of Genesis 10's illustration of the repopulation of the world through Noah's sons: Shem, the patriarch of Asia, Ham of Africa and Japheth of Europe (Thompson and Wajdenbaum 2014: 1–3).

At the close of the ten-fold dynastic succession from Adam to Noah, Genesis 5:32's reference to Noah's succession by Shem, Ham and Japheth forms an envelope structure (Gen. 5:32; 10:1), which marks the fulfilment of the *Book of the Toledoth of Adam* and the use of the flood story to anchor the plotline of the Pentateuch. While the flood story (Gen. 6:5–8:22) is a rewritten version of the Mesopotamian *Atrahasis-Utnapishtim* myth, it structures its reiteration within the Pentateuch with a brief, cryptic introduction to a variation on the Fall of Lucifer legend in Genesis 6:1–4 (Kvanvig 2002; 2004). Reinterpreting the trope of the 'image of God' as 'son of god' in Genesis 5, the Lucifer legend's 'sons of god' interpret the birth of heroes and giants of legend to mark the totality of human corruption as motive cause of the flood. This narrative fragment, rooted in 1 Enoch, also opens a secure path to Genesis 8–9's 'fear and terror' in a covenant story, which serves to prepare the reader for a more comprehensive reiteration of this so enigmatic introduction to the flood story. More than a relatively simple etiology for the *Nephilim* – that nation of terrifying giants in the failed conquest narrative of Israel's first generation in Numbers 13–14, the heroes and giants, born in miscegenation – returns us to a discourse on hubris, which had first been evoked in the garden story and finds its clearest illustration in the allegory of the Tower of Babel as an opening to the patriarchal narratives.

Yahweh's covenant of fear and terror

In contrast to the evil ones of 1 Enoch (Kvanvig 2011: 274–310; cf. Mettinger 2007: 128), Noah was righteous and blameless. Like Enoch himself, he

Sheep without a shepherd   107

walked with God (Gen 6:9; cf. 5:24). A play on the theme of return is evoked in that Noah, like Seth, is chosen to play, as in the Esarhaddon story, the role of surviving remnant from an exile-miming flood (Thompson 2007: 245–46). Narratively speaking, the flood story is part of a chain of exile stories defined by the singularly small, but necessary and stereotypical motif in the Esarhaddon story's thematic element of past suffering brought about by the wrath of the gods in an all-destroying flood, which overwhelms Babylon and casts its people and their king into 70 years of exile (cf. Jer 29:10; Thompson 2007: 245–46). This introductory episode is used to open a leitmotif of divine regret, so central to the Pentateuch and, within the Masoretic tradition, also dominating the plot of Samuels and Kings. Yahweh created mankind, but now regrets what he has created: an unequivocal reiteration of the theme of divine regret which we find in the Atrahasis-Gilgamesh flood narrative. As argued elsewhere, the theme finds its three-fold development in the Mosaic tradition, where Yahweh creates Israel as he had once created mankind, yet only to come to regret what he has made (Ex 32:7–14; Num 11:10–15 and Num 14:13–19; Thompson 2013: 291–304). So too, he both chooses and comes to regret all his eternal choices, as a theme is built that structures the narrative as a whole. The eternal, transcendent election of the eldest sons of Israel's highpriest (Lev 8:10–12; Thompson 2013: 192–93) is reiterated to inaugurate a failed succession, which moves from Eli to Samuel, to Saul and David, confirming the successive theme of failure of the chosen of Yahweh through 1–2 Kings. Not least important for our understanding of the flood story is the primary motif reiterated from Gilgamesh: the divine regret for destroying mankind (Gen 8:20–22), given that there were, from Ishtar's perspective, other ways of diminishing mankind and its evil! The leitmotif of Yahweh's anger, expressed through the desert motifs of drought and famine, already dominates the Eden and Cain narratives. The Pentateuch's countless variations on Yahweh's anger and burning wrath reiterate classic ancient Near Eastern alternatives to the flood as a solution to the evil of mankind. We first identify such alternatives to the flood in the three disasters projected in Atrahasis and Gilgamesh; namely, plague, famine and war. In Genesis' rewriting of Gilgamesh, such alternative punishments are hardly presented as effective pedagogical tools for mankind's improvement. Hardly effective means of change, they prepare the reader rather for the ultimate disasters of an Esarhaddon-like, Exile-bringing flood to come within the Bible's never-ending narrative (Thompson 2005: 315–21).

Just such a trajectory is also intimated by Yahweh's war covenant in Genesis 8–9, marked as it is by the 'fear and terror' of mankind's third reiteration of having been created in the divine image. As humanity's destructive hubris was set in motion in our story when Yahweh gave mankind all the fruit of all the 'green things in the garden' for their food, *save one*, he now introduces a covenant 'reform' (Gen. 9:1–17), tacitly accepting the human incursion into the divine realm. Now, everything is given to them for their food, *save a single exception* – that food of both gods and giants, flesh with its life in it (cf. Num

108   *T.L. Thompson*

13:32; 14:9!). This reiterated trope from the garden story hardly implicitly holds any greater hope of success! With the three-fold motif of mankind, created in the image of the divine in mind, God blesses Noah and his sons that they might again fill the earth – but this covenant is filled with dissonance. Mankind is to be the 'fear and terror' of all living: a Greek loan of the myth of *Phoibos* and *Deimos,* sons of Ares, the god of war. This implicit citation is supported as Yahweh, in his role as just such a volatile, violent God of war, hangs his bow on the clouds to mark his covenant: an implicit promise to sate all future anger with Holy War. With the figure of mankind set in the image of God opening a new plotline, which promises disasters to come, a second narrative segment (Gen 9:18–27) marks contrasting elements of renewal. Noah's three sons leave the ark and re-open the fertility motif of the narrative, which the flood story had temporarily closed, and successfully re-people the earth (Gen. 9:18–19; cf. above 5:32 and 10:1). This points towards new beginnings and Genesis 10's cartographic extension of the *sepher toledoth 'adam.*

Another narrative segment, however, intrudes (Gen 10:18–27), asserting a curse in place of the primary narrative's fertile blessings. Noah takes up Adam's and Cain's disastrous role as mankind's first farmers (9:20!). In Yahweh's image, he plants his vineyard (cf. Isa 5). Noah's wine, however, is sweet; he drinks of it and falls asleep. While lying drunken and naked in his tent, his son, Ham, sees his nakedness, tells his brothers and humiliatingly exposes his father to implied derision. Noah curses Ham's son, Cana'an, the target for a covenant's holy war: with implicit reference to the Macedonians, "when God will make room for Japheth, who will dwell in the tents of Shem" (Thompson and Wajdenbaum 2014: 1–3). The plot motif of nakedness not only reiterates the 'fear' that Adam discovered, naked and exposed, as he heard Yahweh walking in the garden (Gen 3:8). Elements of the story of Noah and the exposure of his nakedness are also reiterated in the allegory of Lot's fear over Yahweh's destruction of the towns of the Jordan valley (Gen 19:29), which had been a well-watered garden that Genesis likens to Yahweh's vineyard in Isaiah's allegory on Jerusalem and its destruction (cf. Gen 13:10; Isa 5:1–7). This association with Lot creates a three-fold narrative, which ties Lot's choice of the fertile garden of the Jordan in Genesis 13 to the destruction of that garden in Genesis 19 (cf. Gen 9:26; 10:18–19). This narrative line increases in its coherence when we take into consideration possible allusions to Ezekiel 16's curse of the three sisters. Allegorically, they represent Jerusalem, Samaria and Sodom and include the reiteration of rape-oriented motifs of their vulnerable exposure and nakedness creating a relevant discourse on themes of exile and return (Thompson 2011b: 196–98; for a historical commentary, see Thompson 2013b).

Genesis as interpretive allegory

Genesis' primeval history closes with Genesis 10's *toledoth* of the sons of Noah, in the form of a three-fold list of the nations of the world who

Sheep without a shepherd 109

"according to their lands, each with their own language, by their families, in their nations" (Gen 10:5.20.31), spread the nations abroad over the earth after the flood. This segmented *toledoth*, however, reverses the expected succession from the *toledoth* of the eldest son Shem to that of his younger brothers, Ham and Japheth (so Gen 5:32 and 10:1), by placing the *toledoth* of Shem in the very last place in order of succession. This *toledoth* of Shem – with its families, languages, lands and nations – is then, however, secondarily revised in Genesis 11:10–27, in the form of a succession of eldest sons, much as in the segments of *The Book of the Toledoth of Adam* in Genesis 5. The resulting variants of the Shem *toledoth* are then linked by a bridge narrative, in Genesis 11:1–9, which offers an alternative etiology for the spread of languages and peoples across the face of the earth – the story of Babel's exile, as Yahweh confuses the language of all the earth. This short, mythic tale in Genesis 11:1–9 offers an ironic caricature of the Hellenistic empire's efforts to create a world with a single language through its revision of the myth of Lucifer's fall, especially as this is interpreted in Jeremiah and Isaiah and centred on the theme of hubris (Raheb 2014: 120–21). In a lecture to the European Association of Biblical Studies a few years ago, I argued that variant reiterations of this myth in Jeremiah 50–51 and Isaiah 13:1–14:23 were used to interpret Cyrus' conquest over Babylon in accord with Isaiah 45 and allow Genesis 11's scene of the destruction of the tower of Babel and the scattering of the people to be understood messianically, as a destruction which opened the way to a return under Cyrus (Thompson 2011c: 115–19). Genesis 11's revision of the Shem genealogy now links the spreading nations to a Noah-miming Terah, with his three sons: Abram, Nahor and Haran. Terah's move to Cana'an not only opens the stories of the patriarchs, as a celebration of Judah's return from 'the city of the Chaldeans', much as Abram's call from Harran evokes the return of Samaritans from Harran to their home at Shechem's Moreh.

My understanding of Genesis' use of the themes of exile and return as a revisionary introduction to the Mosaic narrative of Exodus-Numbers dates back more than twenty years (Thompson 1992: 353–66), when I first drew the conclusion that Genesis, which had created a variety of tropes reflecting an all-Israel, implicitly held a utopian and eschatological understanding of exile. More recently (Thompson 2011a), I illustrated this in a series of lectures, which dealt with the intertextual implications of a cluster of allegorically motivated motifs of disunity, separation and exile on the one hand and return and reconciliation on the other. This led me on an exegetical journey through Genesis and the interrelated plot development of the stories of Abraham and Lot, of Esau and Jacob and of Joseph and his brothers, to ask whether the interrelated clustering of these motifs reflected a discourse in which motifs of separation and exile project a return that is utopian more than historiographic (further, Nathanson 2013). I would like to turn once again to the function of such motif-clusters of exile and return by concentrating on two very brief but pivotal passages which, closing the narratives of Jeremiah, 2 Kings and 2

110   T.L. Thompson

Chronicles as they do, have had considerable influence on modern scholarship's historical understanding.

Jer 52:31–34 and 2 Kgs 25:27–30: Setting a table in the wilderness – a trope of reconciliation

The closure of the Book of Jeremiah is a nearly verbatim reiteration of the closure of the Book of Kings. Jehoiachin, the last of the sons of David, is invited to the Babylonian King Evil-Merodach's table. Following Jeremiah 50–51's great diatribe against a Lucifer-miming Babylon, this scene of humble reconciliation functions as a saving prophecy, marking the end of exile. It implicitly holds a promise of reconciliation, which, through the Babel story of Genesis 11, opens Terah, Abram and Lot's journey to Shechem, Salem and the Jordan's well-watered valley of Sodom – and, perhaps, even evoking Ezekiel 47's vision of a return to the tree of life. Some such interpretation of Jeremiah's closure, reiterated as it is by 2 Kings, seems suggested by the variation of this scene in 2 Samuel, where David plays Evil-Merodach's role of the reconciling victor, inviting the surviving remnant of Saul's house, Mephibosheth (2 Sam 9), as guest to his table in Jerusalem (Thompson 2005: 311–12). Mephibosheth plays the role of the crippled Jacob, who, with his blind father Isaac, illustrates the utopian trope of 'the poor-man's song', calling for the protection of the lame and the blind. In a later interpretation, Jesus, in Matthew's 'cleansing of the temple' story, enters the city in glory and heals the lame and the blind in the temple, overturning David's curse, which had rhetorically banished the whole of Israel – who are represented by the figures of Jacob and Isaac in Genesis – from both Jerusalem and its temple (Gen. 27:1; 32:31–32; 2 Sam. 5:8; Thompson 2005: 80–88).

2 Chron 36:21–23: New beginnings – a trope of return

Reiterating the opening motif of the Assyrian Esarhaddon narrative, in regard to a divine decree of 70 years for Babylon's exile before Esarhaddon was called to return from his exile by Marduk's mercy in a divinely appointed 11th year of exile, and perhaps inspired by Isaiah 45:1's call to Cyrus as Yahweh's messiah, 2 Chronicles closes its story of Jerusalem's fall with Yahweh's call to Cyrus. This announces a new beginning for Jerusalem in fulfilment of Jeremiah's prophetic curse, which had laid the land fallow for its much-needed 70 year sabbatical. *Yahweh Elohei Shamayim*, in his mercy, calls Cyrus to build him a temple in Jerusalem. The narrative of 2 Chronicles closes on the note of Cyrus' proclamation that all of Yahweh's people may go up. Chronicles' casting of this brief evocation of return, as a new beginning granted by a merciful God, has many elements in common with the biblical tale-type of the birth story, not least with the birth story of Isaac in Genesis 18–21. This begins with the promise of a son to the barren, but laughing, Sara, a reward for Abraham's generosity for laying his table in the wilderness

Sheep without a shepherd 111

for three strangers. This joyful, new beginning of the promise, however, is delayed by scenes of failure and disaster, with motifs of famine, desert and exile, as Yahweh tells Abraham of the evil he is planning against Sodom. Abraham's failed search for ten just men whom Yahweh had required from Sodom as his measure of mercy is a terror-embracing failure that turns Sodom into a city of emptiness (תהו קרית), which intertextually echoes Jeremiah's equally fatal search for but a single such man in Jerusalem. As the narrative line turns away from its joy in new beginnings to stories of destruction and exile (Thompson 2013: 167–78), two disturbingly ambiguous figures challenge the reader: that of Abraham – one through whom the whole world is to be blessed (Gen 18:18) – failing to save Sodom and, even more, the figure of Yahweh, who, as judge of the world, will destroy the righteous with the unrighteous (Gen 18:25). Abraham's question: "Shall not the Judge of the world do right?" carries, as we will see, the burden of the remainder of Genesis' narrative discourse!

Who was the keeper of Abel?

The plot development from Genesis 2–3 to Genesis 4 shifted our attention away from Adam's role as keeper in the garden that we might raise the question of who the shepherd of the people of this world might be! In striking contrast to Isaiah 5's "Song of the Vineyard", in which Yahweh is keeper of a vineyard that brings forth sour grapes – an allegory, in which Yahweh turns in his anger against his garden Israel he has created, to wholly destroy it, together with Judah, his favourite vine (Isa 5:1–7) – the garden story of Genesis 2–3 presents mankind's epitome, האדם, 'the man' as Yahweh's vicar and the keeper of the garden. He is a royal figure, an illustration of the role as 'ruler', with which he is described in Genesis 1:26, and of the comparable role he has been given as dynastic first-born recipient of his father's divine image in the genealogy of Genesis 5. In Genesis 2, האדם is set the royal tasks of 'worker and watcher over the garden' (לעבדה ולשמר), a role which reiterates the role of King Sargon of Akkad in his story, who describes himself not only as 'lover of Ishtar', but also as 'keeper of her father's garden' (King 1907; Lewis 1980). Just as Eve, in her role as the 'mother of all living', illustrates the divine epithets used for Ishtar and Inanna, Adam, as keeper of Yahweh's garden, illustrates the royal functions of gardener and keeper of his divinely chosen kingdom, a close, thematic variant of the ancient Near Eastern stereotype of the good king as servant of his god and shepherd of his people (Thompson 2007: 258–59). This is the metaphor which preoccupies the story of Genesis 4.

The Cain and Abel story opens with Eve's ambiguous declamation on giving birth to Cain (קין) with the classic form of a naming etiology: את יהוה קניתי איש: "I have created a man with Yahweh" (Gen 4:1; cf. Long 1968), suggesting the creation of a demigod. The text knows well Adam's role, but focuses rather on Eve's assertion of parity with Yahweh to present its story's

112   T.L. Thompson

central and stunning thematic motif. The common piety of the role of the divine in the miracle of birth is deftly turned to suggest a hubristic claim to a divine role by Eve.

A second son is born, Abel, with his name's etiology's reference to his short life, from הבל (but 'a breath'), the 'shepherd' and 'keeper of sheep' (רעה צון). His elder brother Cain was a 'farmer' (עבד אדמה 'a servant of the ground'), reiterating together the two-fold role of mankind in Yahweh's garden (cf. Gen 4:2 with 2:15). The continuity with the garden story is strengthened by the progressive intensification of the role of the motif of the soil (ha'adamah). As the man and his wife are banned from the garden, Adam, in his role as gardener, is judged by Yahweh's curse and becomes the servant of a now cursed soil. Yahweh drives him from the garden, condemned "to work the land from which he had been taken" (לעבד את האדמה אשר לקח משם; Gen 3:23; cf. 2:15)! Such reiterative continuity, evoked by the story's language, intensifies awareness of the significance of the continuity of the the fate-determining role of the curse. The language stresses the occasional and exemplary nature of storied events: ויהי מקץ ימים. "And so it happened, that Cain, the 'servant of the land', brought its produce as an offering and Abel, likewise, brought of the first-born of his flock and of their fat portions to Yahweh" (Gen 4:3). Yahweh accepts both Abel and his blood sacrifice – the first fruits of his flocks – but, dominated by his curse of the land, Yahweh accepts neither Cain nor the offering from his produce and labour. Cain became very angry and his face fell.

With its cryptic and demanding introduction, this doublet of the garden story engages a central theme of Genesis' primeval narrative: Cain joins his mother to challenge the divine. With its recurrent ironic reiterations, the creation story's three-fold motif of a mankind created in God's image (Thompson 2009) takes yet another illustrating turn. Cain's head hangs in anger, preparing for its reversal in a Yahweh-miming hubris: that uplifting rage which strikes his brother down. He is a man able to take what his mother has created. Having accepted Abel and his offering but not Cain and his, Yahweh turns philosophical and questions Cain's 'burning anger' with a question which again allows the reader to recognize the miming of Yahweh and his attributes that dominate this story's central discourse on murder and revenge (Thompson 2011b). Cain's anger is in the image of the violence-threatening Yahweh we find in Job 42:7–8 (Guillaume and Schunk 2007)! So Cain's uprising imitates the divine recklessness and irascibility dominating the Pentateuch, as in Exodus 32, Numbers 11 and Numbers 13–14 (Thompson 2009). As Eve created a man's life in giving birth to Cain, her son now takes a man's life. Interpreting this challenge to the divine prerogative over life and death, Yahweh projects a mythic struggle with sin for Cain's reflection. Unresisted, sin 'lurks', 'lies in wait' or 'crouches' at the door' – like a snake, a jackal or a lion (חתאת רבץ; cf. Isa 34:13; 35:7). It 'desires' (תשוקתו) Cain. In this first illustration of mankind's now eternal struggle with the snake, prophesied in the curse of Genesis 3:15, Cain is counselled by Yahweh to 'master' (תמשל) his anger (Gen 4:7) with yet another narrative allegory: "Be rather slow to

Sheep without a shepherd 113

anger than a hero; for it is better to master one's spirit than capture a city" (Prov 16:32)! Cain, however, himself the founder of the first city (Gen 4:17), hardly shares such humility with the author of Proverbs and chooses to mirror Yahweh. In a divine-like fury, not with mastered anger but an upraised fury, Cain kills his brother (Gen 4:8; cf. Num 24:9–10; Isa 2:19,21; 14:22). It is only at the very close of its long narrative that the Pentateuch finally responds to the hubris of both Eve and her son in Deuteronomy 32:39's decree that there is no other God than Yahweh: He, alone, kills and lets live.

After Abel's death and after his blood had cried out to Yahweh from the ground, Yahweh asks Cain where his brother is. The question is hardly idle. The audience knows that Yahweh already knows – even as they do. However, it is Cain's answer that is the heart of the matter and bears the weight of the story's plot to open the central core of the story's allegory. Cain answers with a counter-question: "Am I the keeper of my brother?" – השמר אחי אנכי. As reader, one is reminded of Adam's original failure as 'keeper of the garden' (Gen 4:9; cf. 2:15). Reiterating Adam's failure, Cain, the 'servant of the ground', asks his question, but his brother's profession draws irony into the question, as Cain asks of the 'shepherd'! Indeed, his question might well be heard as complaint: Who is his brother's keeper? Indeed, Cain – he and his offering rejected by Yahweh – has no keeper! רעה צאן is the title of one who watches sheep: a royal and divine title of patronage. Kings and gods, in both narrative and myth, are shepherds of their people: keepers and guardians. The story's plot nurtures an unbearable problem: Yahweh had accepted Abel and his sacrifice, even as he had rejected Cain and the offering from his cursed ground, but what can it mean that Yahweh accepted Abel? Abel, the shepherd, however acceptable he and his burnt offering may have been in storied fact, was left unprotected by his patron (I. Hjelm, personal communication). What does Yahweh's acceptance matter? Though the flood story makes it clear that Yahweh likes the smell and savour of a sacrifice, being a patron requires reciprocity and being a shepherd requires sheep that are alive! The Cain story's figure of Yahweh hardly lives up to the divine shepherd of Psalm 23! The all-too-quickly-passing Abel did, in fact, need a patron and keeper. If that keeper were Yahweh, what kind of question does he put to Cain? As a shepherd, Abel brought his sheep to Yahweh and offered them with piety and thanksgiving. But as a sheep, himself, his shepherd was entirely absent!

It is Cain whom the story eventually uses to bring Yahweh to accept his role as divine patron and shepherd. The irony is striking, and the tragedy of Abel's death is exposed as Cain takes upon himself the role of this world's sheep, without a shepherd. His question: "Am I my brother's keeper?" is a question hardly either rhetorical or arrogant. It expresses self-recognition, incapacity and loss. His uncertain fate as fugitive, in exile from his land and his God, forces Cain to protest his fate as the victim of anyone he should happen to meet (Gen 4:12–14). This singular motif of the fugitive is an allegory on Israel in its exilic role, whose suffering is the occasion of Yahweh's vengeance against Babylon, carried out by the Persian Cyrus. Israel is

114   *T.L. Thompson*

presented as one "whose land no longer yields its produce. Israel is a wanderer and fugitive on the earth" (Gen 4:13–14). Jeremiah presents his interpretation, his *pesher*: "Her land is made a desolate waste, with no one living there. ... My people were lost sheep, whose shepherds let them stray ... they wandered from mountain to hill ... any who happened upon them, devoured them ... saying, 'we have no guilt'" (Jer 50:3–7; Thompson 2010: 47–49). Israel too, like Abel and Cain, was a sheep without a shepherd.

Yahweh, in Psalm 23, plays the quintessential role of the good shepherd – a role which comes into play in Genesis 4, when Cain addresses Yahweh in his desperation in the wilderness. It is there, in response to Cain's recognition that his punishment is too great to bear, that Yahweh finally takes up his defining responsibility as Cain's 'keeper'! Yahweh learns to forgive and marks Cain with his patronage. Yahweh's acceptance of his role as Cain's 'good Samaritan', his role as all the world's keeper (שׁמר), marks Cain's life with the sign of his protection and patronage: a life protected by the threat of vengeance (Gen 4:15). This, however, as we quickly learn, is but a passing promise as fleeting and insubstantial as had been his acceptance of Abel. Lamech's overtrumping revenge mocks this would-be shepherd (Gen 4:23–24)!

A great distance lies between Jeremiah's presentation of the fall of Babylon as the beginning of Israel's saving return and the Cain story's classic ancient Near Eastern discourse on revenge and blood guilt, retribution and atonement. The specific motif of Yahweh's revenge, with a trajectory that moves towards Jeremiah 50, as I have previously argued (Thompson 2010; Thompson 2011c), sets Yahweh in the role of the messenger, who is to keep watch over Israel through the wilderness (לשׁמרך בדרך; cf. Ex 23:20–33). This messenger's simultaneous, Janus-faced qualities of protecting Israel in its obedience, and, at the same time, threatening never to forgive its rebelliousness, implicitly portrays Yahweh as the reckless and irascible God of Exodus 32 and Numbers 11 and 13–14. Two other central elements in Cain's allegory – namely, 'the land turned to desert' and 'the wandering of a fugitive' – had both taken their point of departure already in the story of the garden. On the one hand, the land was cursed (Gen 3:17–19) and, on the other hand, mankind was driven from the garden and settled east of Eden (Gen 3:24). In Cain's story, the curse was intensified. The land became his accuser and he was cursed by the ground he himself had worked. He was driven from it to become a fugitive and wanderer on the earth (Gen 4:12–14). He settled east of Eden, in the land of *Nåd* (בארץ נוד; a pun on his fate of 'wandering': Gen 12:16). In the story's closure, Yahweh was not simply shamed with Lamech's overtrumping lust for blood-revenge. His original shepherd was dead and his farmer was a fugitive, without land. The creation was a failure! Mankind must begin anew! And so, 'Adam knew his wife again' and she bore Seth because God gave to her (שׁת לי) yet another seed, and to him – with markedly less hubris – was born 'a man' (Gen 4:26: *'enosh*, a synonym of *'ish* as in Gen 4:1). In illustration of Psalm 8, people begin to call on the name of Yahweh (Ps 8:2–7; Thompson 2002). The problem of the land which has been cursed finds its most immediate resolution in the ironic, etiological interpretation of Noah's name in the Book of Adam's *toledoth*. He will bring us 'relief' (נחם) from our work and from the labour that has come on us because Yahweh 'had cursed the ground', a relief which Noah's flood quickly carries out (Gen 5:29; cf. 7:23).

Sheep without a shepherd

The figure of Cain, representing the helpless, scattered and lost sheep of mankind – those without a shepherd to guide, protect and correct them on their way – opens what has developed into at least three distinct, though polemically interrelated, figures of the divine shepherd. Most typical for the Pentateuch is the generic role of God as shepherd and (guardian) angel. This figure we find in Genesis, for example, in Israel's blessing of Joseph, when he speaks of *ha'elohim* ('the god'), "before whom my fathers, Abraham and Isaac walked, the god who has been my shepherd from my birth until today, the angel who redeemed me from all evil" (Gen 48:15–16) or, indeed, in Jacob's description of the "Mighty One of Jacob" as "the shepherd, Israel's rock" (Gen 49:24). While both Isaiah (e.g., Isa 40:9–11; 53:4–9) and the Psalter (e.g. Ps 23:1–4; 74:1; 95:7; 100:3; 121 *passim*; 140:1–6) reiterate this image of the divine shepherd and keeper, it is also to this figure that the role of Abraham in Genesis, both as *ger* (גר; Arabic: *jar*, with connotations of both stranger and fugitive: one defined as needing protection and compassion) and as keeper of the covenant (אתה את בריתי תשמר ואתה וזרעך אחריך לדרתם; cf. Gen 17:1–14; esp. 17:9–10) can be linked within a piety of 'imitation' (Thompson 1998). Such figures of the divine shepherd, which the patriarchal narratives offer, easily function as narrative reiterations, reflecting Yahweh as humanity's ultimate shepherd, much in the manner of a divinely evocative, imitative model which, e.g. Yahweh's 'messiah' and 'son' reflect (cf. Ps 2; 110; Thompson 2005: 315–21). It is this figure in the role of Israel's shepherd which defines the figure of Moses as played out in Numbers and Exodus. In regard to plotline, however, the mirroring, imitative function of Moses' role quickly develops an implicit polarity and competition with the figure of the irascible Yahweh, as presented in these two books of the Pentateuch.

The figure of Yahweh as guardian and protector seems closely related to the narrative of Yahweh's self-definition, which marks him so distinctively and critically as the god who is 'with Israel' (אהיה עמך; "I shall be with you"; Ex 3:12; Thompson 2013: 119–32). In his role, however, as Irascible God, evoking as it does both the anger and violence of the flood, Yahweh is one for whom the reader must ever be uncertain how he will be 'with Israel', for both good and evil: a narrative core, which, rooted in the defining violence of Exodus 32, Numbers 11 and Numbers 14, has its trajectory firmly aimed towards the stories of the rejection and destruction of Samaria and Jerusalem! The most singularly clarifying biblical text, in my mind, which exposes the logic of this figure of Yahweh best, is the brief, but – for the Book of Isaiah – genre-defining tale of the call and sending of the prophet by Yahweh:

116 *T.L. Thompson*

Go and say to this people: "Hear and hear, but do not understand; see and see, but do not perceive. Make the heart of this people fat and their ears heavy. Shut their eyes! Lest they see with their eyes and hear with their ears and understand and turn and be healed!" And I asked: "How long? O Yahweh" and he answered: "Until cities lie waste, uninhabited and houses without men and the land is entirely desolate"

(Isa 6:9–13)

The story of Samaria's and Jerusalem's destruction is not a story of a past Israel and a past Judah's fall from grace. It is rather an allegory for the instruction of the reader. For that story, one does not want a repentant-ready, Nineveh-like Jerusalem from the Jonah story! Those within the story do not hear and understand and are not wanted to – that is the role of a reader. It is within such an understanding that an irascible Yahweh truly becomes Isaiah's Immanuel figure: indeed, the god as he had been with Samaria and Jerusalem. And it is from their suffering, destruction and exile that such a god might learn compassion and mercy!

An awareness of such an interpretive key for the Pentateuch's narrative, though first suggested in the story of the burning bush (Ex 3:12), becomes transparent in the figure of the messenger whom Yahweh promises to send with Moses (Ex 23:20–33; Ex 33:1–6.15). This messenger of Yahweh, who will be with Israel, is, unfortunately, never clearly realized within the plot in the form of a saving figure until Joshua is given the saving role his name demands in the scene in Numbers 27, in which Moses is to be replaced as Israel's shepherd. Yahweh chooses Joshua to take charge over the assembly and lead them into war and home again – a necessary succession that the assembly not become "like sheep without a shepherd" (Num 27:16–17; cf. Thompson 2009). Moses is told to lay his hand on Joshua, to give him a share in Moses' spirit of wisdom (Num 27:18–19; cf. Deut 34:9).

The motif of the death of the shepherd, causing the sheep to be scattered in Numbers 27, finds its most direct parallel in a reverse reiteration of this trope in the story found in I Kings and 2 Chronicles, in which Yahweh's spirit speaks truthfully through Micah and guides an Aramean soldier's luck-shot arrow to kill Israel's King Ahab. In this fulfilment of Yahweh's curse on the bad shepherd, Ahab, Israel's sheep without a shepherd are – rather than scattered – able to return home in peace (1 Kgs 22:1–40; 2 Chron 18:1–34). Micah had a vision of 'the whole of Israel, spread over the hills like sheep without a shepherd'. Yahweh, rather, gives the story's counterargument: that they now have no master and might return home in peace (1 Kgs 22:17; 2 Chron 18:16). The figure of the king as shepherd is implicit in this ironic narrative of retribution. It is also found in the prophets, especially in Zakariah's judgments of shepherds, good and bad (Zach 10:3–11.17; 11:1–17; cf. Jer 23:1–4; 25:34–38; Ezek 34:1–31; 37:24–28), a paradigm that sketches the tragedy of Israel's story in the rhetorical spirit of 1–2 Kings' account of good kings and bad.

Sheep without a shepherd 117

The complex interrelationship of this theme in such prophetic texts surely needs a chapter of its own. Here, I can only briefly sketch the overall structure of this trope in the prophets. Its use in Zachariah is central to the prophetic book and is oriented towards chapter 12's and 13's vision of the cleansing of Jerusalem through suffering. The people must suffer because they have no shepherd or, alternatively, they must suffer because they have bad shepherds. Yahweh's anger is directed against the shepherds and *Yahweh Zebaoth*, himself, will play the role of shepherd for his flock. He will be Judah's shepherd (Zach 10:2–3). He, himself, will scatter the sheep, calling on the sword to "strike the shepherd, that the sheep be scattered" (Zach 13:7). With echoes of the surviving remnant of Isaiah's exile, two thirds will perish, but a third will survive as remnant, finding salvation through the suffering of exile. They will go through the fire and be refined as silver and gold are refined. Using a similar motif, Jeremiah calls Israel's shepherds 'fools' (Jer 10:21) and in Ezekiel, this motif is given a treacherous connotation. His shepherds feed and guard only themselves (Ez 34:3–10). Again, in Jeremiah the sheep, having lost their way, are scattered (Jer 23:1–4), suffering for lack of a shepherd. As in Zachariah and the Cain story, in both Jeremiah and Ezekiel, Yahweh, himself, becomes the shepherd and watches over the people (Jer 31:7–14; Ez 11:15–25; 34:11–31). He will gather them and save them and return them to their own land. In Ezekiel 34, as in Isaiah, David will be their king and they will have but one shepherd (Ezek 37:24–28). The remnant will be gathered from all the lands into which they have been scattered (Jer 23:1–4). Jeremiah's shepherd is sketched in Yahweh's image (Jer 3:15; Hjelm 2004: 280). With echoes of 2 Samuel 12 and I Kings 5, Yahweh will give them a shepherd after his own heart (cf. 2 Sam 12:25; Ezek 34:23–24) and bring him to guard Israel with knowledge and insight (cf. 1 Kings 5:9). In this, Jeremiah's allegorical figure of the shepherd overlaps and competes considerably with the more mythic figure of Yahweh's messiah.

In returning to the dubious figure of Yahweh as Cain's shepherd, after the death of an unprotected Abel, the central ambivalence of the theme of 'sheep without a shepherd' – a portent of disaster in both Genesis 4:9 and Zechariah 10:2 (reiterated in Matt 9:36; Mk 6:34) – is also an integral motif in Ezekiel 34's great diatribe against Israel's herders, prophesying a messianic role for David as good shepherd. This seems strikingly helpful in coming to terms with the breadth and diversity of the shepherd motif, not least as it seems to support an alternative to Psalm 23's figure of Yahweh, himself, in the role of David's shepherd. This is a divine role, which parallels well with Ezek 34:11–12's figure of Yahweh as the good shepherd, who, because of the failure of Israel's kings, gathers his scattered sheep (cf. var. Jer 23:2–3). The Cain story has subverted this representation of Yahweh as thoroughly as the irony of Lamentations 3:1–6's anti-Psalm 23, with its figure of Yahweh as anti-shepherd – that lurking bear and lion in hiding (Lam 3:10; Van Hecke 2002; cf., also, Van Hecke 2000; Renkema 1998) – so acutely complicates Psalm 23's pious figure of the good shepherd and provides a critical contribution to the Old

118　*T.L. Thompson*

Testament's discourse on justice and mercy, from which Cain's tale nowhere distances itself (see also Hos 13:5–8; Jer 25:36–38; 49:19–20; 50:44–45).

The wife/sister stories and the reconciliation of shepherds in conflict

I feel it necessary at this time to return briefly to the story of Lot's daughters and to the motif, so pivotal to the story, of the daughters' deceptive and incestuous use of their drunken father, when no other possibility of continuing the family seemed available (so, explicitly: Gen 19:31). It is an extraordinary situation, supporting an extraordinary departure from social laws and ethics. In fact, commentaries feel repeatedly compelled to assume that the narrative must imply an anti-Moabite and anti-Ammonite ethnocentric defamation. Yet no such critique is either explicit or likely. Rather, the narrative closes with well-recognized, standard tropes of celebration and approval; namely, the successful pregnancies and births of sons, their naming etiologies and a declaration of their destiny as the ancestors of two great nations of the Transjordan 'to this day' (Gen 19:36–38). The implicit approval of the desperate decision of the daughters' departure from social laws and ethics is remarkable in a story whose introductory episode stresses themes of justice and righteousness (Gen 18:19) and centres on Yahweh's role as "judge of all the earth" (Gen 18:25)!

This provocative dissonance opens a considerable chain of narratives in which both Yahweh and his 'prophet' Abraham occupy a moral ground that is far from either just or righteous! Reiterating themes from the story of Abram in Egypt in Gen 12:10–20 (Thompson 1987: 51–59), Genesis 20 pits the innocence, piety, righteousness and generosity of Abimelech, king of Gerar, against his deceitful and unjustly bigoted guest, Abraham (Gen 20:11), whose divine patron not only threatens this good king with death, but sends a plague against his innocent city. This story's just king even takes upon himself the vindication and protection of Sarah from future mistreatment by her husband (Gen 30:16)! Not Yahweh, but Abimelech is given the role of righteousness's epitome in this most nuanced variation of Genesis' three-fold narrative of the patriarch as stranger, who presents his wife as a sister to be courted (Gen 12:10–20: 20:1–18 and 26:6–11). The complexity of the narrative increases considerably as each of these variations finds its closure in a progressively more peaceful reconciliation of shepherds in conflict, opening with a close variant of Jacob's separation from Esau (Gen 36:6–8) and closing in a three-fold covenant of peace (Gen 13:2–12; 21:22–32 and 26:12–33; Thompson 1987: 56–59). The conflict story of Genesis 20 closes with God healing Abimelech's wife and female slaves, whose wombs had been closed by Yahweh (Gen 20:17–18; Thompson 2013a: 119–32). This healing is immediately illustrated by Sarah's conceiving and giving birth to Isaac (Gen 21:1–3), deftly evoking the fulfilment of the prayer of Hezekiah for the remnant that is left and an end to the day of distress "of rebuke and disgrace, when children have come to the birth and there is no strength to bring them forth" (Isa 37:1–4; Hjelm 2004: 142, 224).

Sheep without a shepherd 119

The dissonant tension on the theme of justice and righteousness continues throughout the patriarchal chain-narratives, marking them with a recurrent reiteration of themes of conflict and abuse, followed by scenes of peace and reconciliation. Consider the mistreatment and abandonment of Ishmael by Sarah, supported by Yahweh and a feckless Abraham (Gen 21:8–21), Yahweh's demand that Abraham sacrifice his son, Isaac, and Abraham's acquiescence to that demand (Gen 22:1–18). The whole of the complex Jacob narrative centres on such themes of conflict and reconciliation. His chain narrative opens with the three-fold conflict of Jacob and Esau from the womb (Gen 25:19–34) and develops a chiastic envelope structure around Jacob's conflict with Laban (Gen 29:15–30; 30:25–31:24), which, in turn, holds that of Leah's and Rachel's conflict intact (Gen 29:31–30:24), before the author finally turns toward a three-fold chiastic closure with its variant scenes of reconciliation (Gen 30:14–19; 31:25–55; 32:3–21; 33:1–17; see Thompson 2013a: 55–66). While the narratives draw on the theme of conflict leading to reconciliation, so appropriate to an understanding of the patriarchal narratives as projecting the utopian myth of return, the recurrent injustice of the story's divine and patriarchal protagonists begs clarification.

"Should he treat our sister as a whore?" (Gen 34:31)

This recurrent riddle on the theme of justice and righteousness in Genesis is once again provoked in the three short narratives centering on the figures of women and the theme of sexual abuse, which go into forming a narrative bridge that binds the Joseph story to the Jacob narratives. The first of these short narratives finds its context within the reiteration of Bethel theophanies introducing the reconciliation doublets of the Jacob and Esau conflict story (Gen 32:24–32 and 35:9–15). Jacob, with his family, arrives safely in the city of Shechem and purchases land from Hamor, Shechem's father (Gen 33:18–20). The story of Dinah's rape (Gen 34:1–35:5) begins in conflicting, but, nevertheless, clear detail:

> And so it happened that Dinah went out to visit "the women of the land", and Shechem ... the prince of the land, saw her, took her, lay with her and defiled her. ... His soul was bound to Dinah, Jacob's daughter and he loved the girl and spoke to her with his heart. So, Shechem asked his father to get the girl for him as wife.
>
> (Gen 34:1–4)

The scene seems to be sketched entirely in accord with the *torah*'s demands in regard to situations in which a man seduces an un-betrothed virgin (Ex 22:16; Deut 22:28–30). Shechem's great love for Dinah requires from her a necessary passivity, however, as it allows the author to raise an interpretive to imagine other than that of rape, if one is to see the woman as innocent of extramarital intercourse. On the one hand, both Shechem and his father ask for Dinah in

120   *T.L. Thompson*

marriage and not only offer the *torah* requirement of a large bride-price and gifts, but they will also open the land to Jacob and his family (Gen 34:5ff.). On the other hand, Jacob's sons defend the issue of shame and purity! Accordingly, they – drawing on Genesis' covenant story (Gen 17:13–14) – expand the *torah* and, deceitfully, lay a trap for Shechem and his father. They demand that all the men of the city be circumcised for they look on it as necessary for purity (Gen 34:14)! Not only Hamor and Shechem, but the whole city accepts: so great was Shechem honoured, who loved Dinah so much! Two days later, the murderous trap is closed. All of Shechem's men were sick with fever and Levi and Simeon entered the city and slaughtered them. The sons of Jacob plundered the defenceless city and took all its riches, women and children, "because their sister had been defiled" (Gen 34:27)!

The story of conflict and rape brings disagreement and disunity. Jacob, fearing for the small few which are his family, all strangers in the land, complained to Levi and Simeon that they had brought the 'people of the land' to hate them (Gen 34:30; cf. Gen 49:5–7). His sons respond to his rebuke rhetorically: "Should he treat our sister as a whore?" (Gen 34:31). The dissonance, however, is followed by a brief parable on 'fear' and 'awe', exposing the narrative's key. The small few of Jacob's sons – with their fear of the people of the land – are sent by God to Bethel, while piety's first principle, the 'fear of God' (חתת אלהים) is spread over all the surrounding villages, such that none pursued Jacob and his sons (Gen 35:5)! Genesis 35 then offers a *pesher* (interpretation) by referring back to the scene of Jacob at Bethel in Genesis 28:16, where the 'fear of God' had gripped Jacob, and overcome the fear he had of Esau (Gen 38:8,12). Those foreigners, Canaanites and Perizites, are given the interpretive role of reflecting wisdom's beginning (Prov 1:7).

"He thought that she was a whore" (Gen 38:15)

The second narrative of this bridge, Tamar's story, finds its structural variant in the Book of Ruth. Like Dinah's story, Tamar's tale opens by setting the legal context for the plotline clearly and distinctly structured on the *torah's* fictive law of the 'levirate' (Irvin and Thompson 1968). Judah marries the daughter of Shua, a Canaanite and begets Er, Onan and Shela. Er marries Tamar. He, however, was evil in Yahweh's view so he killed him. Deuteronomy's understanding of the levirate requires that if brothers live together and one dies, the wife is to be married to her brother-in-law to bear a child for the deceased (Deut 25:5–10). When Onan, however, refuses to fulfil his obligation and spills his seed, Yahweh kills him too. Judah sends Tamar home to her father "until Shela grows up" (Deut 38:1–11).

Time passes and Tamar learns that Shela has grown up and, when Judah travels to Timna to the sheep-shearing feast, Tamar is determined to see the *torah* fulfilled and disguises herself with a veil and sits by the roadside on the way to Timna. When Judah, coming by, sees her so veiled, 'he thought that she was a whore' and asked her to lie with him. When Tamar asked the price he was willing to pay, he offered a young goat, giving his signet ring and staff as caution. Tamar became pregnant, went home and took off her veil, dressing herself in her widow's clothes once again. When Judah discovers she is pregnant, he accuses her of prostitution, demanding that she be burnt (Gen 38:12–24)! When, however, she is brought out, she sends her father-in-law word that the owner of the ring and staff she has is the child's father. Judah acknowledges the justice of Tamar's action: "She is more righteous than I" (Gen 38:26)! An expansive reiteration of birth and naming etiologies celebrates her role as guardian of the *torah*.

"He left his garment with me" (Gen 39:15)

The third story of our trilogy lies within the Joseph story, taking up a very interesting problem of narrative strategy as it presents the wife of a great man who plays the whore. The closest parallel to this tale is an Egyptian *Story of Two Brothers*, which condemns with outrage the licentious and adulterous wife (Wilson 1969). Anubis, the elder brother, was married and his younger brother, Bata, lived with him and played the role of keeper of the house and the fields with great success. There was no one like him. One day, when the brothers were out in the field sowing, Anubis sent Bata to the house for more seed. When he came to the house his brother's wife was combing her hair, so Bata fetched the seed himself, loading himself with barley and emmer. His brother's wife, admiring his strength, took his arm and asked him to lie with her. Bata argued: she was like a mother and Anubis like a father to him! Though he promised her not to tell of this to anyone, the wife was afraid that he would tell her husband, so she greased herself and pretended she had been raped and when her husband found her, she accused Bata that he had beat her and tried to rape her, threatening suicide if her husband allowed Bata to live. When Bata, however, brought the cattle home, the first cow warned him that his brother was waiting to kill him. When the second repeated the warning, Bata ran and Anubis chased after him with his lance. Bata called upon Re-Har-akhti, 'who judges the wicked from the just'. Re-Har-akhti heard his prayer and miraculously saved Bata, who then told his brother what happened, cutting off his phallus to prove the truth of his story. Afterwards the elder brother killed his wife and threw her body to his dogs, while he sat in mourning for his brother.

The story of Joseph and Potiphar's wife in Genesis 39 distinguishes itself from this earlier tale by its marked disinterest in the punishment of the adulterous wife. While the Egyptian story develops the opposing figures of the innocent and loyal keeper of the house versus the guilty, licentious wife and moves its plot towards the tragic mourning of the innocent and the punishment of the evil, Genesis – while stressing the integrity and innocence of Joseph, the unshakably trustworthy keeper of Potiphar's house, as well as the recklessness of the licentious seductress much in the spirit of the Egyptian story – departs sharply from the *Story of Two Brothers* by markedly ignoring

122   T.L. Thompson

the dominating scene of judging the innocence and guilt of the crime. Potiphar's wife's guilt hardly functions in the story, save as a means for translating Joseph to the prison where he can reiterate his role as impeccable and loyal keeper of the house (Gen 39:2–6). Rhetorically, the story of Joseph in Potiphar's house never quite becomes a story about innocence and guilt. It is, rather, the first of a three-fold narrative on the faithful keeper of his master's house, who ever trusts in a divine providence, turning wrong to right. In this three-fold, reiterative tale, all that Joseph does, Yahweh makes a success – until Joseph, released from his prison, becomes Egypt's vizier, with responsibility for all that was to be done in all of Egypt. The coherence of the Joseph narrative resides in a transvaluation of values. The justice of Yahweh, the Judge of the whole world, is not rooted in the theology of the way, with its judgment of evil and success of righteousness (Ps 1:1–6: Thompson 1998). Rather Yahweh is a god, who does what he sees to be right (Thompson 1996).

It is not until the very final chapter of Genesis that our Joseph story takes up explicitly the theme of righteousness and justice as it is understood implicitly in the patriarchal narratives, as they move through themes of exile, return and reconciliation, themes which Abraham's challenge to Yahweh in Genesis 18's debate over the fate of the innocent of Sodom had first exposed:

> Far be it for you to kill the innocent together with the guilty so that the innocent and guilty suffer a common fate! That cannot be. Must not the Judge of the whole world do what is right?
>
> (Gen 18:25)

It is this debate which ever plagues our narrative. The, for the patriarchal narratives, ever central themes of exile and return are ever delayed, building a tension that threatens coherence. In Genesis 50, the brothers lie about their father's dying wish; namely, that he had asked Joseph to forgive his brothers for what they had done to him (Gen 50:15–17). Although Joseph clearly recognizes that his brothers lied to him, his response reiterates the scene of reconciliation in Genesis 45:5–7. "Do not be afraid. Do I stand here in God's place? You meant to do evil against me, but God meant it to be good! ... He comforted them and spoke to them with love" (Gen 50:18–21). The story closes with an echo of Solomon's prayer in I Kings 8:33–34. He judges not with a measured justice, but with unmeasured forgiveness: a new ethic, which embraces the evil of Potiphar's wife. Like Joseph's brothers, she meant evil against Joseph, but God turned it to good. It is a judgment which is appropriate to Judah's unpunished crime against Tamar – and so, too, Levi's and Simeon's murderous deception in Dinah's story. And what with Lot's daughters? What shall the judge of the whole world create? Is it on righteousness or on the mercy and forgiveness of Solomon's prayer (1 Kgs 8:46–53) that the patriarchal allegory of return hangs?

Bibliography

Guillaume, P. and M. Schunk. 2007. "Job's Intercession: Antidote to Divine Folly". *Biblica* 88: 457–72.

Hjelm, I. 2003. "Brothers Fighting Brothers: Jewish and Samaritan Ethnocentrism in Tradition and History". In *Jerusalem in Ancient History and Tradition.* T.L. Thompson and S. Jayyusi (eds). London: T&T Clark: 197–222

——2004. *Jerusalem's Rise to Sovereignty: Zion and Gerizim in Competition.* London: T&T Clark.

Irvin, D. and T.L. Thompson. 1968. "Some Legal Problems in the Book of Ruth". *Vetus Testamentum* 18: 79–99.

King, L. 1907. *Chronicles Concerning Early Babylonian Kings II.* London: Luzac and Co.

Kvanvig, H.S. 2002. "Genesis 6:1–4 as an antediluvian Event". *Scandinavian Journal of the Old Testament* 16/1: 79–112.

——2004. "The Watcher Story and Genesis: An Intertextual Reading". *Scandinavian Journal of the Old Testament* 18/2: 163–83.

——2011. *Primeval History: Babylonian, Biblical and Enochic: An Intertextual Reading.* Leiden, Brill.

Lewis, B. 1980. *The Sargon Legend: American Schools of Oriental Research, Dissertation Series* 4. Missoula: Society of Biblical Literature.

Long, B.O. 1968. *The Problem of Etiological Narrative in the Old Testament* (Beiheft zur Zeitschrift für die alttestamentliche Wissenschaft, 108). Berlin: de Gruyter.

Lundager Jensen, H.J. 2000. *Den fortærende ild.* Aarhus: Aarhus Universitetsforlag.

Mettinger, T.N.D. 2007. *The Eden Narrative: A Literary and Religio-Historical Study of Genesis 2–3.* Winona Lake: Eisenbrauns.

Nathanson, M. 2013. *Between Myth and Mandate: Geopolitics, Pseudohistory and the Hebrew Bible.* Bloomington: AuthorHouse.

Pfoh, E. 2009. *The Emergence of Israel in Ancient Palestine: Historical and Anthropological Perspectives.* London: Equinox/Acumen.

——2012. "Jesus and the Mythic Mind: An Epistemological Problem". In *Is This Not the Carpenter? The Question of the Historicity of Jesus.* T.L. Thompson and T.S. Verenna (eds). Durham: Acumen: 79–94.

Pritchard, J.B. (ed.). 1969. *Ancient Near Eastern Texts: Relating to the Old Testament,* 3rd edition. Princeton: Princeton University Press.

Raheb, M. 2014. *Troen og Imperiet: Biblen Set med Palestinensiske Øjne.* Frederiksberg: Unitas.

Renkema, J. 1998. *Lamentations: Historical Commentary to the Old Testament.* Kampen: Kok.

Speiser, E.A. 1969. "Akkadian Myths and Epics". In *Ancient Near Eastern Texts Related to the Old Testament.* J.B. Pritchard (ed.). Princeton: Princeton University Press: 60–119.

Tengström, S. 1981. *Die Toledotformel und die literarische Struktur der priesterlichen Erweiterungschicht im Pentateuch.* Uppsala: Coniectania Biblica.

Thompson, T.L. 1987. *The Origin Tradition of Ancient Israel: The Literary Formation of Genesis and Exodus 1–23.* Sheffield: Sheffield Academic Press.

——1992. *Early History of the Israelite People From the Written and Archaeological Sources.* Studies in the History of the Ancient Near East 4. Leiden: Brill.

124   *T.L. Thompson*

——1996. "He is Yahweh: He Does What is Right in His Own Eyes". In *Tro og Historie: Festskrift til Nyls Hyldahl*. L. Fatum and M. Müller (eds). Copenhagen: Museum Tusculanum: 246–63.

——1998. "Salmernes bogs 'enten-eller' spørgsmål". In *Teologien i Samfundet: Festskrift til Jens Glebe-Møller*. T. Jørgensen and P.K. Westergaard (eds). Frederiksberg: Anis: 289–308.

——1999. *The Bible in History: How Writers Create A Past*. London: Jonathan Cape.

——2005. *The Messiah Myth: The Ancient Near Eastern Roots of Jesus and David*. London: Jonathan Cape.

——2007. "A Testimony of the Good King: Reading the Mesha Stele". In *Ahab Agonistes: The Rise and Fall of the Omri Dynasty*. L.L. Grabbe (ed.). London: T&T Clark: 236–92.

——2009. "Imago Dei: A Problem in Pentateuchal Discourse". *Scandinavian Journal of the Old Testament* 23/1: 135–48.

——2010. "Reiterative Narratives of Exile and Return: Virtual Memories of Abraham in the Persian and Hellenistic Periods". In *The Historian and the Bible: Essays in Honour of Lester L. Grabbe*. P.R. Davies and D.V. Edelman (eds). London: T&T Clark: 46–54.

——2011a. "Genesis 4 and the Pentateuch's Reiterative Discourse: Some Samaritan Themes". In *Samaria, Samarians, Samaritans: Studies on Bible, History and Linguistics*. J. Zsengeller (ed.). Berlin: de Gruyter: 9–22.

——2011b. "Memories of Esau and Narrative Reiteration". *Scandinavian Journal of the Old Testament* 25/2: 174–200.

——2011c. "Memories of Return and the Historicity of the Post-Exilic Period". In *The Reception and Remembrance of Abraham*. P. Carstens and N.P. Lemche (eds). Piscataway, NJ: Gorgias Press: 103–30.

——2013a. *Biblical Narrative and Palestine's History: Changing Perspectives 2, Copenhagen International Seminar*. London: Acumen Publishing.

——2013b. "Your Mother was a Hittite and Your Father an Amorite: Ethnicity, Judaism and Palestine's Cultural Heritage". *Scandinavian Journal of the Old Testament* 27/1: 76–95.

Thompson, T.L. and T. Verenna (eds). 2011. *Is This Not the Carpenter? The Question of the Historicity of the Figure of Jesus*. London: Equinox/Acumen.

Thompson, T.L. and P. Wajdenbaum. 2014. "Making Room for Japheth". In *The Bible and Hellenism: Greek Influence on Jewish and Early Christian Literature*. London: Acumen Publications.

Van Hecke, P.J.P. 2000. *"Koppig als een Koe is Israël, en JHWH zou het moeten weiden als een schaap in het open veld?" (Hos 4:16). Een cognitief-linguistische analyse van de religieuze Letteren* (unpublished Ph D thesis).

——2002. "Lamentations 3:1–6: An Anti-Psalm 23". *Scandinavian Journal of the Old Testament* 16/2: 264–82.

Wilson, J.A. 1969. "The Story of Two Brothers". In *Near Eastern Texts Related to the Old Testament*. J.B. Pritchard (ed.). Princeton: Princeton University Press: 23–29.

Wyatt, N. 1996. *Myths of Power: A Study of Royal Myth and Ideology in Ugaritic and Biblical Tradition*. Münster: Ugarit Verlag.

——2001. "The Mythic Mind". *Scandinavian Journal of the Old Testament* 15: 3–56.

——2005. *The Mythic Mind: Essays on Cosmology and Religion in Ugarit and Old Testament Literature*. London: Equinox.

8 Idol-taunt and exilic identity

A Dalit reading of Isaiah 44:9–20

Dominic S. Irudayaraj

Crisis in human life begets surprising reactions and ramifications. In crises – real or imagined – people scamper for immediate resolutions. When expected resolutions do not seem to come by, the process of seeking answers is not abandoned; people continue to seek other ways and means. This chapter aims to underscore one such episode from the prophetic literature of the Hebrew Bible.

The idol-taunt in Isaiah 44:9–20 sounds problematic from an image-rich Indian Christian perspective (on idol, see Westermann 2001: 148; on idolatry in the Bible, see Greenspahn 2004). This chapter explores other ways of appropriating this difficult text. A Dalit reading can be apt for such a venture. Dalit literature itself stems from a crisis-ridden context. Hence, a Dalit reading of idol-taunt can help situate the struggle of a prophet who attempted to construct the identities of a 'defeated' deity, a dispersed community, and a de-centred prophet during a time of crisis, namely the exile.

The problematic: Double trouble

The first trouble – insensitivity to Hindu religiosity

Of the many characteristic features of India, countless representations of gods and goddesses in the Hindu temples draw much attention of even passing visitors.

On the one extreme, "Hinduism is sometimes said to be the religion of 330 million gods" (Pandit 2005: 35). Such an exaggerated account is counter-balanced by the view that "each living being is a unique expression of God. In ancient times it was believed that there were 330 million living beings. This gave rise to the idea of 330 million deities or gods" (Verma 2009: 68). In a similar vein, "*Vedas* [the primary texts of Hinduism] proclaim that the one *Brahman*, call it the Truth or Reality, is manifested as so many different *devatās* or deities" (Fitzgerald 2008: 49; on *Vedas*, see Verma 2009: 98–101).

On the other extreme is the Hindu philosophical system of *Advaita*, meaning 'non-dual' or 'not two', which advocates absolute monism. All that exists is *Brahman* or the Ultimate Reality. Even the perception of oneself as an individual being is *māya* ('illusion', see Chattopadhyaya 2000: xvii) because in

126   *D.S. Irudayaraj*

"the depth of my being, which is not 'mine,' is Reality" (Deutsch 1969: 50). Therefore, *Advaita* proposes that salvation is through *aham brahmāsmi* ("I am *Brahman*," see Śaṅkarācārya 1992: 57), namely the realization of one's identity of the inner self as *the Brahman*, the Ultimate Reality. To such a nuanced religious tradition of Hinduism, a cursory reading of idol-polemics in Isaiah sounds insensitive and insulting.

The second trouble – offence to Indian Christian religiosity

Much like the image-rich Hindu places of worship, the Christian churches in India house various and appealing icons and statues. There is also considerable overlap in the way the feasts of these two religions are celebrated (see Meibohm 2002: 67). Spectacular car processions, dramatic animal sacrifices, cooking and offering of freshly harvested rice mark the feasts of these two religions. To an Indian Christian who grows up in a religion wherein statues and icons play a key role in promoting individual and communal devotion, the idol-polemic – which derides iconic representations as 'nothing' (*tōhû* Isa 44:9; cf. Gen 1:2) – sounds both thoughtless and offensive.

Options of appropriation

Scholars offer a variety of reasons to appreciate and appropriate the prophetic taunt. Most scholars resonate with the dismissive tone of the text and offer reasons for the prophetic scoff. For some, the taunt song is a general critique of iconic representation of any divine being because an idol can create a barrier between God and God's people (see von Rad 2001: 340). Others opine that the prophetic deriding has to do with the Israelite faith stance that Yahweh's holiness cannot be idolized. Therefore the prophetic attack is aimed at the iconic worship of Yahweh (see Davies 2000: 104; for a contrary view, see Smith 2003: 186–88).

Israel's faith stance, in addition, underscored the incomparability of Yahweh, which eventually paved the way for the question of the existence of only one God. Read in this way, some scholars interpret the anti-idol sentiments as monotheistic spill over (see Soares-Prabhu 2000). In such interpretation, the exile is perceived as the fertile ground for solidifying an emergent monotheism (see Smith 2002: 43–61). Still others inquire if the dismissive tone has to do with an editorial insertion because most of the idol-polemics are found in Isa 40–48 and they are "considered to belong to late editorial strata" (Blenkinsopp 2002: 240). Claus Westermann instead finds no oddity with the passage in terms of its genre: "The poem makes idolatry out to be coarser than it is. This is due to the nature of the taunt-song" (2001: 151), which has to be dismissive, deriding and denigrating.

Although this list of scholarly appropriations is only representative, the variety of opinions underscores that no single perspective can account for the presence and rationale of these anti-idol sentiments. Nor can anyone claim to provide 'the way' to arrive at the text's meaning. Acknowledging that every attempt at explaining the passage can at best be provisional, this chapter attempts a Dalit reading of Isa 44:9–20.

Dalit literature: A discourse of identity

Nathaniel B. Levtow proposes that Deutero-Isaiah's "earliest kernels originated in Babylonia" (2008: 57). The Babylonian exile was a time of crisis from socio-religious-political perspectives. Uprooted from their homeland, stripped of their religious centre and with no kings, Israel-in-exile was indeed Israel-in-trauma. Any prophet who was operative at that time could not but address the crisis at hand. And the immediate concern of the prophet was to reaffirm the identities of the deity and the people. The proposed Dalit reading would argue that the idol-taunts are the prophetic attempts at constructing the identities that are at stake for the exilic audience.

Much like the exilic experience, Dalit history is marked by experiences of trauma. Dalits have been denied their rightful place within the Indian social system. Relegated to the periphery of society, perceived as polluted and polluting, and therefore deemed untouchables, Dalits have endured crises for centuries (for a historical survey, see Rajawat 2005; on Dalit struggle, see Shinde 2005; and for a case study, see Elangovan 2008: 283–88). Dalit literature embodies features such as 'resistance', 'ridicule' and 'reversal', which not only protest against the hegemonic discourses, but also construct Dalits' fractured and fragmented identity. Dalit literature evidences what happens when a marginalized group's repeated attempt to regain its denied status meets with disappointments. The group then resorts to what is within its power to do. It seeks to formulate counter-discourses. Through these discourses, the group's hopes and anxieties are often given expression.

Features of Dalit literature

A violent and protesting tone dominates Dalit literature because the writers "attempt to be true to their lived experiences … Their vehicle is often brutal, coarse and crude language of the slum" (Kumar 2007: 127–28; on Dalit literature and Dalit hermeneutics, see Prasad and Gaijan 2007; Massey and Prabhakar 2005; Clarke et al. 2010; Brueck 2014). The violence is directed toward the hegemonic structures inherent in existing myths, such as the theory of *Manu* (see Verma 2009: 241–52). Through counter-narratives, Dalit literature attempts to demolish the dominant paradigm of the high castes. As a result, the tone is invariably crude and violent. Their poetic expressions bear these marks vividly (see Kumar 2007: 121–36). In addition to subversion, their counter-cultural literature aims to affirm the identity of Dalits and thereby underscore their human dignity. These purposes are achieved simultaneously by constructing counter-narratives that 'resist', 'ridicule' and 'reverse' the hegemonic meta-narratives.

128   *D.S. Irudayaraj*

Resistance

"Dalit literature is one of the major sites of their resistance and creativity" (Valmiki 2008: xxxii). It is a response to their experience of social exploitation and marginalization. As such, Dalit literature is a 'Resistance Literature' with a two-fold aim:

> Dalit writers regard themselves as inserting their previously silenced voices into the hegemonic canon of Indian literary history through the twin projects of creating a body of new literature along strict theoretical and aesthetic principles and turning their own critical gaze on canonical Indian literary texts.
>
> (Brueck 2011: 347–68)

Such a literary resistance is expressed in many and varied ways focusing on: "Gods and goddesses who condemn caste and preach a religion of common human values; rituals denouncing caste; many anti-brahminical proverbs; [and other] evidence [which] shows that Dalit communities [have access to] gods and temples" (Rajkumar 2010: 47). These features appear frequently in Dalit literature's resistance to hegemonic myths. In short, "the Dalit literature movement was designed to develop a counterhegemonic ideology against the logic of the caste system" (Downing 2010: 154).

Ridicule

As a discursive discourse, Dalit literature embodies a tone of ridicule, scorn or mockery. Such belittling goes hand in hand with its protest tone. For example, the Marathi Dalit literature does not even spare the sacred poets (on sacred poets, see Roy and Sivaramkrishna 1996; also Ranade 1983). Daya Pawar's poem scorns "the legend of Dyaneshwar, who produced the sacred *Vedas* from the mouth of a buffalo" (Paswan and Jaideva 2002: 30). Such an audacious depiction clearly undercuts and makes a mockery of the Hindu notion of eternal *Vedas*. Also free-flowing words and colloquial expressions fill Dalit literature: "the language used was often deliberately provocative, blasphemous, and even obscene, designed to scandalize dominant caste values" (Downing 2010: 154).

Reversal

If 'resistance' and 'ridicule' are aimed to undercut the dominant worldview of the high caste, 'reversal' is employed to both critique the hegemonic narratives and, in the process, construct a narrative that infuses a different and meaningful perspective to the same reality. Accordingly, Dalit literature constructs "their identity by reversing the symbols that defined them as low and/ or polluted into symbols of their culture and the positive identity" (for a field study, see Chockalingam 2007). For example, the drum has been largely associated with Dalit community. Hence, a condescending look is cast after the way the high caste people perceive the drum and drum-playing. But Dalit literature has constructed counter-discourses to extol the drum and drum-playing (see Rajkumar 2010: 48). Another compelling example is the Dalits' habit of eating beef. In South Indian societies, beef-eating is a sign of pollution and a characteristic mark of an outcaste. Various legends attempt to explain how the outcastes came to this despicable state of eating beef. However, a South Indian Dalit community has created counter-discourse to applaud its habit of beef-eating (Chockalingam 2007: 213–27).

The discussion so far has sought to view Dalit literature as a 'discourse of identity from the edge' that aims to construct and affirm the identity of a marginalized group. It was also observed that 'resistance', 'ridicule' and 'reversal' are characteristic marks of these subverting discourses. In the following section, the idol-polemic in Isa 44:9–20 is seen from a similar vantage point in order to underscore the prophetic attempt at constructing the identities of a deity, a community and the prophet.

Idol-taunt in Isaiah 44:9–20

I here present the text of Isaiah 44:9–20 in NRSV's translation.

9   All who make idols are nothing, and the things they delight in do not profit; their witnesses neither see nor know. And so they will be put to shame.

10   Who would fashion a god or cast an image that can do no good?

11   Look, all its devotees shall be put to shame; the artisans too are merely human. Let them all assemble, let them stand up; they shall be terrified, they shall all be put to shame.

12   The ironsmith fashions it and works it over the coals, shaping it with hammers, and forging it with his strong arm; he becomes hungry and his strength fails, he drinks no water and is faint.

13   The carpenter stretches a line, marks it out with a stylus, fashions it with planes, and marks it with a compass; he makes it in human form, with human beauty, to be set up in a shrine.

14   He cuts down cedars or chooses a holm tree or an oak and lets it grow strong among the trees of the forest. He plants a cedar and the rain nourishes it.

15   Then it can be used as fuel. Part of it he takes and warms himself; he kindles a fire and bakes bread. Then he makes a god and worships it, makes it a carved image and bows down before it.

16   Half of it he burns in the fire; over this half he roasts meat, eats it and is satisfied. He also warms himself and says, "Ah, I am warm, I can feel the fire!"

17   The rest of it he makes into a god, his idol, bows down to it and worships it; he prays to it and says, "Save me, for you are my god!"

18   They do not know, nor do they comprehend; for their eyes are shut, so that they cannot see, and their minds as well, so that they cannot understand.

130   *D.S. Irudayaraj*

19   No one considers, nor is there knowledge or discernment to say, "Half of it I burned in the fire; I also baked bread on its coals, I roasted meat and have eaten. Now shall I make the rest of it an abomination? Shall I fall down before a block of wood?"

20   He feeds on ashes; a deluded mind has led him astray, and he cannot save himself or say, "Is not this thing in my right hand a fraud?"

Exilic origin

Levtow situates the origin of the icon-parody in the Babylonian exile (2008: 57–58). Naturally, the text is filled with the concerns of that time. Without centralizing features such as king, land or temple, and having been scattered in a foreign land, the question of identity must have been crucial, especially when measured against the backdrop of "the empire and its control over the exiles' identity" (Cuéllar 2008: 69). This can be observed in Isaiah's message, when, for example, Isa 47 depicts Babylon as disempowered and unprotected daughter, mother and widow. The text projects the belief that Babylon will endure a suffering similar to the fate of the women of Jerusalem, before and during the exile. Such a tone also finds expression in Isa 43:14, which describes the awaiting disaster of Babylon. The desperate longing for a reversal of fortunes underscores the existing dominance of the Babylonian empire over the exiles (see Cuéllar 2008: 69).

Discourse of power and social formation, re-inscribing the identity of people

Icon parodies are situated "within discourses of power and processes of social formation in late exilic and early postexilic Israel" (Levtow 2008: 40). In contrast to the lived experience of disempowerment among the exiles, the prophet develops "innovative yet authoritative reformulations" (Levtow 2008: 43–44). Such prophetic innovation can be found in Isaiah's discussion on the witnesses. Despite the perceivable power of Babylon, Isaiah predicts that the witnesses and worshippers of the Babylonian gods are stupid. They end in shame and are terrified (vv. 9–11) ... even if for an instant they seem to prevail. Such a novel imagination serves a dual purpose: "The ostensible effect is to denude Babylonian confidence; the practical effect, more likely, is to embolden [and] empower Israel" (Brueggemann 1998: 70). The witnesses of the powerful empire are depicted as blind, deaf and uncomprehending and, by doing so, the prophet re-inscribes the identity of the exiles as those who can 'see, hear and understand' the workings of Yahweh (cf. 44:8).

A prophet away from the Holy Mountain, salvaging the identity of the prophet

Dispersed in a foreign land, the exiles had to grapple with profoundly troubling questions: Is Yahweh still powerful? Even if powerful, the question arises: Has Yahweh deserted them? Such questions about the identity of the exiles and the power of their God have serious implications for the identity of the prophet, who is an intermediary between them. Understandably, the prophet begins by stressing that Yahweh's "might is not constrained by location". Nevertheless, "they may suspect a person claiming to be a prophet of Zion's God when that person does not speak on or even near the holy mountain" (Sommer 1996: 165). But Isaiah declares that Yahweh's words can be revealed anywhere in the world. Accordingly, neither is the prophetic work constrained by location (Sommer 1996). Thus, the prophet seems to salvage his/her identity.

Contrast, reclaiming the identity of God

"The central icon parody in vv. 9–20 is surrounded by hymnic verses running through vv. 1–8 and 21–28 that extol the creative and redemptive power of Yahweh" (Levtow 2008: 62). Perceivable themes alternate between the greatness of God and the nothingness of idols. Against this backdrop, the depiction of idol-makers as 'nothing' and idols as profit-less (cf. v. 9) makes a curious contrast. The passage, when read together with the surrounding verses ("the Lord who made you, who formed you" v. 2; "I formed you" v. 21), shows a contrast between a performing Yahweh and idle idols (Davies 2000: 103). Within the Ancient West Asian (i.e. Near Eastern) perspective which attributed the defeat of a nation to its deity, the list of contrasts that the prophet paints makes an audacious attempt at reclaiming the identity of a 'defeated' deity, who is now said to be in control of not only the nation but also its destiny (cf. vv. 7–8).

Resistance

Brueggemann opines that "sub communities of grief and hope … engage in resistance and alternative" (2001: 121). Cuéllar echoes that sentiment: "The prophet's poetic quest to recover a marginalized cultural identity represents an act of resistance. It is a resistance to the imperially imposed identity through the forging of an ancestral awareness" (Cuéllar 2008: 67). Against the dominant and influential presence of the Babylonian empire, Isaiah's immediate task was to resist the kingdom's powerful impact. Such an act of resistance requires a powerful imagination, such as is characteristic in Isaiah's idol-parody.

The detailed description of idol-making such as the work of the ironsmith in v. 12 and the carpenter's work in vv. 13–16, the categorical rejection of idols as "an image that can do no good" (v. 10), and the futile work of the idol-makers ("nothing and … will be put to shame" v. 9; "his strength fails" v. 12; "bows down before the carved image" v. 15; "no knowledge or discernment" v. 19) are juxtaposed with Yahweh who not only creates (cf. vv. 2, 21, 24) but also is in control of history (cf. v. 8). Through such bold projection of failure, the prophet resists the pervasive presence and persuasive appeal of

132   *D.S. Irudayaraj*

the empire. Therefore, much like the Dalit literature, the icon parody in Isaiah is an apt instance of 'Resistance Literature'.

Ridicule

The prophet highlights that the "shapers of images and the images in which they delight are equally empty and valueless" (Goldingay and Payne 2006: 345). Thus, in one stroke the author dismisses both the maker and the made. A tone of ridicule can be sensed in the rhetorical question: "Who would fashion a god or cast an image that can do no good?" (v. 10). The prophet denigrates the long and laborious process of idol-making (vv. 12–17) by highlighting its dual effect: the long process leaves the idol-fabricator fatigued (v. 12) and the end result profits no one (v. 9).

The idol-worshipper is portrayed as feeding on ashes owing to a deluded mind. Thus, the prophet underscores the worshipper's lack of discernment. As a result, the idolaters do not realize the lie in their right hands (cf. v. 20). A dismissive scorn marks the entire taunt song. In short, "the prophet caricatures idol worship in such a way that any worshiper of Yahweh would be forced to laugh at the foolishness of Babylonian worship" (Light 2001: 77).

Reversal

In addition to 'resistance' and 'ridicule', the prophetic discourse is characteristic of at least three discursive 'reversals'.

Firstly, the prophetic depiction brings the idol's essence back to its origin as a planted tree:

> [T]he tour of the idol factory (vv. 12–14) is retrograde: one begins with the blacksmith who prepares the plating (v. 12), moves to the carpenter's shop where the wooden core is shaped (v. 13), moves behind the carpenter's shop to the forest where the tree is cut down and indeed to the nursery where the tree has been planted (v. 14).
>
> (Holladay 1997: 212)

Secondly, and more spectacular, is the way the prophet reverses Ancient West Asian discourses of war (Levtow 2008: 64). These discourses associate honour with the victorious and shame with the vanquished. Frequently, the vanquished are shamed through public rituals. But the creative re-imagination of Isaiah associates shame with the victors ("idol-makers will be put to shame" v. 9; "devotees will be put to shame" v. 11; "the artisans … will be put to shame" v. 11). Thus, as Levtow observes, "by conferring shame on the icons and iconodules of Babylonia, the authors of icon parodies invert the expected relationship between victorious and defeated peoples" (2008: 65).

Thirdly, the surrounding texts of this idol-taunt make reference to themes of creation ("The Lord who made you" v. 2; "I formed you" v. 21). Levtow reads this as prophetic 'presencing' of the God of Israel in contrast to the mouth-washing (*mīs pî*) ceremony of the idols (on *mīs pî*, see Dick 1999). Such ceremonies were aimed at 'presencing' the gods through the idols. But the idol-taunt depicts that the end result is just a block of wood and a lie (cf. vv. 19–20). By such a novel literary depiction, the prophet reverses the dynamics of 'presencing' and 'absencing'. Levtow remarks that 'presencing'/'absencing' is not a distinction based on ontological categories. "The denial of the power of cult images to eat, walk, and otherwise act in cultic contexts rejects the social power of these local iconic cults." (Levtow 2008: 169, n.22). Thus the idol-taunts' "mode of *absencing* Babylonian deity ... was intertwined with their mode of *presencing* Israelite deity through the Yahwistic hymns" (Levtow 2008: 170). As a result, Isaiah's depiction of Yahweh's 'presence' looms large against his 'absencing' Babylonian idols!

The discussion so far has underscored that when it is seen through the characteristic features of Dalit literature, Isaiah's idol-parody bears remarkable features of 'discourses of identity from the edge'. While the bold prophetic re-imagination dares to resist the appeal of a dominant empire, its deriding tone undercuts an otherwise appealing religious feature, namely, the centrality of the empire's cultic images. The prophetic vision seeks to reverse the empire's ideology such as its honour-shame rhetoric of war and reinterpret the 'presencing' and 'absencing' dynamics of the Babylonian cult in contrast to Yahweh's absolute sovereignty. By such means, the prophet seeks to affirm the identities of an apparently 'defeated' deity and a scattered community whose faith in that deity is put to test because of its traumatic experience of the exile. By reclaiming the identities of the deity and the people, the prophet – as the intermediary between God and God's people – rediscovers and reiterates his or her own identity. Thus, a Dalit reading of idol-taunt helps to appreciate the identity construction that is at work in a marginalized setting by a community that perceives itself disempowered.

Conclusion

Jim W. Adams declares that "the language of Isa 40–55 is performative" (2006: 91). In a way, this chapter set out to appreciate and appropriate this performative nature of idol-polemic in Isaiah from a Dalit perspective. It was proposed that when this prophetic text is juxtaposed with Dalit literature, characteristic features such as 'resistance', 'ridicule' and 'reversal' stand out. These features are not the essence of the texts, but they are means towards strengthening the otherwise fragmented identity of their audience. A sympathetic reading of anti-idol passages helps situate the text in its literary provenance, which I believe is the exile. Essentially, the discourse was aimed at building a cohesive community among the people scattered in a foreign land.

The chosen focus on the identity construction helps to tone down the anti-iconic sentiments within the idol-taunt, especially for someone who reads it

134   *D.S. Irudayaraj*

from the image-rich Indian perspective. In addition, a Dalit reading of idol-taunt offers several merits:

- It helps to understand and appreciate the struggle of a prophet in his/her attempt to construct the identities of a deity, a community and a prophet – especially in a traumatic time such as the exile.
- Identity – in prophetic time and now – is rarely a standalone entity. Identity makes sense only in a network of relationships. The Dalit reading emphasizes the inextricable connection of a prophet's identity with those of God and God's people. The prophet can hope to redeem his/her identity only in proportion to his/her task of redeeming other related identities. Identity construction in the context of interconnectedness has greater appeal for marginalized people, especially against the perception of their fragmented identities.
- The Dalit reading invites its readers to sympathize with the struggle of Dalits in their attempt to construct a worldview of equality and human dignity. Going further, it calls us – the readers – to open our eyes to the continued struggles of contemporary siblings of Dalits as well as exiled peoples and to value their identity-affirming discourses.

Despite these merits of the attempted Dalit reading of Isa 40:9–20, the sympathetic reading can hardly stop here. Nor can it afford to turn a blind eye to some of the later interpretive excesses. The same identity-affirming and cohesion-oriented prophetic text, when received by the believing communities and made normative in later periods, has led to an interpretive history that sought to employ exclusive measures. For example, the text in the hands of the returning community, which was at odds with those who had remained in *Yehud*, and in the interpretive traditions of Christian missionaries, who felt the strong urge to purge India of its 'idol-perversion', bear clear marks of exclusion (see Irudayaraj 2012). Therefore, a sympathetic reading of idol-taunt as a 'prophetic construction of identity' needs to be complemented by paying due attention to other interpretations. Revisiting the problems with which this chapter began, for an image-rich and multi-religious Indian reader, neither the sympathetic reading of idol-parody as a 'prophetic construction of identity' nor its complementary outlook as a 'construction of prophecy' seems sufficient. Breaking beyond these binaries of 'prophetic construction'/'construction of prophecy', a reading that is attentive of religious sensibilities and promotes an amicable living is the need of the hour.

And so, let such construction(s) continue!

Note

I gratefully acknowledge Profs. Ingrid Hjelm and Anne Katrine de Hemmer Gudme for their invaluable comments and suggestions and Prof. Gina Hens-Piazza for her scholarly advice.

Bibliography

Adams, Jim W. 2006. *The Performative Nature and Function of Isaiah 40–55*. New York: Continuum International.

Blenkinsopp, Joseph. 2002. *Isaiah 40–55: A New Translation with Introduction and Commentary*, 1st edn. New York: Anchor Bible.

Brueck, Laura R. 2011. "Marking the Boundaries of a New Literary Identity: The Assertion of 'Dalit Consciousness' in Dalit Literary Criticism". In *Religion and Identity in South Asia and Beyond: Essays in Honor of Patrick Olivelle*. Steven E. Lindquist (ed.). New York: Anthem: 347–68.

——2014. *Writing Resistance: The Rhetorical Imagination of Hindi Dalit Literature*. New York: Columbia University Press.

Brueggemann, Walter. 1998. *Isaiah 40–66* (2 vols). Louisville, KY: Westminster John Knox.

——2001. *The Prophetic Imagination*, 2nd edn. Minneapolis: Fortress.

Chattopadhyaya, Shyama Kumar. 2000. *The Philosophy of Sankar's Advaita Vedanta*. New Delhi: Sarup & Sons.

Chockalingam, Arun Joe. 2007. *Constructing Dalit Identity*. Jaipur: Rawat.

Clarke, Sathianathan, Deenabandhu Manchala and Philip Vinod Peacock (eds). 2010. *Dalit Theology in the Twenty-First Century: Discordant Voices, Discerning Pathways*. Oxford: Oxford University Press.

Cuéllar, Gregory Lee. 2008. *Voices of Marginality: Exile and Return in Second Isaiah 40–55 and the Mexican Immigrant Experience*. New York: Peter Lang.

Davies, Andrew. 2000. *Double Standards in Isaiah: Re-Evaluating Prophetic Ethics and Divine Justice*. Leiden: Brill.

Deutsch, Eliot. 1969. *Advaita Vedānta: A Philosophical Reconstruction*. Hawaii: University of Hawaii Press.

Dick, Michael B. 1999. "Prophetic Parodies of Making the Cult Image". In *Born in Heaven, Made on Earth: The Creation of the Cult Image in the Ancient Near East*. Michael B. Dick (ed.). Indiana: Eisenbrauns: 1–53.

Downing, John D.H. (ed.). 2010. *Encyclopedia of Social Movement Media*. California: Sage.

Elangovan, R. 2008. "Atrocities Against Dalits and Human Rights Violations in Tamil Nadu". In *Human Rights Challenges of 21st Century*. V.N. Viswanathan (ed.). Delhi: Gyan: 283–88.

Fitzgerald, Michael Oren. 2008. *Introduction to Hindu Dharma: Illustrated*. Indiana: World Wisdom.

Goldingay, John and David Payne. 2006. *A Critical and Exegetical Commentary on Isaiah 40–55* (2 vols). New York: Continuum International.

Greenspahn, Frederick E. 2004. "Syncretism and Idolatry in the Bible". *Vetus Testamentum* 54(4): 480–94.

Holladay, William L. 1997. "Was Trito-Isaiah Deutero-Isaiah After All?" In *Writing and Reading the Scroll of Isaiah: Studies of an Interpretive Tradition*. Craig C. Broyles and Craig A. Evans (eds). Leiden: Brill: 193–218.

Irudayaraj, Dominic S. 2012. "Idol-Taunt in Isaiah 44:9–20: Prophetic Construction/ Construction of Prophecy? A Dalit/New Historicist Reading". Licentiate Thesis, Jesuit School of Theology, Santa Clara University.

Kumar, Raj. 2007. "Dalit Literature: A Perspective from Below". In *Dalit Assertion in Society, History, and Literature*. Imtiaz Ahmad and Shashi Bhushan Upadhyay (eds). Delhi: Deshkal: 121–36.

136 *D.S. Irudayaraj*

Levtow, Nathaniel B. 2008. *Images of Others: Iconic Politics in Ancient Israel.* Indiana: Eisenbrauns.

Light, Gary W. 2001. *Isaiah.* Louisville, KY: Westminster John Knox.

Massey, James and Samson Prabhakar. 2005. *Frontiers in Dalit Hermeneutics.* Delhi: BTESSC/SATHRI/CDSS.

Meibohm, Margaret 2002. "Past Selves and Present Others: The Ritual Construction." In *Popular Christianity in India: Riting between the Lines*, Selva J. Raj and Corinne G. Dempsey (eds.). New York: State University of New York Press: 61–84.

Pandit, Bansi. 2005. *Explore Hinduism.* Loughborough: Heart of Albion.

Paswan, Sanjay and Paramanshi Jaideva (eds). 2002. *Encyclopaedia of Dalits in India.* Delhi: Gyan.

Prasad, Amar Nath and M.B. Gaijan (eds). 2007. *Dalit Literature: A Critical Exploration.* New Delhi: Sarup.

Rad, G. von 2001. *Old Testament Theology: The Theology of Israel's Prophetic Traditions*, 2 vols. Louisville, KY: Westminster John Knox.

Rajawat, Mamta. 2005. *History of Dalits*, vol. 1. Delhi: Anmol.

Rajkumar, Peniel. 2010. *Dalit Theology and Dalit Liberation: Problems, Paradigms and Possibilities.* Vermont: Ashgate.

Ranade, R.D. 1983. *Mysticism in India: The Poet-Saints of Maharashtra.* New York: State University of New York Press.

Roy, Sumita and M. Sivaramkrishna (eds). 1996. *Poet Saints of India.* New Delhi: Sterling.

Śaṅkarācārya. 1992. *A Thousand Teachings: The Upadeśasāhasrī of Śaṅkara*, Sengaku Mayeda (ed. and trans.). New York: State University of New York Press.

Shinde, Prem Kumar (ed.). 2005. *Dalits and Human Rights: The Broken Future.* Delhi: Gyan.

Smith, Mark S. 2002. *The Early History of God: Yahweh and the Other Deities in Ancient Israel*, 2nd edn. Michigan: Wm. B. Eerdmans.

——2003. *The Origins of Biblical Monotheism: Israel's Polytheistic Background and the Ugaritic Texts.* New York: Oxford University Press.

Soares-Prabhu, George M. 2000. "Laughing at Idols: The Dark Side of Biblical Monotheism (An Indian Reading of Isaiah 44:9–20)". In *Reading from this Place: Social Location and Biblical Interpretation in Global Perspective* (2 vols). Fernando F. Segovia and Mary Ann Tolbert (eds). Minneapolis: Fortress: 109–31.

Sommer, Benjamin D. 1996. "Allusions and Illusions: The Unity of the Book of Isaiah in Light of Deutero-Isaiah's Use of Prophetic Tradition". In *New Visions of Isaiah.* Roy F. Melugin and Marvin Alan Sweeney (eds). Sheffield: Continuum International: 156–86.

Valmiki, Omprakash. 2008. *Joothan: An Untouchable's Life*, Arun Prabha Mukherjee (trans.). New York: Columbia University Press.

Verma, Rajeev. 2009. *Faith and Philosophy of Hinduism.* Delhi: Gyan.

Westermann, Claus. 2001. *Isaiah 40–66*, David M.G. Stalker (trans.). Philadelphia: Westminster John Knox.

9 Exile and emergent monotheism
Learning loyalty from Jeremiah 42–44

Rob Barrett

Introduction

The Old Testament Book of Jeremiah is a book of failure and disaster.[1] The people of Judah have failed as YHWH's people. That the book's audience knows of the resulting disaster is clear even from the book's opening verses: the prophet's activity runs "until the captivity of Jerusalem" (1:3).[2] Accordingly, the book ends with a rehearsal of the fall of Jerusalem (52:1–30). Even the hopeful image of Jehoiachin at the table of the king of Babylon (52:31–34) does not dull the pain, however much this might indicate that failure and disaster are not final, by the grace of YHWH.

It is hope for a future that drives the gathering, writing, disseminating and treasuring of this book's presentation of failure. This is no disinterested, disembodied recounting of dispassionate history. Rather, it is both a forensic analysis of something that went horribly wrong and potent rhetoric that points forward to something right. Through a literary recollection of a failed past, a successful future can be imagined.

The rhetoric of the book of Jeremiah functions by pitting the protagonist prophet against a range of opponents. The reader of the book is assumed to stand with Jeremiah and against these opponents. As the various antagonists reject Jeremiah's message from YHWH, the book's rhetoric presses the audience to form themselves in contrast to these odious literary rebels. In sociological terms, Jeremiah's opponents function as 'reference groups', that is, groups against which people evaluate their own attitudes, circumstances, values, and behaviour (Hyman and Singer 1968). People belong to their own in-group and understand themselves in contrast to any number of out-groups. These out-groups might be real and present or they might be literary constructions reflecting real counterparts. For those receiving and accepting this literary tradition, it is the textual rebels against Jeremiah and YHWH, not the historical figures who may lie behind them, that the readers are to take to heart and define themselves against. The receiving community is to form itself in opposition to the characteristics the text highlights in this literary out-group.

It is common for scholars to note the negative portrayals of various groups in the book and discern the rhetorical purpose of rejecting the post-destruction

138   *R. Barrett*

remnants in Judah and Egypt, with the purpose of favouring those in Babylon (for example, McKane 1996: 1091 and throughout). Such a concern is made explicit in the image of the good and bad figs in chapter 24. However, expressing a preference for one post-destruction group over another does not exhaust the rhetorical goals of these texts. Often left unexplored are the literary developments of the characteristics of these out-groups and the shaping effect of these portrayals on the reading audience. There is more happening than arbitrating between existing groups as the legitimate continuation of YHWH's people. The audience is not simply pressed to identify itself with one historical in-group and to dismiss other historical communities as illegitimate out-groups. The literarily-constructed out-groups, as conceptual reference groups, provide a rich example of rejected attitudes, values and behaviours against which the readers continually draw upon in order to reshape themselves as the in-group. As they reflect on the characteristics of those condemned in the text, the receiving community learns to censure these same objectionable characteristics they discover within their own ranks (Stets and Burke 2000: 225–26). This book's audience, by attending to the portrayals of the literary out-groups and recoiling from their featured failings, follows the lead of the rhetorical text. They adopt the book's literary in-group as their own and consider themselves to have lived out the story of Jeremiah as members of this faithful remnant, regardless of what they and their community did at the time. The readers are pressed to understand themselves as those who did not and do not do the sorts of things ascribed to the rebellious remnant.

Broadly speaking, the primary negative behaviour of the book's various out-groups, the ones who provoked YHWH to bring Babylon against Jerusalem and who continued to provoke him afterwards, is their pursuit of 'other gods'. This has been noted in Leslie Allen's observation of four passages that adopt a 'now' timeframe over and against the 'then' of the destruction (Jer. 5:19; 9:12–16; 16:10–13; 22:8–9; Allen 2008: 14–15). These temporal shifts move the rhetorical focus from the people of Jeremiah's day to its exilic readers. The text voices the cries of the displaced refugees who demand an explanation for the trauma. Each time they ask "Why?" they receive an explanation, which focuses on Judah's abandoning YHWH and going after other gods.[3] This rationale behind the destruction accords with the programmatic explanation found in Jeremiah's call narrative (1:16).

If following other gods is the characteristic of the out-group to be avoided at all costs, the message for the in-group seems clear: fidelity to YHWH alone. But this point is in itself insufficient for constructing a life in exile where the receiving community can live by such fidelity to YHWH. They might legitimately ask, "What does such faithfulness look like for us?" Simply anathematizing the following of 'other gods' leaves at least two significant gaps for building a positive programme. First, there is a gap between the social setting of the book's audience and that of the portrayed pre-destruction Judahites. The predominant setting of the book is in a settled (if tumultuous) life in Judah, while the post-destruction audience of the book is living the displaced life of the exiled. A second gap results from the difficulty of moving from a negative example – 'do not follow other gods' – to a positive programme for life. This difficulty increases with the widely malleable idea of abandoning YHWH for other gods in Jeremiah.

The post-destruction narratives of chapters 42–44 significantly narrow both of these gaps. The first gap is narrowed because the rebellious remnant is already threatened with displacement in ch. 42 and actually displaced in chs. 43–44. This brings them closer to the exilic audience's social situation. Furthermore, after the assassination of the Babylon-appointed governor Gedaliah in chapter 41, the remnant faces the spectre of Babylonian reprisals and comes face-to-face with their utter vulnerability. This is also a key characteristic of the book's exilic audience. In Louis Stulman's description of their situation, the

> disenfranchised refugees living in Babylon had to come to grips with a past that was gone and a future that was not yet inscribed. They found themselves living on the edge, eking out an existence and negotiating a new world after the old one had been dealt a deathblow.
>
> (Stulman 2005: 6)

The book's audience stands powerless as their previous social structure lies in shambles. They face the social responsibility of defining the foundation from which they will protect themselves in their condition of defencelessness in the presence of a hostile world. This responsibility encourages provisional sympathy with the plight of the rebellious out-group in the narratives of chapters 42–44, but the rhetorical condemnation of the out-group presses the receiving community to develop an alternative, positive way forward. They must not become like the rebels portrayed here.

The second gap in building a positive programme out of negative examples is bridged by the presence of two parallel narratives in these chapters.[4] In the first narrative, Jeremiah fails to convince the remnant that they must stay in Judah when they are intent on fleeing to Egypt (chs. 42–43). In the second, after their flight to Egypt, Jeremiah fails to convince them that they must abandon serving the Queen of Heaven (ch. 44). The value of attaching meaning to narrative analogies like this is helpfully demonstrated by Robert Gordon (1980). He notes the tendency to laconicism in biblical narrative, which places a heavy burden upon the interpreter to discern the intended structures and emphases (Gordon 1980:42). Modern readers expect considerably more guidance about the author's intention than is often found in such narratives. But by attending to the ways such narrative analogies are interlinked, the reader might discern the author's intended emphases. Gordon demonstrates this sort of analysis by drawing an analogy between 1 Samuel 24–26's figure of Nabal with Saul (Gordon 1980: 43). In the case of Jeremiah 42–44, the analogy can be represented in an equation of Egypt with the Queen of Heaven. The rebellious remnant seeks first the political protection

140 *R. Barrett*

of Egypt and then the divine protection of the Queen of Heaven. I follow Gordon's general method here, though without further citation, in order to disclose the particular emphases in these negative examples that guide the exilic audience in forming their identity around the idea of remaining loyal to YHWH alone.

Egypt and the Queen of Heaven: A narrative analogy of security

I explore the narrative analogy in Jeremiah 42–44 in three ways. First, I highlight three important common elements in the narratives' plots. Second, I explore the narratives' explicit cross-references and common language. Third, I move from commonalities between the narratives to differences, exploring how the development from the first narrative to the second sharpens the message of the entire section.

Plot elements

The narratives have three elements in common: the remnant is fearful because of its vulnerability; the prophet demands that they resist seeking security from others than YHWH, though this demand is rejected; and YHWH expounds his own reinterpretation of events that urges the remnant to fear him alone and heed the prophet's message. I examine each of these elements in the Egypt narrative (chs. 42–43) and then move on to the Queen of Heaven narrative (ch. 44).

The Egypt narrative

In the Egypt narrative, the post-destruction community must navigate their vulnerability before Babylonian power. They have a well-founded fear of Babylonian reprisals after the assassination of Gedaliah, which the narrator affirms unequivocally (41:18). They know from tragic experience that resisting Babylon's retributive power is futile, and this was so even before the destruction, when they were much stronger. Things are worse now, "for there are only a few of us left out of many, as your eyes can see" (42:2). Their fear of the Babylonians, though utterly reasonable, suggests an impending crisis with YHWH, for fear in the book of Jeremiah should be reserved for YHWH alone.[5]

In light of their fearful vulnerability, the remnant seeks a word from YHWH. They apparently intend to put themselves under YHWH's care and therefore they approach the prophet: "Be good enough to listen to our plea, and pray to YHWH your God for us … Let YHWH your God show us where we should go and what we should do" (42:2–4). They swear to obey YHWH "in order that it may go well with us when we obey the voice of YHWH our God" (42:6). Though seemingly acknowledging their utter dependence upon YHWH (Stulman 2005: 333), they are simultaneously predisposed to seek security in Egypt regardless of YHWH's command. Jeremiah exposes their unspoken logic: "[W]e will go to Egypt where we shall not see war or hear the sound of the trumpet

Exile and emergent monotheism 141

and we shall not be hungry for bread" (42:14). They are making a pragmatic choice to avoid disaster. So when YHWH tells them through Jeremiah to remain in Judah, they reject his message, call it a lie, and flee to Egypt (43:1–7). For the rebellious remnant, it is clear that logical security from Egypt trumps trusting Jeremiah's challenging message from YHWH.

But YHWH does not demand that they abandon all logic; rather, proper logic must account for YHWH's own supreme power over their life. Jeremiah delivers this message: "Do not fear the king of Babylon, the one you are fearing; do not fear him, says YHWH, for I am with you to save you and to rescue you from his power" (42:11).[6] As at Jeremiah's call scene at the beginning of the book, YHWH's presence is determinative and other threats are inconsequential (1:8), such is also the case in this scene of ch. 42, when YHWH's presence trumps both Babylon's military power and the imperial policy of violent retribution for treachery. The remnant might cite their recent traumatic experience of Babylon's retributive violence in the destruction of Jerusalem, but YHWH offers an alternative version of the story: he maintains that he was the determinative will behind the destruction of the city: "If you will only remain in this land, then I will build you up and not pull you down; I will plant you, and not pluck you up; for I am sorry for [נחמתי אל; perhaps better: I have changed direction concerning] the disaster that I have brought upon you" (42:10). But even if YHWH caused the previous disaster, does this mean that the remnant can safely ignore Babylon's response to Gedaliah's assassination? The Babylonian king is still a menacing threat, but YHWH asserts his power over him: "I will grant you mercy, and he will have mercy on you" (42:12). The point is not that the king is impotent – such would be difficult to argue – but that the king's potent sword is subject to YHWH's will, for YHWH can shape the king's will.[7] This works in the opposite direction also for disobedience – staying in the land will lead YHWH to incite the king of Babylon to come against them in Egypt: "If you are determined to enter Egypt and go to settle there, then the sword that you fear shall overtake you there … and there you shall die" (42:15–16). In this case, the king will be YHWH's violent agent: "They shall have no remnant or survivor from the disaster that I am bringing upon them" (42:17). The logic of YHWH's people must involve YHWH, who drives history forward and wields (or quiets) the sword of the mighty.

The Queen of Heaven narrative

The second narrative, in which those who have fled to Egypt serve the Queen of Heaven, bears the same key plot features. The remnant must navigate the vulnerability stemming from their self-imposed exile in Egypt and they seek security through cultic service to the Queen of Heaven.[8] They have analyzed their previous experience – as they did in their decision to flee the king of Babylon in the first narrative – and have concluded that this course of action will lead to their preservation. When they worshipped the Queen of Heaven in

142   R. Barrett

Judah, they experienced that they "had plenty of food, and prospered, and saw no misfortune" (44:17). In a likely reference to Josiah's cultic reforms (Allen 2008: 447), they observed, "From the time we stopped making offerings to the Queen of Heaven ... we have lacked everything and have perished by the sword and by famine" (44:18). Therefore logic dictated a re-establishment of the lapsed cult with the expectation that these offerings will provide security. Their emigration to Egypt exercised political logic to gain security and their worship exercises cultic logic to the same end.

Jeremiah's response to serving the Queen of Heaven is not surprising. YHWH's anger over his people's turning to other gods runs throughout the book. Here YHWH recalls his appeal to those living in Jerusalem before the destruction, when he said concerning the offerings, "I beg you not to do this abominable thing that I hate!" (44:4). But they did not listen or change their behaviour (44:5). A similar demand is now made of the remnant in Egypt (44:9–10), but it refuses the message.

As in the first narrative, YHWH here provides a counter-rationale for them that subverts their logic and discloses that they are making the same mistake by turning to the Queen of Heaven rather than fearing YHWH (44:10). The reasonable fear resulting from their vulnerability is being quieted in the wrong way. YHWH presents an irreconcilable alternative interpretation of history that leads to an alternative course for the remnant to secure their survival. When, however, the remnant insists that it was the cessation of the cult of the Queen of Heaven that brought their destruction, YHWH claims that it was the cult itself that caused it. As with the flight to Egypt to avoid Babylon's sword, which only served to provoke YHWH to wield Babylon's sword against them, cultic service to the Queen of Heaven will only provoke YHWH's anger against them (44:8). It will do nothing to secure them, but only produce the opposite effect of what they seek. YHWH swears that he will destroy the entire remnant in Egypt – apart from a few escapees – by the sword of Pharaoh's enemy (44:26–30). The Queen of Heaven cannot deflect Babylon's sword any more than Egypt can.

The plotline of the two narratives is the same, with Egypt and the Queen of Heaven alternately put in the role of potential protector. The vulnerable remnant of Jerusalem's destruction uses logic based on past experience to justify seeking security apart from YHWH. When YHWH forbids this, the people reject the prophetic command. Finally, YHWH provides an alternative interpretation of history, which underlines that his overruling power implies an overruling logic for the remnant's pathway to security. The key difference between the two narratives lies in the object of the remnant's hope as either political protection in Egypt or divine protection from the Queen of Heaven.

Cross-references and common language

Since appeal to thematic connections can be idiosyncratic, it is helpful to complement the previous analysis with an analysis of the narratives' linkage of thematic and linguistic features. The narratives make explicit reference to

Exile and emergent monotheism   143

each other's concerns, which in both narratives is presented in marked linguistic phrases that highlight their emphases.

There is a reference to the primary concern of the second narrative at the end of the first. In the reversal of the remnant's logic of flight, YHWH envisions summoning Nebuchadrezzar to exercise destructive power over Egypt, undercutting the seeming security of this land and destroying the fleeing Judahite remnant. Nebuchadrezzar will "ravage the land of Egypt" (43:10–11). This will nullify the false security of the first narrative. But Nebuchadrezzar's destruction then extends so far as to "kindle a fire in the temples of the gods of Egypt" (43:12; also v. 13). The gods of Egypt have played no prior role in chapters 42–43, but this added detail points forward to YHWH's judgment on the remnant's misplaced confidence in the Queen of Heaven, which first appears in chapter 44.

The second narrative also refers back to the first. The worshippers of the Queen of Heaven are referred to as those who have "entered to sojourn there [that is, in Egypt]" (לגור שם באים; 44:8 and, with slight variations, 44:12, 14, 28). That this is an explicit cross-reference is clear by the author's use of the same two verbs and locative adverb in the first narrative (42:15, 17, 22; 43:2). This pattern appears nowhere else in the Hebrew Bible. The rebelliousness of the flight is enhanced by saying that the remnant "set their face" to come to the land of Egypt (שׂמו פניהם לבוא; 44:12). This combination of terms was used also in the first narrative (42:15, 17). While this description of the remnant's flight is functional within the plot of the first narrative, there is no obvious reason to identify the worshippers of the Queen of Heaven in these terms except to highlight the connection between the two narratives of seeking security apart from YHWH. These cross-referencing devices fall outside the inner logic of each narrative in order to pull them together.

Additional common language between the two narratives guides the reader to discern two important points of connection between them. First, in the discourse about loyalty, the source of the previous disaster is made a key question as either the king of Babylon, the Queen of Heaven or YHWH. In both narratives, YHWH takes full credit: "My anger and my wrath were poured out" (42:18; 44:6). Although the order of the nouns and the stem of the verb are not exactly the same, it is striking that these three terms (נתך, חמה, אף) appear together in only one other place in Jeremiah (7:20), and nowhere else in the Hebrew Bible. This is remarkable in light of the number of references to YHWH's action against Judah and Jerusalem in Jeremiah.[9] Both narratives also use similar and rare forms to refer to "the disaster I [YHWH] have brought" (Jer 42:10; 44:2; cf. 42:17) against the disobedient.[10] The pivotal point in these parallel locutions is not the simple fact of disaster, but that it is YHWH who has caused and will cause disaster. The role of Babylon is only that of YHWH's puppet. Any surmised activity by the Queen of Heaven is delusion. YHWH is the only power that matters.

Second, verbal repetitions point to the depth of destruction YHWH causes. The remnant plays a high-stakes game. The triple threat "by the sword, by

144   *R. Barrett*

famine, and by pestilence" is raised against the disobedient in both narratives (בחרב ברעב ובדבר; 42:17, 22; 44:13).[11] In both cases it results in becoming a curse (קללה; 42:18; 44:8, 12, 22), a waste (שמה; 42:18; 44:12, 22), an oath (אלה; 42:18; 43:1, 10; 44:12), and a reproach (חרפה; 42:18; 44:8, 12, 13). Allen (2008: 446) suggests that 44:12 has been 'crammed with echoes' of 42:15, 17 in order to enhance the similarities between the judgments (see also 44:14). Finally, both narratives highlight the totality of YHWH's destruction by referring to no survivor or escapee (שריד, פליט; 42:17; 44:14). These two nouns are nowhere else conjoined in Jeremiah and appear together only in three other instances in the Hebrew Bible. These repetitions mark the parallel and utter destruction YHWH prepares for those making the wrong choice.

Narrative development

The plot, cross-referencing, and verbal connections between the two narratives highlight their commonality. But beyond the commonalities is a development from the first to the second narrative that sharpens the resulting construction.

I will present three developments, the first of which is the most striking, namely the way the remnant interacts with the prophet over the question of how to secure itself. In the first narrative, they seek out Jeremiah to inquire of YHWH about what they should do in a clear self-understanding of their vulnerability (42:2–3). They commit themselves to obedience, regardless of YHWH's instructions (42:5–6). The narrator shows no interest in exploring their inner psychology, whether they speak with integrity or not, although their prior intention to go to Egypt (41:17-18) and their continuation along this course in the midst of Jeremiah's report (42:21–22) raises suspicions. While they might have had the best of intentions in their request, their final rejection of Jeremiah and his message from YHWH display a disregard for the outcome of the inquiry (43:1–7). The second narrative extends this disregard for YHWH's will as there is no pretence at all about seeking YHWH's approval concerning their argument in favour of the Queen of Heaven. In asking for YHWH's blessing for the flight to Egypt, the remnant might have imagined that they could get Egypt's protection along with YHWH's full blessing. This, however, turns out to be incorrect. In the second narrative, the remnant avoids inquiring of YHWH about offering cultic service to the Queen of Heaven. Therefore the second narrative has Jeremiah proactively confront them, though to no avail. The trajectory from the first to the second narrative signals a fading regard for YHWH's will. The subtle replacement of security from YHWH with security from Egypt gives way in the narrative sequence to a complete exchange of loyalty to YHWH for loyalty to another deity.

My second example of progressive plotlines between the two narratives concerns the reality of the power of security which the remnant seeks. In the first narrative, Egypt's political power is undoubtedly real. There seems to be no question that the remnant can gain protection within Egypt's borders.

Exile and emergent monotheism 145

Even if refugee status leaves some vulnerability, their situation would be less precarious than waiting, with no defence, for Babylon's unchecked reprisals for the assassination of Gedaliah. But if Egypt might be a realistic choice of protective power, the Queen of Heaven has no ability whatsoever to secure the remnant. In the book of Jeremiah, no other god apart from YHWH acts in such a way. In a grammatical opposition to the common idea that other gods have power, the book does not even go so far as granting any god apart from YHWH the honour of being the subject of an active verb. While the book stresses over and again the people's attraction to other gods, the rationality of this is more than suspect: it is ludicrous, for only YHWH acts. So within the world of the book, there is absolutely no power of protection from the Queen of Heaven. The remnant has moved from a seemingly rational engagement with Egypt to a meaningless trust in another deity. Of course, even if Egypt wields some measure of true power, YHWH still overrules, thus dashing the remnant's hopes, but their hope in protective power from the Queen of Heaven is a non-starter.

The remnant's fading confidence in Egypt's power provides my third example of narrative progression. Those fleeing to Egypt had confidence in Egypt's power to protect them from war and famine, but even after their arrival in Egypt, their sense of vulnerability remains. They still fear war and famine (44:17–19) as their initial confidence in Egypt's power to provide security has mysteriously evaporated after their arrival. However, their persisting fear is left unexplained in the text. It is not a result of YHWH's promised dispatching of the king of Babylon to wield the sword against Egypt for this has not (yet) happened. In their continuing need, they are now just as confident that the Queen of Heaven will protect them as they formerly were confident in Egypt. The implicit message is clear: security apart from YHWH is always partial and incomplete. They are attributing power to powerless things and refuse to recognize YHWH's superior power. Life is precarious, especially when one's group sojourns in a foreign land. The exilic readers of the book will face insecurity from many sides. Whenever YHWH's security is deemed insufficient, the never-ending search for a more complete protection will continue. The 'other gods' take many forms, whether political Egypt or the cultic Queen of Heaven or some other, but they cannot provide the security the remnant seeks.

What is the implication of these developments in the narrative analogy? A central message of the book of Jeremiah is the impotence of other gods in comparison to YHWH. The analogy brings this point home with Jeremiah's discourse about the Queen of Heaven. She is powerless. But what can be said about Egypt? By juxtaposing the narratives, the dangerous suggestion is made that YHWH overrules not only questionable deities but the unquestioned political reality of Babylonian reprisals over Gedaliah. The analogy moves from the political sphere to the divine sphere. It is made clear throughout the Book of Jeremiah that YHWH is sovereign in heaven and that other cults are off limits to the remnant. By means of the analogy, the narrative construction presses a more striking claim, namely that YHWH also has sovereignty over political

146 *R. Barrett*

powers on earth. A sympathetic reader of the book who endorses its argument for the fall of Jerusalem as resulting from worshipping other gods is urged to receive a much harder message: YHWH confounds *Realpolitik*. The narrative analogy carries the book's message about the divine realm into the political. YHWH overrules and thereby nullifies other undeniable, real-world powers. Doubting Babylon's will or military ability to punish treachery against its appointed governor would have been ludicrous to suggest. But Jeremiah's YHWH insists on a different calculus for the heirs of these texts.

Implications

In this closing section, I will discuss the implications of these texts both in terms of their construction of a form of 'monotheism' and in regard to the political possibilities for the exilic audience.

Jeremiah's paired discourses might be judged a noteworthy contribution to the development of Jewish monotheism as a central identity marker, which grew in prominence and definition from the experience of exile. These chapters shape their exilic audience as a monotheistic people in a particular way that exalts YHWH over other purported powers. It is increasingly recognized that monotheism is not a single concept – the denial of the existence of all deities but one – but takes on a variety of forms. Varying movements and developments emphasize different monotheistic constructions. Konrad Schmid (2011: 289) has argued that the expression of a monotheistic God requires creativity in order to develop received traditions into a new set of ideas and structures. He has examined the post-exilic Priestly Code in order to develop "a better understanding of 'its' particular monotheism", joining into a single entity identified with the term אלהים the God of creation, the God of the ancestors, and the God of the Exodus. Schmid's question about the monotheizing moves made by the authors of the Priestly Code can be applied to Jeremiah also. Earlier reflection on this question has sought a binary yes/no answer to questions of whether Jeremiah is monotheistic or not. Henry Saggs observed that Jeremiah has tied YHWH's role as cosmic creator to exerting power over all the nations also (1978: 42). So also Ernst Axel Knauf (1991: 61–62), who, referring to Jeremiah 2:11, found that Jeremiah has claimed YHWH a universal deity over all nations. Mark Smith (2000: 153) pointed to Jeremiah 16:19–20 as evidence of Jeremiah's monotheism, while Robert Gnuse (1997: 270) declared the prophet "virtually monotheistic", since with him YHWH rises to the level of "international deity with universal concerns". It is obvious that Jeremiah's engagement with imperial politics asserts YHWH's power over all nations and thus over their gods also.

On the other hand, Nikiprowetzky (1975: 82, 88 n. 40) resisted labelling Jeremiah as monotheistic since it magnified YHWH's incomparability without actually denying the existence of other gods. Indeed, the presence of 'other gods' – including the Queen of Heaven – within the book of Jeremiah suggests that the book falls short of envisioning a truly monotheistic world.

Jeremiah's world contains 'other gods' of some sort. Rather than fixating on whether Jeremiah is fully monotheistic or not, it is perhaps more helpful to ask what kind of world the book constructs as it plays out the nature and interrelationship between YHWH and 'other gods'. It would miss the point of Jeremiah's rhetoric to think that, by allowing the category of 'other gods', YHWH is merely able to overpower the other gods of the cosmos as the first among many gods. The narrative analogy in chapters 42–44 offers a helpful example of the book's subtle argument about YHWH's uniqueness. As demonstrated by the parallel between the remnant seeking protection from Egypt and the Queen of Heaven, the book of Jeremiah creates a conceptual category for alternative powers to YHWH. In this case, the alternatives include other gods and political powers. However, the narratives argue that entrusting oneself to any of these powers means abandoning YHWH. The issue at hand is not whether these alternatives really exist. It would make no sense to deny the ontological reality of protective Egypt or ominous Babylon. The point is not about the existence or not of alternatives to YHWH, but that it is a fatal mistake to grant these powers autonomy besides YHWH, and to think that other powers can be played-off against YHWH or that concessions should be made to them.

Jeremiah is able to accomplish something that an ontological denial of the existence of other gods could not. The world of Jeremiah contains other powers, but it rejects the idea that they can resist YHWH. This move creates a wide-ranging, practical monotheism, if not a pure, theoretical one. In particular, Jeremiah's portrayal of YHWH's superintendence over the remnant's life displaces not only other deities by denying them 'reality' in the sense of having no bearing on life, but also and at the same time displaces even undeniable political powers such as Egypt and Babylon. These potencies, Jeremiah dares to claim, are as much no-things as the do-nothing other gods. It may seem foolish to deny the autonomous reality and power of the Babylonian king, but, in Jeremiah's conceptual world, submitting to such a power without regard for YHWH only provokes to anger the one, true, and dangerous power with whom the remnant must reckon. So while Jeremiah may not advocate a pure, conceptual monotheism, it constructs a strong, practical monotheism.

Two direct implications for the formation of the exiles' understanding become readily apparent. First, by reducing Babylon's influential political power to a tool safely held in YHWH's hand, the exilic audience can allow the possibility of submitting to Babylon's imperial reign. If foreign powers are not really 'foreign', since they are under YHWH's control, the exiles need not necessarily resist such powers as opponents. This perspective provides a positive pattern for the later deference to Persian power that is so evident in the post-exilic period. The book of Jeremiah constructs a theological possibility for the compatibility of submitting to imperial power yet properly fearing YHWH.

Second, the people of YHWH face social pressure to adopt the cultic practices of surrounding cultures, especially in a vulnerable exilic condition. The literary out-group of chapter 44 embraced such a cult and the book's audience

148   R. Barrett

was pressed to reject them. Participation in such cults confers social benefits even apart from any alleged action by the served deities. These social benefits are not inconsequential, yet Jeremiah 44 impugns the pursuit of such benefits as offensive to YHWH, who has the ability to reverse the apparent logic of maintaining well-being through assimilating to the local cultural conventions. The monotheism of these chapters asserts that YHWH's power to bless supersedes even undeniable social powers. But this demands loyalty to him alone. It is possible to remain distinctly YHWH's, even as a dispersed people in a foreign land.

In conclusion, the two narratives of Jeremiah 42–44 present two negative examples for their exilic audience. Their analogy draws together political dependence upon Egypt and cultic dependence upon the Queen of Heaven as similar offences against YHWH, both in motivation and in threatened outcome. The result is to marginalize powers other than YHWH, whether the intimidating and undeniable power of Babylon, the apparently protective power of Egypt, or the socially conventional power of local cults. For the community formed by these texts, a community facing destabilizing vulnerability, commitment to YHWH demands difficult decisions with real implications. By observing these negative narratives and the way the analogy functions rhetorically to define the contours of improperly directed fear and disloyalty to YHWH, Jeremiah's audience is guided beyond rejecting the rebellious character of these reference groups to re-define their own in-group character as those fearing YHWH alone. The result is a form of monotheism that does not deny the theoretical existence of all but one deity. However, on a practical level, it goes much further by denying the independent reality of a broad range of powers that might tempt the people of YHWH into disloyalty towards their superintending God. By taking the two narratives together, loyalty to YHWH can include both an ability to acquiesce to the reigning political powers subjected to YHWH and a refusal to assimilate with the power claims embedded in the prevailing socio-cultic norms which conflict with Yahwistic demands. The resulting synthesis offers a way of maintaining loyalty to YHWH beyond the vulnerable state of exile.

Notes

1 A portion of this research was written within the Sofja Kovalevskaja project on early Jewish monotheisms, supported by the Alexander von Humboldt Foundation and the German Federal Ministry of Education and Research.
2 All references are to the MT; the LXX is not considered in this work.
3 The people variously abandon YHWH (5:19; 16:11), YHWH's law (9:12) and YHWH's covenant (22:9).
4 Louis Stulman (2005: 343–46) observes and develops connections between these two narratives in somewhat different directions than the present work.
5 Jer. 1:8; 3:8; 5:22, 24; 10:7; 17:8; 23:4; 30:10; cf. 10:5; 26:19; 32:39.
6 Escape to Egypt out of fear of a human king has also yielded destructive consequences in the past (26:21–23).

Exile and emergent monotheism   149

7 Stulman (2005: 335) notes similarly that the prophetic message "call[s] into question geopolitical logic" and adds Jeremiah's challenge follows in the footsteps of Isaiah's response to Assyria (Isa 31:1; cf. Ps 146:3, 5).

8 The Queen of Heaven is most likely to be identified with Astarte, possibly in syncretism with her Mesopotamian equivalent Ishtar (Day 2002: 144–50).

9 Nahum 1:6 combines the three terms in a different way.

10 42:10 uses the root עשׂה rather than בוא.

11 'Pestilence' appears only in MT, enhancing the parallel.

Bibliography

Allen, L.C. 2008. *Jeremiah: A Commentary.* Louisville: Westminster John Knox.

Day, J. 2002. *Yahweh and the Gods and Goddesses of Canaan.* Sheffield: Sheffield Academic Press.

Gnuse, R.K. 1997. *No Other Gods: Emergent Monotheism in Israel.* Sheffield: Sheffield Academic.

Gordon, R.P. 1980. "David's Rise and Saul's Demise: Narrative Analogy in 1 Samuel 24–26". *Tyndale Bulletin* 31: 37–64.

Hyman, H.H. and E. Singer. 1968. *Readings in Reference Group Theory and Research.* New York: The Free Press.

Knauf, E.A. 1991. "From History to Interpretation". In *The Fabric of History: Text, Artifact, and Israel's Past.* Edelman, D.V. (ed.). Sheffield: JSOT Press: 26–64.

McKane, W. 1996. *Jeremiah: Volume 2: 26–52.* Edinburgh: T&T Clark.

Nikiprowetzky, V. 1975. "Ethical Monotheism". *Daedalus* 104(2): 69–89.

Saggs, H.W.F. 1978. *The Encounter with the Divine in Mesopotamia and Israel.* London: Athlone.

Schmid, K. 2011. "The Quest for 'God': Monotheistic Arguments in the Priestly Texts of the Hebrew Bible". In *Reconsidering the Concept of Revolutionary Monotheism.* Pongratz-Leisten, B. (ed.). Winona Lake, IN: Eisenbrauns: 275–93.

Smith, M.S. 2000. *The Origins of Biblical Monotheism: Israel's Polytheistic Background and the Ugaritic Texts.* Oxford: Oxford University Press.

Stets, J.E. and P.J. Burke. 2000. "Identity Theory and Social Identity Theory". *Social Psychology Quarterly* 63(3): 224–37.

Stulman, L. 2005. *Jeremiah.* Nashville: Abingdon.

10 The return from exile in Ezra-Nehemiah

Roberto Piani

Ezra-Nehemiah's multifaceted portrait of post-exilic Judah

A key issue in dealing with exile and identity is represented by narratives about the 'return from exile'. This event, certainly at least partially historical even if not directly accessible through the biblical accounts, has played a major role in the identity discourse of the Israelites. The way in which the authors of return narratives represented the coming back from the Babylonian captivity often evokes other founding myths of the Israelite past, such as the exodus stories.

The biblical account in Ezra-Nehemiah constitutes an essential stopover for an intellectual enterprise interested in reconstructing how identity has been shaped around the event of the exile, and particularly focusing on the subsequent returning groups. Indeed, the interpretation of that account and of its key features has been quite different through the centuries. The focus of this contribution will be the peculiar portrait of one of the main protagonists of the return from exile according to the Books of Ezra and Nehemiah, namely, Ezra.

The biblical narrative presents Ezra as the leader of a second stream of returnees. His role has been interpreted in seemingly different ways. It is astonishing to observe how much importance is given to Ezra in post-biblical literature, when compared with the limited relevance he has in the biblical texts. In 4 Ezra, for example, he is portrayed as a 'second Moses'. Talmudic sources even claim that "Had Moses not preceded him, Ezra would have been worthy of receiving the Torah for Israel" (Halivni 1997: 15). Probably this image influenced later interpretation of Ezra as "the founder of Judaism", (Koch 1974) and often as a sort of 'second Moses'. Under his guidance, the return from exile could therefore be read as a 'second exodus'.

The parallel between the return from exile and the exodus is of key importance in understanding the purpose the authors had in mind when writing these narratives. Of course, as others have noted (Williamson 2007, Throntveit 2012, Japhet 2006), there are some elements in Ezra-Nehemiah that could be read in connection to the exodus theme. For example, in the incipit of the book, describing the offering of gold and silver, the author/editor remembers the spoiling of the Egyptians and the role of the Levites during the journey being similar to their role during the wandering in the desert. Other points will be addressed later. It seems important to ask ourselves whether we have solid elements in the biblical books that narrate Ezra's story. Is the second exodus paradigm really the most important one in these books? Or are references to one of the foundation myths of Israel only a later development thanks to post-biblical narratives?

This kind of question has significance not just for a better understanding of the character of Ezra. Whether these narratives of the return from the exile are understood as a 'second Exodus', or even as a radical novelty – the foundation of a 'new religion', Judaism – this has of course important implications for issues of exile and identity, and particularly for the focus of this chapter.

Scholarship on the role of Ezra is rich. It was Klaus Koch, in his 40-year-old essay, which remains valuable, who identified Ezra as the key figure for the foundation of Judaism (Koch 1974). Other scholars (Garbini 1988, Kratz 2000, Pakkala 2004) have stressed the artificial nature of this figure and so decisively diminished his historical value. And again other scholars (Blenkinsopp 1989) compared Ezra and Nehemiah to other Persian officials in charge of their own people, such as the 'Persian-Egyptian' official Udjahorresnet in Egypt.

Previous scholarship has indeed tried to compare the story of the post-exilic period as narrated in Ezra-Nehemiah with other biblical paradigms. Thus we have those who regard it as a 'second exodus' such as Koch, Blenkinsopp and, to a certain degree, Williamson; or those who label it under the genre of 'pilgrimage literature' such as Knowles (2004). Still others – such as Reinmuth (2008) – emphasized the connection with other key events in the biblical narrative, have such as those narrated regarding Joshua or Josiah.

In regard to Ezra, a promising approach in order to clarify possible inspiring paradigms seems to be an analysis of intertextual links. In this contribution, I want to briefly discuss some of the main arguments proposed in the past to describe Ezra, and then suggest other possible ways of understanding Ezra and the overall image of the return from exile presented in these narratives.

General patterns in Ezra-Nehemiah

Examining biblical narratives, one must repeatedly redress questions of possible paradigms that might have inspired a biblical book – either as a whole or only in one of its sections or supposed redactional layers. In the following I sketch some of the major interpretive lenses used to better understand Ezra-Nehemiah.

Ezra-Nehemiah as a second exodus

Among scholars engaged in an analysis of the relationship between Ezra and the exodus narrative, Koch might be have been the first to suggest how, in the

152 *R. Piani*

book of Ezra, and especially in the chapters regarding the Ezra character, we find elements, which present his travel from Babylon to Yehud as a 'second exodus' and a partial fulfillment of prophetic expectations (Koch 1974: 184–89). This is one of three summarizing theses that he develops in his article.[1] I will focus first on his general idea and then on some particular points useful for the overall aim of this article.

The Ezra narrative is interpreted by Koch as a fulfilment of the exilic prophets' oracles about 'a marvelous return of the exiles', namely, a 'second exodus'.[2] He therefore suggests possible passages in which the Ezra/exodus connection should be evident. He interprets, for example, the need for Levites (Ezr 8:15–20) as a link to the exodus narratives in the sense that also the return from Babylon to Jerusalem should follow "the order of the march through the desert after the original Exodus" (see Num 1, 2, 10:13 ff.). In the same way, the guidance of a priest (Ezra) reminds one of "the role of Aaron and Eleazar and the anti-royalist attitude of P" (Koch 1974: 187). One must, however, notice that the role of the Levites is especially relevant in only one of the exodus traditions; that is, in the wilderness and Sinai narratives in Numbers. In the traditions preserved in the book of Exodus their role seems not as prominent as Koch emphasizes. He offers no further elements to link Ezra to Aaron and Eleazar, other than their being priests. In the Ezra narratives there is scant trace of priestly activities or prerogatives exercised by Ezra.

Koch further considers the actions undertaken by Ezra when he arrives in Jerusalem – for example, the separation of the returning exiles from the peoples of the country, or the new way of celebrating the Feast of Tabernacles – and finds them comparable "to the occupation of the promised land after the first exodus" (Koch 1974: 188). Interpreting Ezra's deeds as the fulfilment of exilic prophets' oracles is therefore connected by Koch to the events narrated by the Bible *after* the entrance into the Promised Land, namely with what Joshua accomplished. Such events can and cannot be included among a typical exodus paradigm, depending on how broadly one considers the exodus event (for instance, was it only the exit from Egypt? Did it include the wandering in the desert or even the actual conquest of the land?).

Some of Koch's suggestions certainly seem interesting on a general and thematic-structural level, but they need a firmer textual foundation. Particularly when he includes events of the conquest narrative in his discussion of Ezra as a participant of or leader of a 'second exodus': his main argument risks becoming too general.

Other scholars (Coats 1968, Williamson 2007) find a possible parallel with exodus in the beginning of Ezra-Nehemiah, which seems to evoke a famous motif of the exodus narratives, namely the plundering of the Egyptians. The allusion, underscored by Ackroyd (1991), seems to rely semantically only on the quite common terms 'golden and silver vessels', as the following table illustrates.

Maybe more interesting for the present discussion are the contrasting views of the foreign king in Ezr 1:4–6 compared to Exodus 3 and 11. The Exodus

The return from exile in Ezra-Nehemiah 153

Table 10.1 The pairing of "gold and silver" is quite frequent in the Hebrew Bible: there are at least 78 occurrences of the expression כסף זהב

Ezr 1:4		Ex 3:22; 11:2	
וכל־הנשאר מכל־המקמות אשר הוא גר־שם ינשאוהו אנשי מקמו <u>בכסף ובזהב</u> וברכוש ובבהמה עם־הנדבה לבית האלהים אשר בירושלם	And let all survivors, in whatever place they reside, be assisted by the people of their place with silver and gold, with goods and with animals, besides freewill offerings for the house of God in Jerusalem.	^{3:22} ושאלה אשה משכנתה ומגרת ביתה <u>כלי־כסף וכלי</u> <u>זהב</u> ושמלת ושמתם על־בניכם ועל־בנתיכם ונצלתם את־מצרים	Each woman shall ask her neighbor and any woman living in the neighbor's house for jewelry of silver and of gold, and clothing, and you shall put them on your sons and on your daughters; and so you shall plunder the Egyptians
		^{11:2} דבר־נא באזני העם וישאלו איש מאת רעהו ואשה מאת רעותה <u>כלי־כסף וכלי זהב</u>	Tell the people that every man is to ask his neighbor and every woman is to ask her neighbor for objects of silver and gold.

Ezr 1:6		Ex 12:35-36	
וכל־סביבתיהם חזקו בידיהם <u>בכלי־כסף בזהב</u> ברכוש ובבהמה ובמגדנות לבד על־כל־התנדב	All their neighbors aided them with silver vessels, with gold, with goods, with animals, and with valuable gifts, besides all that was freely offered.	³⁵ ובני־ישראל עשו כדבר משה וישאלו ממצרים <u>כלי־כסף</u> <u>וכלי זהב</u> ושמלת ³⁶ ויהוה נתן את־חן העם בעיני מצרים וישאלום וינצלו את־מצרים	The Israelites had done as Moses told them; they had asked the Egyptians for jewelry of silver and gold, and for clothing, and the LORD had given the people favor in the sight of the Egyptians, so that they let them have what they asked. And so they plundered the Egyptians.

narrative is composed around the theme of a divine promise and its fulfilment, which in the Ezra narrative is formed rather as the king's commandment and its realization. Of course, the divine initiative is put to the fore also in Ezra-Nehemiah, since Cyrus has been 'stirred up' by God, but it seems evident that the author(s) wanted to underscore a positive portrait of the Persian administration, at least at the incipit of the book. The contrast is even more striking if one compares the Persian kings with the corresponding

154　*R. Piani*

negative image of Pharaoh in the exodus narratives. The more Pharaoh hardens his heart in refusing to allow the Israelites to depart, the more Cyrus is depicted as not only permitting a departure, but even instigating the return of the exiled Jews to rebuild their temple in Jerusalem. The strategic position at the beginning of the Ezra-Nehemiah narrative allows hypothesizing a possible echo of the exodus's motif of the plundering of the Egyptians. Nonetheless other paths can be followed in the interpretation of Ezr 1:4–6. For example, one could detect a possible allusion to Hag 2:7 or Isa 60, where all the nations will bring their precious gifts to the mountain of the Lord. Along this line, Koch has hinted at the possibility that the Ezra narrative could have been intended as a realization of eschatological prophecies of a new exodus. However, one may ask whether it is possible to draw intertextual connections when the shared lexemes are so few.

Ezra-Nehemiah as a pilgrimage

Another key issue for those who argue for an Ezra-Nehemiah/exodus parallel regards the verb עלה, 'go up', significantly present in Ezra and Nehemiah. Already the Talmud used the occurrence of that verb to draw a parallel between Moses and Ezra: "Of Moses it is written, And Moses went up unto God, and of Ezra it is written, He, Ezra, went up from Babylon" (b.Sanhedrin 21b). Knowles (2004), who discusses and criticizes the exodus parallels, argued instead that this verb is of key importance to understanding Ezra-Nehemiah as manifesting a 'pilgrimage pattern'. Her position, however, seems to be too much dependent on the interpretation of the verb עלה. In this regard, the observations made by Dyma (2009) seem more convincing. He disagrees that עלה is a *terminus technicus* for taking part in a pilgrimage due to its various uses in secular and especially military contexts. Moreover, some arguments of Knowles seem to me a bit strained: for example, the בני הגולה are not coming back to Babylon, as a normal pilgrimage pattern would imply. Also the pilgrimage connotations she argues for another very common verb, בוא, seem not fully convincing.

In sum, it looks like Ezra-Nehemiah could represent echoes of exodus narratives, some clearer, some more debatable. But the attempt to describe it as a pilgrimage account does not provide a good fit either. It looks as though the exodus or pilgrimage patterns provide just one tile of a more complex mosaic.

Ezra-Nehemiah as a second conquest of the land

Another paradigm referred to in the interpretation of these texts is that of the conquest narrative. Koch finds the actions undertaken by Ezra when he arrives in Jerusalem – for example, the separation from the 'people of the countries' and the new way of celebrating the Feast of Tabernacles – "comparable to the occupation of the promised land after the first exodus" (Koch 1974: 188). These enterprises Koch sees as a fulfilment of exilic prophetic oracles by Ezra, paralleling the events narrated in Joshua *after* the entrance into the Promised Land, rather than the exodus from Egypt. The same parallel between Ezra-Nehemiah and the conquest narrative is pointed out by Abadie (1998) who looks for structural connections between Ezr 1–6 and the Pentateuchal narratives. With regard to the conquest, he argues that Ezr 2 parallels the entrance into the Promised Land, while the conflict with the '*am ha'aretz* of Ezr 3–4 might echo the conflicts with the local populations we find in Deut 7. Also, the liturgical assistance of priests and Levites in Ezr 3:10–11 can be compared to the warrior's liturgy of Jos 6. For Abadie, the celebration of the Passover in Ezr 6:19–22 represents a structural parallel with Jos 5:10–12, that is, the first Passover after the entrance into the Promised Land.

The structural similarities noted by Abadie and the thematic similarities emphasized by Koch indicate possible allusions to conquest themes. Nonetheless, as regarding the exodus parallels, also in this case, one must demand further elements than just those cited in order to state strong intertextual connections. To see Ezra-Nehemiah modelled only on Joshua's conquest narratives gives a partial image.

Ezra-Nehemiah as a re-establishment of the status quo ante

What are the arguments for interpreting Ezra-Nehemiah as a re-establishment of the status quo ante, that is a pre-exilic status?

Koch has reasons to see the cultic emphasis as one of the driving forces in Ezra-Nehemiah. In that sense, it is true that one of the leading threads of the narrative is the re-building of the temple, which is the main focus of the so-called Cyrus edict. The vicissitudes of its reconstruction occupy the main section of Ezr 1–6 which has its epilogue in the festive dedication of the "second temple" (Ezr 6:16 ff.). A single reference is also made to the "first house of God" (Ezr 3:12) in an emotionally charged scene of regret about the lost glory of the first building. The reiterated quotation of the Cyrus decree (Ezr 6:3–4) even gives precise indications about the measurements of the temple to be rebuilt (see the dimensions of Solomon's Temple in 1 Kings 6:2). The cultic emphasis seems, however, to progressively fade away after the first six chapters. While an emphasis on the temple vessels is still present in Artaxerxes' letter (Ezra 7), issues of community identity and delimitation come to the fore (Ezra 8–10). Later the rebuilding of the city walls and other social reforms find more space in the narration (Nehemiah 1–13). If the rebuilding of the temple could represent a re-establishment of the status quo ante, the dynamic of the final text in Ezra-Nehemiah leads in other directions. So, what would be a more suitable image to express the aim of these texts?

An alternative view: Ezra as one of the agents of the Torah

In order to answer the question, this contribution will focus on Ezra as one of the main characters of the central section of the book of Ezra-Nehemiah. He

156   *R. Piani*

exemplifies the different interpretive lenses used to understand the book of Ezra-Nehemiah as a whole. Through his characterization we may receive useful clues to the paradigms that inspired Ezra-Nehemiah in its overall framework and aim. Of course, the results cannot be absolutized, since there are other elements and characters (Nehemiah especially) that should also be taken into account.

Kratz (2008) suggested that a useful procedure is to look at the *Wirkungsgeschichte* of the figure of Ezra. From apocryphal texts (4 Ezra), Talmudic literature (b.Sanhedrin 21b par) and even Qur'anic sources, one gets an astonishing image of Ezra. He is considered a second Moses, a new founder of Jewish religion, the mediator of a newly revealed Torah to his people and comparable (according to the Qur'an) to the Messiah. It seems that the link between Ezra-Nehemiah and exodus, pointed out by some scholars, is confirmed and further developed by post-biblical portraits of Ezra. However, one must ask whether these post-biblical developments are free interpretations of Ezra's 'original' characteristics, or whether there are elements in Ezra-Nehemiah that allow this hermeneutical move.

Ackroyd's reflections on the character of Ezra link Ezra to the wilderness narratives (e.g. Ex 17:8–17; Num 20:14–31). In Ezr 8:21 ff., Ezra is reluctant to ask the king for a military escort for his group, because he had proclaimed to the Persian ruler that God's hand would protect them. According to Ackroyd, this recalls the dynamics of the wilderness episodes, where a dialectic between God's protection, symbolized e.g. in Exodus 13–14 and Numbers 9–10 by the cloud guiding the Israelites, and the people's (and leaders) unfaithfulness is at stake. Ackroyd (1991: 297) sees here a common feature between Ezra and Moses/Aaron as the leaders of Israel during the wanderings through the desert, and he comments: "Here Ezra is depicted, almost with humor, as the leader who has proclaimed his absolute faith, but who secretly doubts the power and protection of God."

It is not so clear how Ackroyd came to this conclusion, as Ezra is, in fact, presented in 8:23 as coherent with his proposals. He proclaims a fast and observes how that pious act found a hearing from God. As other scholars have noted, there might here be an intentional comparison with Nehemiah, who in Neh 2:9 is escorted by the army of the Persian king.[3] Ezra, on the other hand, shows his faith and confidence *soli Deo*, the results of which are confirmed in Ezr 8:31.

Besides the link Ackroyd argued for, Abadie (1998: 23) notes further possible connections between Exodus and Ezra. For example, he asserts that in Ezr 1:4 with the expression גר־שם there should be an implicit reference to the name of Moses' first born (Ex 2:22). The argument seems weak, since it is based only on a lexical similarity and other possible connections are absent. Rather, it should be noted how the absence of the גר in Neh 8, opposed to its parallel occurrences in Deuteronomy, is more significant for the interpretation of these passages.

Finally, it seems that clear, direct connections between the characters of Moses and Ezra are not well enough grounded in Ezra-Nehemiah. A direct connection between Ezra and Moses, in fact, does not emerge from the text itself. The connections proposed by scholars such as Ackroyd and Abadie seem not entirely convincing.

The more evident links seem to be those that relate Ezra to other key moments of the Israelite history such as told in the narratives about Joshua and Josiah. This is especially clear in Nehemiah 8, to which we will now turn.

Ezra and Joshua

A strong hint of a textual relation between Ezra and Joshua is the explicit reference to Joshua in Neh 8:17: "And all the assembly of those who had returned from the captivity made booths and lived in them; for *from the days of Joshua son of Nun* to that day the people of Israel had not done so".

Important, both from a lexical and a thematic point of view, is the expression תורת משה את־הספר (the Torah scroll recurs in Neh 8:1, 2, 3, 18). The scroll of the Torah becomes progressively the focus of attention in Neh 8, as happens also in Jos 8:31 (the renewal of the Covenant after the capture of Ai) and Jos 23:6 (Joshua's exhortation to the people before another renewal of the Covenant in Jos 24). The words used by Joshua in his last exhortation to the Israelites (Joshua 23) recall what he heard directly from God in 1:7–9, which also refers in other words to the centrality of the Torah.

The differences between the quoted texts are relevant. While in Nehemiah 8 the emphasis is on the *reading* of the Torah, in Joshua 1 it is on *writing*. Joshua will be charged with the reading of the Law in chapter 8. The probably secondary insertion of Levites explaining the Torah (absent in the Septuagint), gives the passage of Nehemiah 8 further remarkable characteristics: now the Torah must be *explained* to the people, a need that is not explicitly recognized in the Joshua passages. The contrast is especially strong with Joshua 8's emphasis on a faithful reading by Joshua of exactly what Moses commanded.[4]

Another common feature shared with the Joshua narratives is the emphasis on the role of the people, who are the main focus of the narrative in the sections that have Ezra as the main character. In Nehemiah 8 this is evident from the beginning, when עם occurs fourteen times and קהל twice. The concentration of these terms here and in Ezr 7–10 (six times) substantiates the significant role of the people, especially when compared with a lower concentration of the terms in Ezra 1–6 and the remainder of Nehemiah. Furthermore, as has been underscored by Tamara Eskenazi (1988), the people take the initiative by gathering and asking Ezra to read from the Torah (Neh 8:1–2; and, through people's representatives, 8:13). Yet another hint at a possible construction of Ezra having in mind Joshua is given by the circumstances in Ezr 9:3, which recall a similar reaction in Joshua in 7:6.

Ezra and Josiah

Interesting connections can be argued also between Nehemiah 8 and 2 Kings 22–23. Besides the repetition of the expression ספר התורה in 2 Kings 22:8, a scribe with his abilities also plays the main role, much as Ezra in Nehemiah 8.

158 *R. Piani*

Table 10.2 2 Kings 23:22 and Nehemiah 8:17

2 Kings 23:22	Neh 8:17
כי לא נעשה כפסח הזה מימי השפטים אשר שפטו את־ישראל וכל ימי מלכי ישראל ומלכי יהודה	ויעשו כל־הקהל השבים מן־השבי סכות וישבו בסכות כי לא־עשו מימי ישוע בן־נון כן בני ישראל עד היום ההוא ותהי שמחה גדולה מאד
No such Passover had been kept since the days of the judges who judged Israel, or during all the days of the kings of Israel or of the kings of Judah;	And all the assembly of those who had returned from the captivity made booths and lived in them; for from the days of Jeshua son of Nun to that day the people of Israel had not done so. And there was very great rejoicing.

The closest parallelism is expressed in an explicit reference to past events in 2 Kings 23:22, such as was the case also in Neh 8:17 (see Table 10.2): "No such Passover had been kept since the days of the judges who judged Israel, or during all the days of the kings of Israel or of the kings of Judah".

I recognize in this reference an intention to create a network of the founding events in Israelite history. From Nehemiah 8 one can draw several lines that connect it with the time of Joshua, the role of the Levites, and Josiah's reform. These texts hold in common especially one element, namely the Torah scroll.

Concluding remarks

After a brief review of the main interpretative patterns applied to Ezra-Nehemiah, I focused, as a case study, on Ezra as a character. I have argued that Ezra is not presented (as post-biblical literature does) explicitly and exclusively as a second Moses in the biblical texts. This is especially true of Nehemiah 8. The image provided in post-biblical texts seems to have resulted from an over-interpretation of the biblical figure of Ezra. If some – though weak – general allusions to the exodus themes can be found, especially in the first part of the Book of Ezra, no explicit connection between the characters of Moses and Ezra can be identified in the texts. As a consequence, the overall image of the return from exile as depicted in Ezra and Nehemiah seems not to be just that of a second exodus. Rather, I propose seeing Nehemiah 8, especially, as a text that offers the possibility of understanding Ezra as one of the agents of the Torah. Sure, he is a legitimate successor to Moses, but much closer to Joshua, Josiah and the Levites than to a Pentateuchal figure of Moses. Biblical traditions emphasize for each of these characters distinctive aspects of the Torah: Moses with its revelation, Joshua and Josiah with its (faithful) transmission, and Ezra (and the Levites) with its transmission and interpretation.

Interesting dynamics emerge between the characters Moses, Joshua, Josiah and Ezra as examined in this chapter. If Moses received the Torah directly from God, Joshua was commissioned to write down a copy of it and read it faithfully and completely to the people. Ezra (and the Levites) as described in

The return from exile in Ezra-Nehemiah 159

Table 10.3 Nehemiah 8:1, Joshua 8:31; 23:6; 1:7–9

Neh 8:1

ויאספו כל־העם כאיש אחד אל־הרחוב אשר לפני שער־המים ויאמרו לעזרא הספר להביא את־ספר
תורת משה אשר־צוה יהוה את־ישראל

All the people gathered together into the square before the Water Gate. They told the scribe Ezra to bring the book of the law of Moses, which the LORD had given to Israel.

Josh 8:31

כאשר צוה משה עבד־יהוה את־בני ישראל ככתוב בספר תורת משה מזבח אבנים שלמות אשר
לא־הניף עליהן ברזל ויעלו עליו עלות ליהוה ויזבחו שלמים

Just as Moses the servant of the LORD had commanded the Israelites, as it is written in the book of the law of Moses, "an altar of unhewn stones, on which no iron tool has been used"; and they offered on it burnt offerings to the LORD, and sacrificed offerings of well-being.

Josh 23:6

וחזקתם מאד לשמר ולעשות את כל־הכתוב בספר תורת משה לבלתי סור־ממנו ימין ושמאול

Therefore be very steadfast to observe and do all that is written in the book of the law of Moses, turning aside from it neither to the right nor to the left,

---

Josh 1:7-9

רק חזק ואמץ מאד לשמר לעשות ככל־התורה אשר צוך משה עבדי אל־תסור ממנו ימין ושמאול ⁷
למען תשכיל בכל אשר תלך
לא־ימוש ספר התורה הזה מפיך והגית בו יומם ולילה למען תשמר לעשות ככל־הכתוב בו כי־אז ⁸
תצליח את־דרכך ואז תשכיל
הלוא צויתיך חזק ואמץ אל־תערץ ואל־תחת כי עמך יהוה אלהיך בכל אשר תלך ⁹

Only be strong and very courageous, being careful to act in accordance with all the law that my servant Moses commanded you; do not turn from it to the right hand or to the left, so that you may be successful wherever you go. This book of the law shall not depart out of your mouth; you shall meditate on it day and night, so that you may be careful to act in accordance with all that is written in it. For then you shall make your way prosperous, and then you shall be successful. I hereby command you: Be strong and courageous; do not be frightened or dismayed, for the LORD your God is with you wherever you go.

Neh 8 had not only to read from the Torah, as the faithful Joshua did, but also to explain it. For the author of Nehemiah 8 a mere mediation and oral transmission seems not enough. The people, the real protagonists in this chapter, need the qualified mediation of the Torah-experts, both to hear it (Ezra) and to understand it (Levites).

The relevant role of scribes and priests, as evoked also in the story about Josiah in 2 Kings 22–23, is nonetheless at the service of the people's understanding of the Torah. For the author of these post-exilic narratives, the transmission and the explanation of the Torah is the decisive core of Israelite identity. In this sense, the Ezra-Nehemiah narratives seem to stress a continuity, which, connected with Joshua and Josiah traditions, emphasizes the Torah as the determining factor of Judahite identity.

160 *R. Piani*

What I have argued may have consequences for our understanding of how the Bible represents Judahite identity after the exile. I attempted to critique the image of Ezra as a second Moses and propose instead that he has to be seen as one of the agents of the Torah. If one follows the first image, the return from exile is that of a radical new beginning. Judahite identity would then take on a revolutionary form with the newly revealed Torah such as 4 Ezra exemplifies. If, on the contrary, Ezra is viewed 'only' as one of the agents of the Torah, a picture emerges that is closer to other biblical traditions. Ezra-Nehemiah's Israel thereby must be seen as shaped in continuity with the past and the Torah as the determining identity factor. Emphasizing the role of the Torah of Moses, the biblical authors achieved a double outcome: a legitimation and authorization of Ezra and his group as successors to Moses, Joshua and Josiah. At the same time, as the discussion of mixed marriages reveals, they also found a subtle way to introduce their own take on social problems. This eventually led to new interpretations of the 'old Mosaic Torah' in light of their situation and, perhaps more importantly, their agenda.

Notes

1 The other two are: "Ezra came to Jerusalem as the real high priest of the family of Aaron. His purpose was to change his people into a 'holy seed' around the holy place, which God had given as a tent-peg and source of life during the times of political servitude" (Koch 1974: 190); and "Ezra was sent to all his 'people beyond the river', including the Samaritans. His aim was to establish one Israel out of all 12 tribes, which explains the later acceptance of the Pentateuch by the Samaritans" (Koch 1974: 193).
2 Koch (1974: 188) refers to Zimmerli (1963, 192–204). See also Anderson (1962, 177–95).
3 Kapelrud 1944: 50–51; in der Smitten 1973: 22.
4 I agree here with Ingrid Hjelm 2000 and 2004 that the emphasis on the need of explanation and interpretation of the Torah by Ezra and the Levites could be the connecting point with the rabbinical idea of Ezra as the giver of the oral Torah. Anyway I find that explicit textual references to the Torah of Moses in Ezra-Nehemiah, and especially in the section with Ezra as the main character, are better documented.

Bibliography

Abadie, P. 1998. "Le livre d'Esdras: un midrash de l'Exode?". *Transeuphratène* 14: 19–31.

Ackroyd, P.R. 1991. "God and People in the Chronicler's Presentation of Ezra". In *The Chronicler in His Age*. P.R. Ackroyd (ed.). Sheffield: Sheffield Academic Press: 290–310. Originally published 1976 with the same title in *La Notion biblique de Dieu: le Dieu de la Bible et le Dieu des philosophes*. J. Coppens (ed.). Leuven: Leuven University Press: 145–62.

Anderson, B.W. 1962. "Exodus Typology in Second Isaiah". In *Israel's Prophetic Heritage: Essays in Honor of James Muilenburg*. B. Anderson and W. Harrelson (eds). New York: Harper & Brothers: 177-195.

Blenkinsopp, J. 1989. *Ezra-Nehemiah: A Commentary*. London: SCM.

Coats, G.W. 1968. "Despoiling the Egyptians". *Vetus Testamentum* 18/4: 450–57.

Dyma, O. 2009. *Die Wallfahrt zum Zweiten Tempel. Untersuchungen zur Entwicklung der Wallfahrtfeste in vorhasmonäischer Zeit*. Tübingen: Mohr Siebeck.

Eskenazi, T.C. 1988. *In an Age of Prose. A Literary Approach to Ezra-Nehemiah*. Atlanta, GA: Scholars Press.

Garbini, G. 1988. *History and Ideology in Ancient Israel*. London: SCM Press.

Halivni, D.W. 1997. *Revelation Restored: Divine Writ and Critical Responses*. Boulder, CO: Westview Press.

Hjelm, I. 2000. *The Samaritans and Early Judaism* (*JSOTS* 303). Sheffield: Sheffield Academic Press.

——2004. *Jerusalem's Rise to Sovereignty. Zion and Gerizim in Competition* (*JSOTS* 404; *Copenhagen International Seminar* 14). London and New York: T&T Clark.

In der Smitten, W.T. 1973. *Esra. Quellen, Überlieferung und Geschichte*. Assen: Van Gorcum.

Japhet, S. 2006. "Periodization between History and Ideology II: Chronology and Ideology in Ezra-Nehemiah". In *Judah and the Judeans in the Persian Period*. O. Lipschits and M. Oeming (eds). Winona Lake, IN: Eisenbrauns: 491–508.

Kapelrud, A.S. 1944. *The Question of Authorship in the Ezra-narrative: a Lexical Investigation*. Oslo: Dybwad.

Knowles, D. 2004. "Pilgrimage Imagery in the Returns in Ezra". *Journal of Biblical Literature* 123/1: 57–74.

Koch, K. 1974. "Ezra and the Origins of Judaism". *Journal of Semitic Studies* 19: 173–97.

Kratz, R.G. 2000. *Die Komposition der erzählenden Bücher des Alten Testaments. Grundwissen der Bibelkritik*. Stuttgart: UTB.

——2008. "Ezra – Priest and Scribe". In *Scribes, Sages, and Seers. The Sage in the Eastern Mediterranean World*. L.G. Perdue (ed.). Göttingen: Vandenhoeck & Ruprecht: 163–88.

Pakkala, J. 2004. *Ezra the Scribe. The Development of Ezra 7–10 and Nehemia 8*. Berlin – New York: de Gruyter.

Reinmuth, T. 2008. "Nehemiah 8 and the Authority of Torah in Ezra-Nehmiah". In *Unity and Disunity in Ezra-Nehemiah. Redaction, Rhetoric, and Reader*. M.J. Boda and P.L.Redditt, (eds). Sheffield: Sheffield Phoenix Press: 241–62.

Smith, M.S. 1997. *The Pilgrimage Pattern in Exodus*. Sheffield: Sheffield Academic Press.

Throntveit, M.A. 2012. *Ezra-Nehemiah*. Interpretation. Louisville, KY: John Knox Press.

Williamson, H.G.M. 2007. "The Torah and History in Presentations of Restoration in Ezra-Nehemiah". In *Reading the Law: Studies in Honour of Gordon J. Wenham*. J.G. McConville and Karl Möller (eds). New York: T&T Clark: 156–70.

Zimmerli, W. 1963. "Der 'neue Exodus' in der Verkündigung der beiden grossen Exilspropheten". In *Gottes Offenbarung: gesammelte Aufsätze zum Alten Testament*. W. Zimmerli. Munich: C. Kaiser Verlag: 192–204.

Index of sources

Hebrew Bible

Genesis
1 106
1:2 102, 126
1:26 111
2–3 111
2:4–3:24 106
2:15 112, 113
3 51
3:8 108
3:15 112–13
3:17–19 6, 101, 114
3:23 101, 112
3:24 114
4 6, 51, 111, 114
4:1 111, 114
4:1–24 106
4:2 112
4:3 112
4:7 55, 112–13
4:8 113
4:9 113, 117
4:10–14 101
4:12–14 113, 114
4:13–14 113–14
4:15 114
4:17 113
4:23–24 114
4:26 114
5 106, 109, 111
5:1 105–6
5:1–32 106
5:24 106–7
5:29 101, 115
5:32 106, 108, 109
6–10 51
6:1–4 106
6:3 79

6:5–8:22 106
6:7 101
6:9 106–7
6:11–12 101
7:23 115
8–9 106
8:20–22 107
8:21 104
8:21–22 101
9:1–17 107
9:2 105
9:18–19 108
9:18–27 108
9:20 108
9:25–27 101
9:26 108
10 106
10:1 106, 108, 109
10:5.20.31 108–9
10:18–19 108
10:18–27 108
11 51, 109, 110
11:1–9 106, 109
11:10–27 109
12–50 55
12:1–4 101
12:1–9 18
12:3 105
12:6–7 58
12:10 56
12:10–20 18, 56, 118
12:16 114
13 108
13:2–12 118
13:10 108
13:13 55
14:18–20 17

Index of sources 163

15:13 56, 57, 79
17 43n11
17:1–14 115
17:13–14 120
18 103
18–21 110
18:18 111
18:19 118
18:20 55
18:25 7, 111, 118, 122
19 108
19:29 108
19:30–38 7, 101–2
19:31 118
19:36–38 118
20 118
20:1–18 118
20:6 55
20:9 55
20:11 118
20:17–18 118
21:1–3 118
21:8–21 119
21:22–32 118
22:1–18 119
25:19–34 6, 101, 119
26:1–11 56
26:6–11 118
26:12–33 118
27:1 110
28:16 120
29:15–30 119
29:31–30:24 119
30:14–19 119
30:16 118
30:25–31:24 119
31:15 56
31:25–55 119
31:36 55
31:39 55
31:45–54 56
32:3–21 119
32:5 56
32:24–32 119
32:31–32 110
33:1–17 119
33:18–20 119
34:1–35:5 119
34:5ff. 119–20
34:14 120
34:27 120
34:30 120
34:31 119–20
35:5 120

35:9–15 119
36:6–8 118
37 55
37–50 55
37:22 55
37:23–36 21
37:26–27 55
38:8 120
38:1–11 120
38:12 120
38:12–24 121
38:15 120–21
38:26 121
39:2–6 122
39:9 55
39:15 121–22
40:1 55
42–45 21
42:22 55
43:8–9 55
44:32 55
45:5–7 122
45:7 56
45:8 56
46 21
46:3–4 56
47:1–12 56, 79
47:4 56
47:9 56, 79
47:19 57, 79
47:25 57, 79
48:15–16 115
49:5–7 120
49:24 115
50:13 56
50:15–17 122
50:17–21 55
50:18–21 122
50:19 57
50:20 56
50:24 55
Exodus
1–15 32, 44n18
1:1–15:21 83–84
1:8–11 79
1:13 57
2:22 156
3 152–54
3:8 30
3:8.10 32
3:12 115, 116
3:17 30
6 43n11
10:26 57

164 *Index of sources*

11 152–54
12:37 81
13–14 156
14:5 57
14:12 57, 79
15:18 45n35
15:22–40:38 83–84
16:3 57, 79
17:8–17 156
19:5–6 84
21:1–22:16 19
22:16 119
22:20 57
22:26 56
23:9 56, 57
23:20–33 114, 116
32 55, 112, 114, 115
32:7–14 103, 107
32:34 80
33:1–6.15 116
Leviticus
1:13 104
8:10–12 107
19:34 57
25:2–7 72–73
25:23 57
25:42 57
26 80
26:3–13 54
26:33 54
26:40–42 55
26:43 54
Numbers
1 152
1:46 81
2 152
9–10 156
10:13 152
11 112, 114, 115
11:5 57, 79
11:10–15 103, 107
13–14 106, 112, 114
13:32 107–8
14 115
14:1–12 54
14:3–4 57, 79
14:8–9 54
14:9 107–8
14:13–19 103, 107
14:22 84
14:24 54
14:27–38 57
14:34 55
16:12–15 54

16:22 103
20:11 80
20:14–31 156
21–24 54
23:22 44n18
24:8 44n18
24:9–10 113
25 81
25:2–3 81
25:7–8 81
25:11–13 81
26:51 81
26:64 79, 81
26.64 54
27 116
27:12–14 80
27:16–17 116
27:18–19 116
28–30 54
31 81
32:10–15 81
32:11–13 79
Deuteronomy
2:7 81
4:5 57
4:27 74
5:12–15 30
6:1 57
6:21–23 30
7 155
8:1 57
10:19 57
11–12 57–58
11:29 58
12:1 57
12:31 83
18:9 57
18:10 83
20:10–15 83
21:10–14 81
22:28–30 119
25:5–10 120
26:1 57
26:5 58, 79
26:5–9 30
27:4 58
28 54, 80
28:1–14 54
28:64 54
30:2 55
31 80
31:24–26 80
31:26 80
31:26–27 80

Index of sources 165

31:29 80
32:39 113
32:50–52 80
34 60, 80
34:4 80
34:6 85
34:9 116
Joshua
1:7–9 157, 159
5:10–12 155
7:6 157
8:31 157, 159
9 22
23 157
23–24 58
23:6 61, 157, 159
24 21, 58, 157
24:26 61
Judges
2:1 30
3:7–11 60
6:7–10 44n17
6:8 32
6:8–9 30
1 Samuel
7:14 38, 39
24–26 139
2 Samuel
5:8 110
6:17–19 104
7:6 82
9 110
12 117
12:25 117
24 104
24:1–25 102
24:16–17 103
24:18–25 104
1 Kings
5 117
5:9 117
6:2 155
8 104
8:22–53 104
8:23–53 54
8:30–32 104
8:33–34 122
8:33–40 104
8:46–53 105, 122
8:54–61 104
8:62–66 104
12:25–33 43n15
22:1–40 116
22:17 116

2 Kings
17 8n1, 72, 94
17:24 2
18:31–32 54
18:32 54
19:35–36 54
22–23 157, 159
22:8 157
23:22 158
24–25 72
25 1–2
25:11–12 93
25:12 67
25:27–30 110
Isaiah
1–39 92
2:19 113
2:21 113
5 108
5:1–7 105, 108, 111
6:9–13 115–16
10:5–11 93
13:1–14:23 109
14:22 113
24–27 92
24:1 102
24:10 102
31:1 149n7
34:13 112
35:7 112
36:16 54
37:1–4 118
37:36–37 54
40–48 126
40–55 66, 92
40:9–11 115
41 92
43:1 97n5
43:3–4 97n5
43:14 97n5, 130
44:1–8 131
44:2 131, 132
44:8 130, 131
44:9 126, 131, 132
44:9–11 130
44:9–20 7, 125, 129–34
44:10 131, 132
44:11 132
44:12 131, 132
44:12–17 132
44:13–16 131
44:15 131
44:19 131
44:19–20 133

166   *Index of sources*

44:20 132
44:21 131, 132
44:21–28 131
44:24 131
44:28 92
45 109
45:1 110
45:1–4 92
47 130
49:22 66
52:3 97n5
53:4–9 115
56–66 66
56:8 66
58:6 66
60 154
60:4 66
60:9 66
61:1 66
66:20 66
Jeremiah
1:3 137
1:8 141, 148n5
1:14–15 67
1:16 138
3:8 148n5
3:15 117
4–5 105
4:23 102
5:1–5 102
5:6–10 105
5:11–17 105
5:19 138, 148n3
5:22 148n5
5:24 148n5
7:20 143
9:12 148n3
9:12–16 138
10 32
10:5 148n5
10:7 148n5
10:21 117
13 32
16:10–13 138
16:11 148n3
16:19–20 146
17:8 148n5
22:8–9 138
22:9 148n3
23:1–4 116, 117
23:2–3 117
23:4 148n5
24 138
24:1–10 70

24:8 67
25:11 93
25:12 66, 68
25:34–38 116
25:36–38 117–18
26:19 148n5
26:21–23 148n6
29:10 66, 68, 107
30:10 148n5
31:7–14 117
31:29 22
32:20–22 30
32:39 148n5
41 139
41:17–18 144
41:18 140
42–44 7–8, 139–48
42:2 140
42:2–3 144
42:2–4 140
42:5–6 144
42:6 140
42:10 141, 143
42:11 141
42:12 141
42:14 140–41
42:15 143, 144
42:15–16 141
42:15–22 56
42:17 141, 143–44
42:18 143, 144
42:21–22 144
42:22 143–44
43:1 144
43:1–7 141, 144
43:2 143
43:10 144
43:10–11 143
43:12 143
43:13 143
44:2 143
44:4 142
44:5 142
44:6 143
44:8 142, 143, 144
44:9–10 142
44:10 142
44:12 143, 144
44:13 143–44
44:14 143, 144
44:17 141–42
44:17–19 145
44:18 142
44:22 144

Index of sources 167

44:26–30 142
44:28 143
49:19–20 117–18
50 114
50–51 109, 110
50:3–7 114
50:44–45 117–18
52 1–2
52:1–30 137
52:31–34 110, 137
Ezekiel
6:14 102
11:13 67
11:14–25 70
11:15–25 117
11:25 70
16 92, 108
23 92
34 117
34:1–31 116
34:3–10 117
34:11–12 117
34:11–31 117
34:23–24 117
37:24–28 116, 117
39:1–2 67
40–48 83
Hosea
2:15 31
12:1 105
12:13 31
13:5–8 117–18
Joel
2:20 67
4:1 76n6
4:1–3 67
4:2 74
Amos
2:10 31
3:1 31
9:7 31
Nahum
1:6 149n9
Haggai
1:12 67
1:14 67
2:2 67
2:6–7 67
2:7 154
Zechariah
1–8 67–68, 76n10
1:7 68
1:12 68
1:14–17 68

2:7 74
6:10 70
7:1 68
7:5 68
9–14 68, 76n10
10:2 117
10:2–3 117
10:3–11.17 116
10:6–12 69
10:9–10 69
11:1–17 116
13:7 117
Psalms
1:1–6 122
2 115
8:2–7 114
23 113, 114, 117–18
23:1–4 115
74:1 115
79 91–92
80 91–92
80:9–10 30
89 91–92
92:10 74
95:7 115
96:1–13 104
100:3 115
105:1–15 104
106:1.48 104
110 115
121 115
137 6, 20, 89–96
137:1 89
137:2 90
137:3 90, 93
137:4 90
137:5 90
137:6 90
137:6–7 89–90
137:7 90
137:8 93
137:8–9 90–91
140:1–6 115
146:3 149n7
146:5 149n7
Proverbs
1:7 120
16:32 113
Job
42:7–8 112
Lamentations
3:1–6 117
3:10 117
4:21 91

168 *Index of sources*

4:22 91
Ecclesiastes
  1:17 105
Esther
  2:5–6 73–74
  3:8 74
  8:5 74
Ezra
  1–6 155, 157
  1:1–4 73
  1:4 156
  1:4–6 152–54
  1:12 68
  2:1 74, 76n15
  2:1–2 67
  3–4 155
  3:8 76n15
  3:10–11 155
  3:12 155
  6:3–4 155
  6:16ff. 155
  6:19–22 155
  7 155
  7–10 157
  8–10 155
  8:15–20 152
  8:21ff. 156
  8:23 156
  8:31 156
  8:35 76n15
  9:1 70
  9:3 157
  9:4 70
  9:7 76n15
  10:7 70
  10:8 70
  10:9 70
  10:16 70
Nehemiah
  1–13 155
  1:2 71, 76n15
  1:2–3 67
  1:3 71, 74
  1:8 54
  2:9 156
  3–4 15
  5:1–13 71
  6 15
  7:6 76n15
  8 8, 156, 157–59
  8:1 157, 159
  8:1–2 157
  8:2 157

8:3 157
8:13 157
8:17 76n15, 157, 158
8:18 157
9:36 77n16
13:23–27 71
1 Chronicles
  5:41 72
  11:1–9 104
  13 104
  15 104
  16:1–3 104
  16:8–36 104
  16:33 104
  21:1–30 102–3
  21:15–17 103
2 Chronicles
  18:1–34 116
  18:16 116
  30:9 77n20
  36:11–21 93
  36:19–20 72
  36:20–22 68
  36:21 73, 93
  36:21–23 110–11
  36:22–23 16, 73, 92
Matthew
  9:36 117
  27:32 61n4
Mark
  6:34 117
  15:21 61n4
Luke
  25:26 61n4
John
  19.30 85
Acts
  2:10 61n4
  6:9 61n4
  11:20 61n4

Septuagint

Exodus
  19:1 30
Numbers
  33:38 30
1 Kings
  6:1 30
Psalms
  104:38 30
  113:1 30

Apocrypha and Pseudepigrapha

1 Maccabees
15:23 61n4
2 Maccabees
2:23 61n4
4 Ezra 150, 156, 160

Philo

De Vita Mosis
2.288 85
Legum Allegoria
III: 224–35 85

Josephus

Antiquitates
12.1 24n20
14.114–16 61n4
14.118 61n4
16.169 61n4
Contra Apionem
I.16ff. 17–18
II, ch. 44 52

Babylonian Talmud

b. Sanhedrin
21b 154, 156

Greek and Roman authors

Apollonius of Rhodes
Argonautica 51–52
Curtius Rufus
Historiae Alexandri Magni **IV, 8–11** 24n18
Diodorus Siculus
Bibliotheca Historica **40.3** 25n26
Hecataeus 18, 25n26
Herodotus
Historiae **IV** 52

Homer
Odyssey 51–52
Livy 14, 23n4
Ab Urbe Condita **V:34–49** 90
Pindar
Pythian Ode 52

"El-Amarna letters" (Knudtzon 1907–15)
45–49 38
106 38
280:30–35 24n7
Hittite Diplomatic Texts (Beckman 1999)
39–40 38
Kanaanäische und aramäische Inschriften (Donner and Röllig 1962–64)
2.168 44n27
Ancient Near Eastern Texts (Pritchard 1969)
255 35
285 93, 97n5
288 24n9, 97n8
318 38
320 44n27

Samaritan sources

The Samaritan Chronicle II
Ms. 1142 59–60
Ms. 1168 59–60
The Kitāb al Tarīkh of Abu' l-Fath (Stenhouse 1985) 57, 58–59
Memar Marqah (Macdonald 1963)
V 3–4 85
V 124 86
V 126.23–26 85
V 128.1–2 85
Tibåt Mårqe (Ben-Hayyim 1988)
258–70 85
261 86

Index of authors

Abadie, P. 155, 156, 157
Ackroyd, P.R. 152, 156–57
Adams, J.W. 133
Ahlström, G. 54
Ahn, J. 1, 9n5
Albertz, R. 65, 71, 76n3
Albright, W.F. 23n1, 23n3, 44n27, 82
Allen, L.C. 138, 142, 144
Alonso-Schökel, L. 30
Alt, A. 20
Altman, A. 61n7
Anderson, B.W. 160n2
Anderson, R.T. 59, 61n13, 62n18, 86n4
Appelbaum, S. 52

Bahn, P. 45n33
Balzer, K. 81
Barkay, G. 2–3
Barrett, R. 7–8
Barstad, H.M. 2–3, 77n19
Becking, B. 2, 3, 70, 73
Ben Dor Evian, S. 41
Ben-Hayyim, Z. 85, 86n4
Ben-Shlomo, D. 28
Ben Zvi, E. 3, 15, 29
Berger, P.-R. 97n6
Berlin, A. 65, 73
Blenkinsopp, J. 126, 151
Blum, E. 43n11
Boccaccio, P. 31
Boisvert, L. 31
Bori, P.C. 43n4
Bowman, J. 59, 60, 61n13, 62n18, 62n21
Brekelmans, C.H.W. 83
Brettler, M.Z. 43n12
Briant, P. 52, 76n1
Bright, J. 23n1, 23n3
Broadie, A. 86n4
Broida, M. 82

Brueck, L.R. 127, 128
Brueggemann, W. 130, 131
Bryan, B.M. 44n20
Budde, K. 82
Burke, A.A. 40
Burke, P.J. 138

Cahill, J.M. 23n5
Carmichael, C. 61n8
Carroll, R.P. 65, 67, 70, 73, 75, 77n19
Carter, C.E. 3
Catastini, A. 43n10
Caubet, A. 41
Cazeaux, J. 52–53
Charlesworth, J.H. 24n21
Charpin, D. 24n10
Chattopadhyaya, S.K. 125
Childs, B.S. 30
Chockalingam, A.J. 128, 129
Clarke, S. 127
Clay, A.T. 24n12
Coats, G.W. 30, 43n12, 152
Coggins, R.J. 61n13
Cohen, R. 41
Cohn, R.L. 86
Collins, J.J. 83
Cowley, A.E. 96
Crane, O.T. 57, 59, 62n18
Cross, F.M. 82
Crown, A.D. 60, 62n21
Cuéllar, G.L. 130, 131

Damgaard, F. 85
Daube, D. 30
Davies, A. 126, 131
Davies, G. 84
Davies, P.R. 44–45n28
Day, J. 149n8
Decker, W. 44n23

Index of authors 171

Delitzsch, F. 82
Deutsch, E. 125–26
Dever, W.G. 38–39
Dick, M.B. 133
Downing, J.D.H. 128
Dozeman, T.B. 31
Dyas, D. 85
Dyma, O. 154

Edelman, D. 95
Eichrodt, W. 76n3
Eissfeldt, O. 13
Elangovan, R. 127
Erll, A. 95
Eskenazi, T.C. 157

Faust, A. 24n8, 38–39
Feldman, M.H. 41
Feldt, L. 84, 86
Fensham, F.C. 81
Finkelstein, I. 14, 23n5, 23n6, 24n7,
    24n15, 45n29, 95
Fitzgerald, M.O. 125
Flight, J.W. 82
Florentin, M. 59, 60
Fohrer, G. 13
Frankena, R. 61n7

Gaijan, M.B. 127
Galambush, J. 83
Garbini, G. 39, 45n28, 151
Gaster, M. 57, 59, 61n13, 62n17
Geertz, C. 28
Gennep, A. van 86
Gertz, J.C. 43n11
Giles, T. 59, 61n13, 62n18, 86n4
Giveon, R. 33
Gmirkin, R.E. 25n23, 61n3
Gnuse, R.K. 146
Goldingay, J. 132
Gordon, R.P. 139–40
Gottwald, N. 83
Grayson, A.K. 54, 61n7
Greenspahn, F.E. 125
Gregory, B.C. 66
Gross, W. 30
Guillaume, P. 112

Halivni, D.W. 150
Halvorson-Taylor, M.A. 54, 61n7, 73,
    74, 76n8, 76n11, 77n24, 81–82
Hasel, M.G. 45n31
Hawkins, R.K. 38–39

Helk, W. 45n30
Hendel, R. 29
Higginbotham, C.R. 40, 44n20
Hjelm, I. 1, 2, 3, 5–6, 8n3, 8n4, 24n20,
    53, 54, 57, 58, 61n9, 61n13, 61n14,
    62n17, 85, 86, 86n4, 97n8, 101, 113,
    117, 160n4
Hoffman, Y. 29
Hofstee, W. 28
Holladay, W.L. 132
Hulster, I.J. de 28, 42n3
Humbert, P. 30, 31
Humphreys, W.L. 77n27
Hyman, H.H. 137

In der Smitten, W.T. 160n3
Irudayaraj, D.S. 7, 134
Irvin, D. 120

Jackson, K.P. 44n27
Jaideva, P. 128
Japhet, S. 72–73, 150
Johnson, W.R. 37
Johnstone, W. 72
Juynboll, T.W.J. 57, 62n18

Kang, S.M. 31, 83
Kapelrud, A.S. 160n3
Keel, O. 32–33, 35–36, 44n22
Kenyon, K.M. 2–3
Killebrew, A.E. 23n5, 45n31
King, L. 111
Klingbeil, M. 28
Knauf, E.A. 2, 82, 146
Knoppers, G.N. 3, 8n2, 8n3
Knowles, D. 151, 154
Koch, K. 150, 151–52, 154–55, 160n1,
    160n2
Kratz, R.G. 151, 156
Kuhn, T. 13
Kumar, R. 127
Kvanvig, H.S. 106

LaBianca, Ø.S. 41
Lawson Younger, Jr., K. 2, 8n1, 15
Leith, M.J.W. 52
Lemche, N.P. 4, 6, 13, 14, 24n19, 25n27,
    25n28, 25n31, 25n32, 94, 97n6
Levenson, J.D. 73, 77n26
Levin, C. 3, 29
Levtow, N.B. 127, 130, 131, 132–33
Lewis, B. 111
Liebowitz, H.A. 33

172   *Index of authors*

Light, G.W. 132
Lipschits, O. 2, 3, 24n8, 24n15, 29, 76n1, 95, 96n3
Liverani, M. 38, 40, 41, 43n8, 44–45n28, 53, 82–83
Long, B.O. 111
Lords, K.V. 40
Lundager Jensen, H.J. 105
Lyon, D.G. 53

Ma, J. 45n32
MacCarthy, D.J. 61n7
Macdonald, J. 57, 59, 62n17, 85, 86n4, 86n5
Magen, Y. 16
Manassa, C. 25n24
Martin, M.A.S. 40
Mason, S. 43n7
Matthiae, P. 32
Mazar, E. 23n5
McConville, G. 84
McKane, W. 137–38
Meibohm, M. 126
Mendenhall, G.E. 61n7
Mendonça, J.T. 43n4
Merrill, E.H. 76n7
Mettinger, T.N.D. 106
Meyers, C.L. 68, 76n7
Meyers, E.M. 68, 76n7
Miller, D.M. 43n7
Miller, P. 44n27
Montgomery, J.A. 61n13
Morris, E.F. 40, 45n31
Mowinckel, S. 13
Mumford, G.D. 41

Na'aman, N. 2, 29n45, 45n29
Nathanson, M. 109
Niccacci, A. 44n27
Niditch, S. 81, 83
Nielsen, E. 17, 25n22
Niessen, F. 57, 59, 62n17
Nikiprowetzky, V. 146
Nora, P. 95
Noth, M. 23n1, 30, 31, 58, 83
Nünning, A. 95

O'Connell, R.H. 44n17
O'Connor, D. 44n23
Oded, B. 2, 15, 53–54, 67, 77n19, 83
Oeming, M. 76n1
Ofer, A. 3
Oren, E.D. 40

Otto, E. 43n11
Oz, A. 43n5
Oz-Salzberger, F. 43n5

Pakkala, J. 151
Pandit, B. 125
Panitz-Cohen, N. 41, 45n31
Parpola, S. 61n7
Paswan, S. 128
Paul, S. 25n29
Payne, D. 132
Pearce, L.E. 3
Pérez-Castro, F. 62n21
Pfoh, E. 38–39, 101
Piani, R. 8
Porzia, F. 4–5, 36, 43n6
Power, C. 5
Prasad, A.N. 127
Pury, A. de 29, 43n8

Rad, G. von 13, 18–19, 126
Raheb, M. 109
Rajawat, M. 127
Rajkumar, P. 128, 129
Ranade, R.D. 128
Reinmuth, T. 151
Rendtorff, R. 30, 43n12
Renfrew, C. 41, 45n33
Renkema, J. 117
Rochberg, F. 82
Röllig, W. 44n27
Rom-Shiloni, D. 29
Römer, T.C. 29, 43n12
Roy, S. 128
Russell, S.C. 31, 43n15, 44n18, 44n19

Saggs, H.W.F. 146
Sanders, J.A. 1
Śaṅkarācārya 126
Schäfer, H. 37, 44n25
Schectman, S. 56
Schmid, K. 29, 43n11, 146
Schunk, M. 112
Schwarz, B. 95
Sham, S.A. 41
Shaw, I. 37
Sherratt, E.S. 41
Shinde, P.K. 127
Silberman, N.A. 14, 24n7
Singer, E. 137
Sivaramkrishna, M. 128
Ska, J.L. 43n9, 45n34

Smith-Christopher, D.L. 65
Smith, M.S. 83–84, 126, 146
Soares-Prabhu, G.M. 126
Sommer, B.D. 131
Speiser, E.A. 103, 104
Spreafico, A. 30
Staubli, T. 33, 44n26
Steiner, M.L. 23n5
Stenhouse, P. 57, 58–59, 60, 61n13,
   62n16, 62n20
Stern, E. 2, 3
Stern, P.D. 83
Stets, J.E. 138
Strawn, B.A. 44n26
Stulman, L. 139, 140, 148n4,
   149n7

Tal, A. 86n4
Tappy, R.E. 24n16
Tengström, S. 106
Thompson, T.L. 6–7, 8n4, 61n3,
   93, 97n7, 101–2, 103, 105–7, 106,
   108, 109, 110, 111, 112, 114, 115,
   116, 118, 119, 120, 122
Throntveit, M.A. 150
Tov, E. 76n3
Tsedaka, B. 86n5

Uehlinger, C. 28, 32–33, 35–36,
   44n22
Ussishkin, D. 23n5, 24n15, 95,
   97n9

Valmiki, O. 128
Van De Mieroop, M. 41, 45n33
Van Hecke, P.J.P. 117
Van Seters, J. 31–32, 96n4
Vaughn, A.G. 23n5
Verma, R. 125, 127
Vilmar, E. 57, 58

Wajdenbaum, P. 52–53, 61n3,
   106, 108
Watanabe, K. 61n7
Weeks, M. 80
Weinfeld, M. 61n7, 76n14, 80–81
Weinstein, J.M. 40
Weippert, M. 86n3
Wellhausen, J. 23n2
Westbrook, R. 25n29, 41
Westermann, C. 125, 126
de Wette, W.M.L. 23n2
Wiese, A. 36
Wijngaards, J.N.M. 30–31
Williamson, H.G.M. 70, 76n13, 150,
   151, 152
Wilson, J.A. 121
Winckler, H. 53
Winter, I.J. 44n21
Wyatt, N. 101

Zadok, R. 3
Zertal, A. 24n8
Zimmerli, W. 76n3, 160n2
Zorn, J.R. 3

eBooks
from Taylor & Francis
Helping you to choose the right eBooks for your Library

Add to your library's digital collection today with Taylor & Francis eBooks. We have over 50,000 eBooks in the Humanities, Social Sciences, Behavioural Sciences, Built Environment and Law, from leading imprints, including Routledge, Focal Press and Psychology Press.

Choose from a range of subject packages or create your own!

Benefits for you
- Free MARC records
- COUNTER-compliant usage statistics
- Flexible purchase and pricing options
- 70% approx of our eBooks are now DRM-free.

Benefits for your user
- Off-site, anytime access via Athens or referring URL
- Print or copy pages or chapters
- Full content search
- Bookmark, highlight and annotate text
- Access to thousands of pages of quality research at the click of a button.

Free Trials Available

We offer free trials to qualifying academic, corporate and government customers.

eCollections
Choose from 20 different subject eCollections, including:
- Asian Studies
- Economics
- Health Studies
- Law
- Middle East Studies

eFocus
We have 16 cutting-edge interdisciplinary collections, including:
- Development Studies
- The Environment
- Islam
- Korea
- Urban Studies

For more information, pricing enquiries or to order a free trial, please contact your local sales team:

UK/Rest of World: **online.sales@tandf.co.uk**
USA/Canada/Latin America: **e-reference@taylorandfrancis.com**
East/Southeast Asia: **martin.jack@tandf.com.sg**
India: **journalsales@tandfindia.com**

www.tandfebooks.com